A publication in
The Adult Education Association
Handbook Series in Adult Education

Developing, Administering, and Evaluating Adult Education

Alan B. Knox
and Associates

Developing, Administering, and Evaluating Adult Education

Jossey-Bass Publishers

San Francisco • Washington • London • 1980

DEVELOPING, ADMINISTERING, AND EVALUATING ADULT EDUCATION
by Alan B. Knox and Associates

Copyright © 1980 by: Adult Education Association
of the United States of America
810 Eighteenth Street, N.W.
Washington, D.C. 20006

Jossey-Bass Inc., Publishers
433 California Street
San Francisco, California 94104

Jossey-Bass Limited
28 Banner Street
London EC1Y 8QE

Library of Congress Cataloging in Publication Data

Knox, Alan Boyd, 1931–
    Developing, administering, and evaluating adult
education.

    (Adult Education Association handbook series in
adult education)
        Bibliography: p. 263
        Includes index.
        1. Adult education.   I. Title.   II. Series: Adult
Education Association. Adult Education Association
handbook series in adult education.
LC5215.K63   374   80-7998
ISBN 0-87589-467-4

Manufactured in the United States of America

JACKET DESIGN BY WILLI BAUM

FIRST EDITION

Code 8027

The AEA Handbook Series
in Adult Education

WILLIAM S. GRIFFITH
University of British Columbia

HOWARD Y. McCLUSKY
University of Michigan

General Editors

Edgar J. Boone
Ronald W. Shearon
Estelle E. White
and Associates
Serving Personal and
Community Needs Through
Adult Education
April 1980

Huey B. Long
Roger Hiemstra
and Associates
Changing Approaches
to Studying Adult
Education
April 1980

John M. Peters
and Associates
Building an Effective
Adult Education
Enterprise
April 1980

Alan B. Knox
and Associates
Developing, Administering,
and Evaluating
Adult Education
October 1980

Foreword

Adult education as a field of study and of practice is not well understood by many literate and intelligent American adults whose exposure to the field has been limited to one or a few aspects of its apparently bewildering mosaic. Since 1926, when the American Association for Adult Education (AAAE) was founded, the leaders of that organization and its successor, the Adult Education Association of the U.S.A. (AEA), have striven to communicate both to the neophytes in the field and to the adult public an understanding of its diverse and complex enterprises. A major vehicle for accomplishing this communication has been a sequence of handbooks of adult education, issued periodically to convey a broad view of the mosaic. In 1934, 1936, and 1948 the AAAE published the first three handbooks. Although the Association had intended to issue a handbook every two years, that plan was not carried out for a number of reasons, including the outbreak of World War II and the termination of support by the Carnegie Corporation. Within three years of the publication of the 1948 handbook the Association itself dissolved in order to establish the AEA, which included the former members of both the AAAE and the Department of Adult Education of the National Education Association. It was nine years before the AEA was able to publish its first handbook, the fourth in the sequence, followed a decade later by the fifth version.

In the early 1970s both the Publications Committee of AEA and the Commission of the Professors of Adult Education (an affiliated organization of the AEA) explored the kinds of handbooks that could be designed to serve the changing nature and needs of the field. They found that different parts of the field were developing at different rates—in some areas information was becoming outdated rapidly, whereas in others a decennial handbook would be adequate to maintain currency. Moreover, the growing literature and the many developments in policies and programs led them to conclude that a single volume of traditional size would not be sufficient to treat the expanding knowledge base, the changing policies and practices, and the controversial topics in adult education. Accordingly, the Publications Committee decided that the next handbook would consist of several volumes, allowing the presentation of an increased amount of information on each of nine selected parts of the field and preparing the way for subsequent revisions of each volume independently on a schedule reflecting the pace of change in each area. The result is The AEA Handbook Series in Adult Education, which is being developed by the general editors with the guidance and assistance of the Publications Committee.

The present volume, *Developing, Administering, and Evaluating Adult Education,* focuses on the increasing importance of the administrator in determining program efficiency and effectiveness. Adult education administration is both qualitatively and quantitatively different from administration in traditional institutions. The range of administrative functions is broad, including scholarly, entrepreneurial, actuarial, and human relations skills—and adult education administrators need specially prepared materials to help them develop these skills. Accordingly, Alan B. Knox and his associates present a comprehensive survey of the literature relevant to such administrative competencies. The authors isolate selected components of the administrator's job and demonstrate how familiarity with these concepts can help the administrator better fulfill his responsibilities. In sum, this book redresses the previous imbalance in adult education literature that emphasized instruction and overlooked the critical significance of administration. In conjunction with the other eight volumes in the series, the book presents the adult education mosaic in a comprehensible and comprehensive manner for both workers in the field and others who seek to understand it.

Preparation of the series required the cooperation and dedicated efforts of scores of chapter authors, Publication Committee chairmen and members, and successive executive committees of the AEA. In bringing together the insights and perceptions of adult education scholars, the series is a major contribution of the Association to the advancement of an understanding of adult education as a field of study and of practice.

September 1980   WILLIAM S. GRIFFITH
                                                      HOWARD Y. MCCLUSKY
                                                      General Editors

Preface

This book provides a comprehensive overview of concepts and practices related to adult education program development and administration. It was prepared for practitioners in the field, especially program administrators who work with adult participants and resource people, such as teachers, discussion leaders, and consultants, in planning and conducting adult education programs in the form of courses, workshops, and guided individual study.

Adult education practitioners work in a wide range of agencies, including schools, colleges, businesses, churches, libraries, and associations. Usually they have had some experience in the field before reading a book like this one to gain a broader perspective on the concepts and practices that have been helpful to other practitioners.

Each practitioner devises distinctive methodologies that reflect procedures typical in the type of agency and the specific agency in which he works. Most practitioners will probably modify but not dramatically change these procedures. This book provides concepts, generalizations, and examples to help adult education administrators develop and modify their program development and administration strategies. It should help practitioners become more aware of their own strategies and discover alternative procedures and concepts from other settings that can be considered in the formulation of more effective strategies.

As used in this book, a distinction is made between concepts and descriptions of actions in which practitioners engage. A concept consists of formulated thought or opinion that expresses the central meaning of something that is known; a concept goes beyond an impression, notion, or passing thought and is a result of insight, reflection, and reasoning. The essence of a concept is that it is an abstract idea about what is or ought to be, generalized from particular instances. The generalization process may be based on insightful observation of practice, philosophical analysis, or analysis of empirical research data. A concept can deal with a dynamic process as well as a static situation, but it is more than a description of a relationship or procedure.

This book begins with an introductory chapter that describes and illustrates a broad and flexible approach to adult education program development and administration. This overview chapter contains highlights of the concepts and practices that are developed and illustrated in greater detail in subsequent chapters. The overview is followed by three chapters on major components of program development—program origins, program objectives and activities, and program evaluation. The next four chapters discuss broad aspects of program administration: participation (marketing and counseling), resources (financial and physical), staffing (recruitment and development), and leadership (including goal setting and coordination). The book concludes with a brief chapter on future directions of policy and research in adult education program development and administration.

The authors have selected concepts and generalizations they deem especially useful for practitioners and have indicated the supporting professional literature to facilitate further reading. Examples are also included to illustrate the actions corresponding to each major concept. This treatment should assist practitioners in their personal efforts to relate knowledge of the field to their own actions.

Urbana, Illinois   ALAN B. KNOX
September 1980

Contents

The Authors

LINDA K. BOCK, program development specialist, Office of Continuing Education and Public Service, University of Illinois, Urbana-Champaign.

DENNIS A. DAHL, associate vice-chancellor for academic affairs and director, Continuing Education and Public Service, University of Illinois, Urbana-Champaign.

ARDEN D. GROTELUESCHEN, associate professor of educational psychology, Office for the Study of Continuing Professional Education, University of Illinois, Urbana-Champaign.

JAMES C. HALL, dean, School of Continuing Education, Pace University.

ALAN B. KNOX, professor of continuing education, University of Illinois, Urbana-Champaign.

PHILIP M. NOWLEN, assistant dean, University Extension, and director, Center for Continuing Education, University of Chicago.

RONALD SZCZYPKOWSKI, president, Magi Educational Services.

JOY REED BELT, administrative assistant to the vice-president, Continuing Education and Public Service, University of Oklahoma.

THURMAN J. WHITE, vice-president, Continuing Education and Public Service, University of Oklahoma.

Developing,
Administering,
and Evaluating
Adult Education

Chapter One

◆◆◆◆◆◆◆◆◆◆◆◆◆◆◆◆◆◆◆◆◆◆◆
◆◆◆◆◆◆◆◆◆◆◆◆◆◆◆◆◆◆◆◆◆◆◆

Approach

◆◆◆◆◆◆◆◆◆◆◆◆◆◆◆◆◆◆◆◆◆◆◆
◆◆◆◆◆◆◆◆◆◆◆◆◆◆◆◆◆◆◆◆◆◆◆

Alan B. Knox

Each adult education administrator devises his own approach to program development and administration. These approaches vary to the extent that they are informed by relevant professional literature and the experience of other practitioners. This book will examine concepts and procedures relevant to adult education program development and administration, based on the relevant professional literature. The concepts and procedures drawn from research and experience can be used by administrators to guide and enrich their practice. Examples of typical and exemplary current practice are provided by the chapter authors as practical applications of the concepts in the daily activities of adult education administrators. Together the summaries of concepts and practices provide a framework for adult education administration.

The practice of adult education is an art based on science. Effective adult education administrators, teachers, and counselors work with adult participants in educational programs to help them achieve certain goals—in this case, learning. Effective practice is an art because it encompasses responsiveness, interpersonal relations, and values. Effective practice is based on science because it draws upon tested knowledge from various scholarly disciplines.

The art and the science of adult education are complementary: The art focuses on the goals and humanistic values that guide professional practice; the science focuses on research-based generalizations and orderly procedures that enable practitioners to perform effectively. Both the art and the science of professional practice depend on experience with people, relationships in specific situations, and concepts from the literature of the field.

A particularly important aspect of the art of professional practice is effective interpersonal relations. Many people and resources upon which adult education practitioners depend are provided voluntarily. This places a premium on persuading the adult participants and on winning and maintaining the cooperation of part-time instructors and of administrators who arrange for part-time use of facilities and assist with referrals and placements. Many program development procedures tend to be collaborative, as illustrated by planning committees composed of participants, resource people, and the program administrator. In these situations, establishing effective interpersonal relations is itself an art.

Adult education practitioners deal with many kinds of values, including client aspirations and life-style, parent organization priorities, societal expectations, and personal beliefs. Recognition, clarification, analysis, and accommodation of these values are important value judgments made by practitioners. Acceptance of differing values and resolution of value conflicts are aided by an openness to the values of others and by effective interpersonal relations.

The science of adult education is based on organized knowledge, including description, espoused theory, and research results. The essential ingredient in science is the data-based generalization that can be used to illuminate, analyze, guide, and interpret professional practice. In adult education, organized knowledge comes from many sources. Some refer specifically to adult and continuing education, such as studies conducted by professors and graduate students who specialize in adult education. Most formal research relevant to adult education comes from disciplines such as psychology or sociology, but often such research does not apply directly to practice or provide a blueprint for decision making by practitioners. Organized knowledge that deals specifically with adult and continuing education is therefore especially valuable in synthesizing and applying research findings from other disciplines.

Part of the scientific base of adult education administration consists of the relationships that are revealed by research findings. Practitioners must make decisions about such relationships as: the likelihood that a given instructional method will lead to learner persistence and achievement; the likelihood that one mix of marketing procedures will be more effective than others in attracting and retaining adult participants; and the likelihood that one approach to the program planning process will be more effective than others in producing a successful program and winning cooperation from relevant experts and groups. Reflecting on past experience can help practitioners make such decisions. Organized knowledge can also enable practitioners to benefit from other people's experience and mistakes. Many research conclusions indicate the likelihood of certain relationships, and some findings even indicate variability from one situation to another, such as rural or urban settings, formal or informal programs, bright or dull learners, receptive or resistent collaborators. Thus, a major contribution of research is to increase the accuracy of the practitioner's estimate that a given relationship will occur. Practitioners who understand and can apply research results related to adult education are better prepared than practitioners who do not utilize this information in their ability (1) to recognize the salient features of a situation at the diagnostic stage, (2) to include and combine the crucial ingredients at the planning stage, and (3) to appreciate the most influential dynamics at the implementation stage.

This introductory chapter provides an overview of the topics to be dealt with in detail in subsequent chapters. These topics deal with program development (origins, objectives, activities, and evaluation) and administration (participation, resources, staffing, and leadership). These sections parallel and highlight the main ideas of the subsequent chapters of the book as a whole.

Program Development

Program ideas may originate informally as adult educators work with current programs, but they may also result from awareness of traditions in the field and from formal procedures such as needs assessment and exploration of future directions. It is usually necessary to select a manageable set of clear and realistic objectives from a range of potential objectives related to a promising program idea and to select and organize learning activities to achieve those objectives. The results must inevitably undergo evaluation. In addition to the informal evaluation that always occurs, formal evaluation increases the likelihood that evaluative judgments are based on adequate evidence and that evaluative judgments will be available to those who can use them. Evaluation activities include planning, selecting, describing, judging, and reporting.

Origins

Most educational programs for adults evolve informally as program administrators contemplate current practices and resources in the sponsoring agency and in similar agencies. More formal procedures can also be used to consider and choose new program directions (McKinley, 1973); including educational needs assessment, reflections on traditions in the field, and exploration of future directions. The use of systematic procedures to draw on multiple sources of program ideas contributes to program responsiveness and effectiveness.

One of the richest sources of new program ideas is an understanding of adults as learners. Familiarity with adult development and learning provides a perspective within which practitioners can plan and conduct educational programs responsive to adult tasks and aspirations (Havighurst and Orr, 1956; Knox, 1977a, 1979b). In addition, needs assessment procedures can identify the most urgent and widespread educational needs on which to focus program development efforts (Bradshaw, 1974; Hertling and Greenburg, 1974; Monette, 1977; Valley and Hamilton, 1976).

Finally, practitioners can generate and refine new program ideas by systematic exploration of likely and desirable alternative futures (Ziegler, 1970). The resulting conclusions can contribute to agency priorities and to the selection and implementation of programs that are most desirable, feasible, and complementary with other agencies and resource allocations. In Chapter Two, Philip Nowlen shows how an insightful program planner can "scan" four settings—individual, group, organization, and community—to improve his ways of identifying promising program origins. In describing the scanning process, Nowlen details how the consideration of traditions, context analysis, needs assessment, and desirable future directions aids the planner in formulating creative program ideas.

Objectives and Activities

Core program development tasks typically include establishing clear and realistic objectives and organizing learning activities to achieve those objectives. Practitioners with program administration responsibilities, such as conference coordinators, often serve as members of planning committees, making decisions about educational objectives and learning activities as well as selecting and working with resource people. Program ideas typically yield a more extensive and diffuse range of potential objectives than can be accommodated in a single educational program with limited time and resources.

The main reason for setting objectives and selecting and organizing learning activities is to enable participants to increase their proficiency in ways suggested by the program objectives (Northcutt, 1973; Wientge and DuBois, 1964). In most educational programs for adults, in addition to striving for the achievement of educational objectives through modification of knowledge, skills, and attitudes, program planners often encourage the application of new learning in the form of changed performance (Knox, 1975b). One purpose of program evaluation is to collect and analyze evidence of the impact of the educational program on participant proficiency and performance, with special attention to the contribution of educational methods and materials. The resulting conclusions can assist subsequent program development.

In Chapter Three, Ronald Szczypkowski discusses a rationale and provides an explanation of the terminology dealing with the administrator's involvement in program development. In doing so, Szczypkowski shows how the skillful administrator considers agency purposes, relevant content, target audiences, framing of objectives, and systematic procedures for the selection of objectives. From these he demonstrates a method for selecting and sequencing learning activities to achieve those objectives.

Evaluation

Program evaluation includes formal internal and external evaluation to supplement the inevitable informal evaluation (Tyler, 1969). Formal evaluation increases the likelihood that evaluative judgments will be based on adequate evidence and that conclusions will be available to those who can use them. Adult education program evaluation is a process of judging program effectiveness in ways that encourage people associated with the program to use the conclusions for program improvement and justification (Knox, 1969).

The program evaluation process can be used to improve program quality, justify and advocate program accountability, and facilitate communication among people associated with the program (Worthen and Sanders, 1973). Program evaluation promotes decision making by learners, teachers, administrators, and policy makers, and it should take into account the various contexts in which they function. Evaluation activities include planning, selecting, describing, judging, and reporting (Grotelueschen, Gooler, and Knox, 1976).

In Chapter Four, Arden Grotelueschen addresses both conceptual and practical aspects of program evaluation. By providing a framework of evaluation purposes, elements, and components, he shows how an evaluator can deal systematically with his tasks. Focusing on the ingredients of program evaluation (objectives, audience, issues, resources, evidence, data gathering, analysis, and reporting) and using examples drawn from adult basic education, religious education, and continuing medical education, Grotelueschen illustrates practical evaluation plans. He distinguishes between research and evaluation, and deals with important issues each program planner must consider in educational evaluation.

Program Administration

Program administration covers a wide range of activities. Initial and continued adult education participation is encouraged by information and counseling services, which relate to both program development and administration (Knox and Farmer, 1977). In addition to recruiting participants and staff, the adult education agency must acquire financial and physical resources, some of which are voluntary contributions. The attraction, selection, and development of teachers, counselors, administrators, and support staff is an especially important function. Administrative leadership undergirds all of these functions and is informed by an understanding of organizational and administrative behavior, program productivity, priority setting, and administrative strategies. The ultimate goal is agency coordination.

Participation

Many influences encourage or discourage adults to begin and to continue participating in an education activity. Two of the most important of these influences are the marketing and counseling practices of the adult education administrator. In Chapter Five, Linda Bock draws from the research on participation to show how age, level of aspiration, reference groups, self-concept, previous education, and sex can be considered in designing marketing and counseling practices to increase both enrollment and retention in adult education programs. Bock explains how marketing efforts can plan recruitment, taking into consideration both the personal and situational factors that enter into the decision making of potential participants. She discusses the complementary counseling roles played by professional counselors, administrators, teachers, and paraprofessionals, especially as they relate to preventing or reducing dropout from educational programs. Using illustrations of effective and innovative marketing and counseling practices, Bock demonstrates how administrators can use an understanding of key concepts to build the supports required to increase recruitment and retention in adult education programs.

Resources

In addition to recruiting participants, the adult education agency acquires a variety of financial and nonfinancial resources. For example, a public school adult education division obtains financial income from participant fees, some reimbursements by employers, ongoing support from state and federal tax funds, subsidy by the local school system, and short-term external grants. Also, cosponsors may make in-kind contributions of facilities, materials, and volunteer services. Other resources (physical facilities, films, and library books, for example) may be purchased or rented with adult education funds.

The image of an agency as worth supporting as well as the number of satisfied participants strongly influence the acquisition of resources, because most adult education agencies—lacking exclusive facilities, full-time faculty, or an automatic flow of participants or finances—must seek new resources every few months. Private manifest demand (individual voluntary registration not subsidized by employers or other sponsors) for adult education by participants reflects the belief that the benefits exceed costs. (In addition to fees paid, total participant costs include participation costs, such as transportation, and opportunity costs, that is, the amount of income an individual loses by spending the time to take a class.) Public demand is a reflection of the public's willingness to support specific kinds of adult education as indicated by tax support for specific programs that may be free to the intended participants. Adult education is considered a public investment when the returns to the community are seen as being greater than the returns to individual participants. These returns may be in terms of quality of life, improved citizenship, reduced welfare costs, and so on.

In Chapter Six, Dennis Dahl discusses the range of both financial and nonfinancial resources needed by adult education agencies to conduct programs. He examines procedures for acquiring resources, influences on the acquisition processes, planning of resource use, and evaluation of alternate uses. In describing current practices, he emphasizes how concepts are applied in a variety of agencies and then explores ways the practices could be improved in the future. As competition increases for these resources among potential providers, as governments and professional associations develop regulations for continuing education, and as the number of clients increases, administrators will find Dahl's insights helpful in their attempt to obtain, and most effectively use, resources in building superior adult education programs.

Staffing

Staffing is one of the most important functions of the adult education administrator. It is through staff members that most of the work of the agency is accomplished, and their proficiency, dedication, and performance are crucial to the success of the program. Accordingly, the staffing function is of strategic importance in maintaining and upgrading the capacity of any agency to conduct exemplary adult education programs.

In Chapter Seven, James Hall decries the ad hoc approach to staffing sometimes found in adult education agencies. He calls for the formulation of policies to set the framework for sound staffing practices. Making use of research in personnel administration, Hall suggests how to define jobs, recruit staff, and develop and retain those who are hired. Writing from the perspective of a practicing administrator, he discusses legal questions and systematic procedures for recruitment and helping the new employee become adjusted to his organization. As he compares orientation and employee development efforts among agencies of varying sizes, Hall calls attention to the discrepancies between typical and ideal practices, showing both how practice can be improved and what results can be anticipated. Finally, Hall effectively demonstrates how staffing sets the context and establishes the limits to organizational development efforts in adult education agencies.

Leadership

Effective agency leadership by adult education administrators reflects an understanding of organizational and administrative

behavior, program productivity, priority setting, and administrative strategies. In addition to proficient planning and implementation of program development, attraction of participants and staff,
and deployment of resources, administrative leadership entails
coordination of these functions so that the individual programs are
conducted in concert and the total agency achieves its objectives
and runs smoothly.

Some features of adult education administration distinguish it from administration in other fields. The main purpose
of the adult education agency is to help adults learn and directly
utilize their increased proficiency in family, work, and community
living. The agency is typically a dependent unit of an organization
with major purposes other than the education of adults. This marginality increases the competition for resources within the parent
organization. Both participants and resource people usually work
part time, which increases the importance of administrative roles
regarding program development. These characteristics, in turn,
contribute to an administrative orientation toward the community
service area as well as toward the parent organization, and for
most agencies this orientation is reflected in strong enrollment
objectives. These characteristics present special challenges to
the administrator who aspires to lead his agency toward the more
effective achievement of its goals while at the same time providing the ideas and challenges that will inspire his staff to superior
performance.

In Chapter Eight, Thurman White and Joy Belt discuss
ways in which the performance of selected leadership functions
influences the ability of an adult education agency to cope with
internal and external needs in a changing environment. Stability
is essential, they argue, and so is change. Noting that few adult
education administrators engage in long-range planning, these observers charge that placing undue emphasis on short-range goals
threatens the long-term stability of the organization. One means of
ensuring that the long-range outlook is given adequate attention is
the establishment of governing and advisory boards that focus on
policies, plans, and objectives. In working with such boards, with
staff, and with the adult clientele of the agency, the administrator
is primarily responsible for stimulating, guiding, facilitating, and

assessing change efforts. He does so through the leadership he provides in planning, organizing, and evaluating. And although all members of the agency, staff, clientele, and boards have an interest in the organization's long-term operation, it is the primary responsibility of a single individual, the administrator, to provide the leadership needed to make change possible without jeopardizing long-term prospects.

The Application of Knowledge

Effective adult education practitioners are able to put their ideas into action, producing results. This book is designed to present some major concepts that practitioners have found useful and to suggest some ways in which these concepts can be implemented. However, this attention to applications can only be illustrative; each practitioner must develop personal strategies for applying knowledge resources to action problems and opportunities.

An administrator of educational programs for adults typically acquires professional proficiency through a gradual socialization process that begins where the predecessor left off and is modified through interaction with people in the agency. A practitioner who reads professional literature or attends professional meetings and courses gains a perspective on professional practices and goals that goes beyond the perspective of the immediate agency setting. This broader perspective, in turn, helps to produce or clarify discrepancies between what is and what might be. Efforts by practitioners to overcome these discrepancies are indicators of professional progress.

The future vitality of adult education may well depend on deliberate attention to discrepancies between current and improved practice. In the past, progress in the field resulted primarily from dedicated amateurs pioneering new programs and practices with little attention to professional literature. Given the low public visibility of the field, benign neglect by parent organizations, and limited contact across segments of the field, this emphasis on isolated innovation and deemphasis on learning from other people was understandable and possibly even functional.

Recently, however, there has been an increasing premium

on a broader perspective on adult education and a sense of direction based on a familiarity with literature and practice elsewhere. Lifelong learning during the adult years has become very visible, policy makers and administrators in parent organizations and government agencies now covet a piece of the action, and demands for accountability and coordination among provider agencies are becoming more insistent. The result is a challenge to the leaders in the field.

The underlying thesis of this book is that vital leadership for adult education entails more than hustle and responsiveness. Effective administration entails a sense of direction based on understanding of goals of individuals, society, and parent organizations as well as mastery of procedures to pursue those goals. The evolving field is too complex, fast moving, and competitive to allow each administrator to discover independently the crucial issues and practices. In the future, success in the field will depend increasingly on the ability to learn from the concepts and experience of others and to apply this new understanding to action problems and opportunities. The authors of this book present a range of concepts and experience as a source to those who are developing, administering, and evaluating adult education today.

Chapter Two

Program Origins

Philip M. Nowlen

"Close to three million years ago," wrote Richard Leakey (1977, p. 8), "on a campsite near the east shore of Kenya's spectacular Lake Turkana, a primitive human picked up a water-smoothed stone and with a few skillful strikes transformed it into an instrument. . . . It is a heart-quickening thought that we share the same genetic heritage with the hands that shaped the tool . . . and the mind that decided to make the tool." Almost three million years after the Turkana tool was used, Michelangelo saw his David in a piece of marble so flawed that it had been cast aside, unwanted by other sculptors. The origins of the tool and the sculpture lay not in the smooth stone and flawed marble but in the minds of the people who fashioned them—minds prepared and disciplined to see technology and sculpture in objects others recognized only as stone.

Likewise, the origins of the continuing education programs lie not simply in evolving life roles, new government legislation, community problems, the increasing employment of women, or additional leisure time but in the minds of adult educators, minds prepared and disciplined by the literature and tradition of the field to see potential programs in events, problems, and expressions that others see only as personal moments of interest or worry.

I use the term *origins* rather than the more familiar *needs assessment* in order to be as inclusive as possible of the influences at work in the disciplined minds of adult educators. Needs assessment is only one of a number of formal procedures instrumental in generating, locating, selecting, or refining program ideas. Other formal procedures include inventories of agency resources, surveys of similar agencies, diagnostic techniques, and the like. Program ideas also appear or evolve informally, even intuitively. Among the influences frequently at play are the values and goals of the parent organization of the adult education agency, the literature and tradition of the field, current thinking on adult education philosophy and procedures, and the personal values of the adult educator. Finally, a specific needs assessment is typically shaped by existing suggestions of program ideas, which the assessment instrument is in part designed to test.

These influences and procedures all contribute to the adult educator's "scanning devices," which view the complex structure of a phenomenon (the economic, environmental, and historical structure of an event, for example) and facilitate the adult educator's probing of each aspect of the infrastructure (life roles, performance of professions, function of systems, and the like). For example, the increasing employment of women is a phenomenon that might be subjected to the following scanning devices: Dewey's doctrine of learner-centered interests and needs prompts the drafting and application of a needs assessment instrument influenced by Knowles (1970). The application of the concept of adult life roles, taken from the social sciences (Havighurst and Orr, 1956), suggests a scan to reveal program ideas that relate generally high motivation for improvement to successful past performance providing the desire for yet better performance. Or, using some of the perspectives brought together by Knox (1977a), one might scan the increasing employment of women for non-work-related program ideas: the broader problem of sex-role stereotyping, family-role stress, and an evolving but still integrated self-concept. Alternatively, one might see in the increasing employment of women the continuing education needs of the employer organizations when one scans through the lens of organization development (Bennis, 1969). Scanning the same phenomenon through the lens of agency resources, one might discover an agency research paper reinterpreting the significance of unemployment statistics as a direct result of increased employment of married women. And here we have a list of scans that only begins to illustrate the possibilities. The number and kind of scans need be limited only by the capability to act upon the results.

Settings for Scanning

Recent surveys of program development among the professions (Pennington and Green, 1976) and among member institutions of the National University Extension Association (Hertling and Greenburg, 1974) as well as descriptions from the late 1950s (London, 1960) reveal that adult education programs occur within one of four broad interpersonal settings, distinguished by interaction patterns between the learner and other program participants. The ideas for these programs also originate within these interpersonal categories.

1. The individual setting
   a. The individual learner has minimal interaction with other adults engaged in the same program.
   b. Examples are correspondence study, television courses, and one-to-one coaching (such as that between farmer and agricultural extension advisor).
   c. The selection of the program and of corresponding materials can be highly responsive to the individual learner. The person developing the educational materials and the program advisor tend to have the controlling influence on program ideas.
2. The temporary group setting

     a. Adults with minimal previous contact with each other, if any, assemble for the program and at the end return to their separate settings and pursuits.

     b. Most conferences and workshops involve temporary groups, as do evening courses.

     c. The planning committee has the major influence on the basic program idea. If there is only one teacher or resource person, he or she also has a major influence on the basic program idea as well as modifications of the program in process. Consensus among participants can be used to modify the program in process as well. The program administrator can exert major influence on generation of the program idea (when the planning committee is interdisciplinary in character) and on refinement of the idea (when there are two or more teachers and resource people).

3. The organization setting

     a. Members of an organization participate in an educational program in which the prior and subsequent relationships among the learners have a major influence on the program.

     b. Organizational development is the main example, but the characteristics are much the same for in-service programs such as those designed for hospital physicians and residents.

     c. Program ideas tend to evolve from major problems and opportunities related to organizational functioning. The generation and implementation of those ideas often reflect the relative political clout of various parts of the organization.

4. The community setting

     a. The educational program focuses on problems and assembles participants who relate to two or more organizations or segments of a neighborhood or community. One of the program purposes, usually designated as most important, is community improvement.

     b. Community development is the main example.

     c. Program ideas tend to evolve from major problems and opportunities related to community functioning. Some ideas arise from events themselves: a court desegregation decision, a sharp rise in unemployment, and the like. Other ideas are selectively chosen as "issues" because a programming agency chooses to treat them as such—for example, infant mortality and morbidity in the ghetto or the impact on private charities of closing federal tax loopholes.

Houle (1972) has developed a detailed eleven-category analysis of program origin settings, and these settings may be linked with one another in complex programs. For example, a nontraditional degree program is obviously expressed in the individual and temporary group settings and may even make use of organizational and community settings. Nevertheless the entire program may be shaped by an individual learning contract and therefore may be seen as primarily determined by the individual setting, with the primary advisor as the most influential resource person. In organizational development, the program may design a special work project team, each member chosen because of his special skills. In this case, the design and primary learning setting will be organizational, although one or another member may require use of a temporary group (such as a workshop offered by an agency outside the organization) as a portion of the overall organizational program. Finally, a temporary group such as a conference on marketing adult education programs may make use of one-on-one coaching opportunities, but the basic design and setting remains that of the temporary group.

Sources of Program Ideas

Hertling and Greenburg (1974) found that most administrators and program planners rely heavily upon their experience and intuitive judgment in generating program ideas. Pennington and Green (1976) characterize this reliance as "flying by the seat of the pants." Experience and intuitive judgment can be the product of careful reflection on the tradition and purposes of the agency. It can represent familiarity with the literature of the field: its philosophy, history, and operating traditions. Informed intuition functions optimally in scanning for program ideas with the aid of the following procedures and influences.

Local Agency Objectives and Strategies

Many contributors to the field of adult education have discussed the influence of an agency's founding instruments, current directions, and operational strategies on the search for program ideas (Houle, 1972; Knowles, 1970; Knox, 1968a; Knox, 1968b). As Houle puts it, "Despite initial limitations, the range of choices open to the founders of an organization or association is usually greater than that available to their successors, who will always have to deal with the tangible and intangible legacies of the past" (1972, p. 117).

The tangible past—such as the founding documents of the agency, its history, and its plans for the future—are inescapable influences on the search for program ideas. Intangible legacies—such as the invisible borders of the "acceptable," the unspoken rules of procedure, and the prevailing ethos—also serve as guides for the practitioner seeking program ideas. Programs generated with these constraints in mind tend to have agency-wide support, because they can be presumed to advance the agency toward unfulfilled objectives or, at least, to be fully in keeping with the agency's spirit and practice. This is true whether an organization's goals and strategies are directly related to continuing education or not. For example, the idea of an "alumni college," broadly defined as a series of experiences designed to refresh alumni intellectually, socially, even spiritually, is an idea strongly supportive of certain agency goals which might spread rapidly through interagency contacts. A more specific example is a medical school that needed to admit more patients who would be promising teaching material. An in-service continuing education program conducted at community hospitals by the medical school faculty created ties of professional respect and personal friendship that resulted in a substantial increase of referrals of the kind desired by the teaching hospital. In yet another case, the mandate given to a secondary school regarding evening programs for adults resulted in that agency's providing a site and coordination for the course offerings of three major universities and one community college. This interinstitutional cooperation is unlikely to have been mandated to each of the institutions of higher learning, yet the coordinated efforts of the institutions added success to the overall program.

In practice, attention to local agency objectives and traditions as a source of new program ideas tends to be implicit and informal. Program directions typically evolve as adult participants, resource people, and program administrators propose new courses or workshops that are outgrowths of familiar programs. However, administrators could use an agency's purposes and traditions for new program ideas more deliberately by analyzing the fit between formal statements of purpose, current program offerings, and emerging realities. This process might occur as part of an accreditation self-study for an educational institution, more modestly as an analysis by an adult education agency staff of program goals and directions, or in a comparison of a current program with the expectations of people associated with the program to identify discrepancies that suggest program modifications (Knox and others, 1974).

The Literature

Beyond local and agency-specific sources of program ideas, practitioners have potential access to accumulated literature on the historical, philosophical, and operational traditions of adult continuing education. Especially valuable to administrators are the differing approaches to generic issues of various sponsoring agencies such as community colleges, labor unions, libraries, universities, and professional associations. Assumptions and values expressed in the literature and current thinking affect the entire program development process but are especially important for the origins of their program directions precisely because they so shape subsequent developments.

Historical Literature. A wide range of program ideas has emerged in the past along with various societal influences and professional initiatives. Knowles (1960, 1977) offers a useful summary of these program ideas (although his studies are limited to adult education in the United States). Knowles emphasizes the importance of vocational and religious instruction during colonial times, followed by an intense search for knowledge triggered by the industrial revolution and the Enlightenment. He emphasizes the development of voluntary associations and agencies and the emergence of a national educational system in the years between the Civil War and World War I. Next, Knowles chronicles the development of quite varied institutions such as the Chautauqua, correspondence courses, agricultural education, workers' education, the tripling of the number of colleges and universities, and the appearance of free public libraries and evening schools. Knowles concludes by observing seven trends (1960, pp. 23–25):

> 1. There has been a pressure toward national integration of adult education activities.
> 2. There has been a drive toward integration of adult education at the local level.
> 3. Large-scale support of adult education by private foundations has developed.
> 4. Government support of adult education has been expanding.
> 5. A distinctive body of knowledge and techniques has begun to emerge.
> 6. The student body of adult education has greatly expanded.
> 7. Adult education has become a conscious and differentiated function of an increasing number of institutions.

Knowles also reports a significant change in the role of the adult educator from "willing amateur to trained specialist." A change in basic theoretical conception has also occurred "from remedial to developmental" (1970, pp. 33, 34).

Studying the history of the adult education movement enriches our scanning for ideas, and reviewing the history of adult education as a distinctive academic field of study reveals widely varying views about the essential nature of that field. Houle (1972) has developed six "credos" that illustrate the various views of the nature of adult education:

1. Adult education is a movement unified by a common effort to achieve a single all-encompassing goal.

2. The task of the educator of adults is to discover what adults themselves know they need to learn and to provide it for them.
3. Educators of adults should adapt the methods of other forms of schooling to fit the requirements of adult students.
4. Powerful, creative leaders are important to the adult education process.
5. General institutional processes must be improved.
6. Educators of adults should stress informality, improvisation, and innovative thinking and methods.

(For a more comprehensive discussion of adult education as a movement and field, see Grattan, 1955.)

Few practitioners are familiar with historical trends in the field of adult and continuing education, because past and emerging trends are usually taught in graduate courses on adult and continuing education but seldom appear in professional association meetings or in casual professional reading. However, adult education administrators who understand major trends in the field can better identify hazards to avoid and influences to utilize and can recognize the relationships between agency developments and societal influences. This kind of historical understanding can be gained through personal reading or through professional development activities conducted by agencies or professional associations.

Philosophical Literature. The values and meanings associated with ideas and practices is the concern of the philosophical literature. This body of research increases both the number of phenomena recognized by practitioners as worthy of careful scanning and the ways in which each phenomenon might yield program ideas. The philosophical influences upon adult education can be configured in various ways, but the major innovators and their contributions are generally agreed upon. Here again, Houle (1972) is of great assistance, and the following overview is essentially his.

Adult educators in the 1920s and '30s found in John Dewey's protest against stifling rigidity and mindless formality a spirit close to their own. Dewey's pragmatic approach provided a rational foundation for their practices in program development. Specific applications of Dewey's thought to adult education were made by Lindeman (1961) and Kotinsky (1933); in fact, Dewey's concepts influenced most of the systems that followed.

Some systems are based on Ralph Tyler's thought. Pennington and Green join Houle in judging most current theoretical formulations of program planning processes to have been heavily influenced by Tyler (Houle, 1972; Pennington and Green, 1976). Tyler (1950) is prescriptive, defining objectives in terms of learners, content specialists, and contemporary life. The results are then screened by philosophy and psychology so as to develop specific objectives to guide instruction; supportive experiences are chosen and organized; and evaluation measures the extent to which means have brought about the specified ends.

A very different approach is set forth by Decker F. Walker (1971). Walker's model is descriptive of actual practice and will surprise the practitioner by revealing the small ratio of explicit planning decisions to decisions reached implicitly.

Social psychology was applied to educational theory in the work of Kurt Lewin. Lewin's conceptions in the 1930s, particularly as applied in the late 1940s by Bradford (1947), resulted in the group dynamics approach. Although opinion is mixed regarding the value of specific procedures (such as the encounter group), the field remains persuaded of the need to deal with the issues of learning in groups. Another application of Lewin (by Verner, 1964, among others) analyzes the processes of interaction between the change agent and individual or group clients. The resultant change theory is of greatest use in the organizational and community settings (Insko, 1967).

Community development is the basis of still another philosophical approach. Similar in strategy to change theory and similar in its problem-solving approach to Dewey, community development is defined by McClusky (1960, pp. 416–417) as "the induction and educational management of that kind of interaction between the community and its people which leads to the improvement of both. Community in this context would be regarded as external, buildings, transportations systems, and the like as well as internal, that is, ideals and values held in common." Perhaps if more adult education agencies in the 1960s had been familiar with philosophers like Richard Poston, who wrote that community development is "a process of self-discovery by which the people learn how to . . . solve their community problems" (1954, p. 194), those agencies would have been more cautious in their assumptions about the solutions that they believed would come from the agencies' interventions in the community. In any event, the community development movement is still recovering from its decline brought on by unrealistic goals, an illustration of the essential correctives the sources have to offer.

Systems analysis has resulted in another approach. Knowles' definition of systems analysis is a procedure "for constructing models of total systems that range from simple graphic portrayals of relationships to highly mathematical abstractions" (1970, p. 261). Lifelong learning could, in this sense, be considered a permanent system and each experience a temporary system. In organizational development, the organization is the permanent system and the continuing education experience is the temporary system.

H. M. Kallen (1962) makes a number of contributions to our understanding of the philosophy of the field that deserve special attention. Kallen points out that although Edward Thorndike was influenced heavily by Dewey, Thorndike broke free of the teaching-learning relationship by treating learning experimentally as an independent variable. This methodology was based on observation of animal learning patterns, and its legacy to adult education was modern educational psychology. Kallen also emphasizes the influence of values in the education process, claiming that the remarkably different program offerings by agencies with almost identical settings, publics, and philosophies must ultimately be attributed to differences in the values of the agencies' leaders. Kallen's sense of values is that the process of being, especially of human being, is liberty, "a chaos of spontaneity," and that order is established by foregathered primal liberties. Applied to adult education, Kallen's values underlie some practitioners' understanding of the liberal education of adults—the identification of closures, walls, bonds of any sort and their elimination through education.

In the 1930s, the American Association for Adult Education included many people such as Eduard Lindeman, Lyman Bryson, and Harry and Bonaro Overstreet, whose orientation was more to social philosophy than to daily administrative concerns of practitioners. However, without adult education graduate programs and professional associations, most practitioners were aware of neither the existence of a field of adult education nor related philosophical issues. During the past two generations, as the qualifications of practitioners in the field have shifted "from willing amateur to trained specialist," there has been a decline in attention to social philosophy as reflected in professional association meetings and publications, but a growing number of practitioners in the field are attending to emerging issues and their implications for programming. The philosophical literature of the field can help practitioners decide to what extent their values are reflected in program emphases.

Operational Literature. Research on actual program operations and participation in field-wide professional associations help practitioners relate program activities elsewhere to new program directions locally. In scanning for ideas, the individual or agency field of vision is crucial. Will centralization or decentralization of a function be more productive? Obviously the way the agency is organized and operates will be one of the key factors, but how does the practitioner decide? Thorough knowledge of the formal and informal structures of the agency as presently constituted, coupled with familiarity with the literature on organizational development, organizational change, and the financial and human costs of change, are essential guides. Bennis (1969) offers an introduction to such considerations, particularly in his references and selected bibliography. After "positioning" the agency for maximum vision of potential ideas, the staffing function should be carefully considered in terms of the different leadership styles demanded by differently structured organizations. The issues that arise in choosing the appropriate operational configuration are reflected in the majority and minority views of organizational arrangements within Michigan State University's Task Force on Lifelong Education (Hesburgh, Miller, and Wharton, 1973).

Hertling and Greenburg's (1974) study of the methods used by National University Extension Association member institutions to determine continuing education needs and interests is an example of useful descriptive operational literature. Their results confirm that most of the research conducted to determine program ideas is done in house by personnel for whom conducting research represents only one of their responsibilities. Only 16 percent of these personnel reported that a university-wide unit did the research, and only 6 percent used private agencies. According to the Hertling and Greenburg study, the sources of information reported by respondents as most frequently used were employer-employee groups, individual members of their faculties, community groups or organizations (such as Rotary and the League of Women Voters), and key individuals in the community. Questionnaires and interviews used to survey present enrollees were judged most effective; surveying the general population was judged least effective. Eighty percent of the respondents reported that their resources for conducting research were insufficient.

The Pennington and Green (1976) comparison of program development processes in six professions identified and described planning strategies. Resulting similarities were analyzed, yielding an identification of six clusters of activities: originating the idea, developing the idea, making a commitment, developing the program, teaching the course, and evaluating the impact. Cluster one, "originating the idea," includes formal needs assessment, request from clients and client groups, the availability of project monies, legislative mandates, and suggestions from academic sources. Typically, ideas originating from the outside clients or client groups were received by either a faculty member or continuing education staff member. A significant finding was the overlap between idea origination and the other five clusters. Consider the implications for the generation of ideas from the four interpersonal settings noted earlier if the influential person or people described in each setting were sensitized to scan for new program ideas in planning, executing, and evaluating educational experiences. The very act of refining a program idea often involves eliminating related notions that might be developed into other programs. Unanticipated questions and issues may arise in the course of an educational activity, signaling possible program ideas to participants. In other words, the program development process serves to create the intended program and to generate a wealth of potential new program ideas if people with influence in the process can be helped to see and record them.

In practice, the two most widespread ways of obtaining new program ideas from current practice are scanning materials from other programs and noting potential spin-offs from current local programs. Many practitioners obtain materials—such as brochures, reports, and articles from other programs—which suggest ideas for new local programs, and even format and procedures for doing so. Conversations with colleagues from other agencies at professional association meetings serve similar purposes. There appears to be less deliberate attention to generating spin-offs from local programs. Participants are sometimes asked to suggest other program topics of interest on evaluation forms. Resource people and program administrators and counselors are less often asked about new program ideas. Administrators can stimulate the generation of new program ideas by summarizing current efforts and by asking agency personnel to explore new program directions creatively.

In addition to the foregoing sampling from the general literature, each segment of the broad adult education field has a rich literature of its own that highlights program ideas, including books, journal articles, and even compilations of research abstracts (Niemi, Grabowski, and Kuusisto, 1976).

Context Analysis

There are two distinct ways in which context analysis can serve as a fruitful source of program ideas. The first approach assumes the object of analysis to be the agency in its various contexts. Thus, the professional interests and personal values of program administrators will be reflected in the generation of new programs. Members of the agency's parent organization—such as professors, congregants, and division managers outside the training department—have specialized experience, professional interests, and personal values that can be used to plan programs not likely to be provided by other agencies. Some agencies have organized internal information systems to provide regular input of this sort; others make only an occasional survey of internal resources. Outside resource people can also be a source of new program ideas, as can the agency's funding sources in government, private foundations, and the like. Social, political, and economic trends in the community and nation—the agency's macroenviron-ment—may also be perceived as an influence on the needs of adults for further education (National Center for Education Statistics, 1976). The identification of program ideas from sources like these, outside the agency, when linked with unique internal expertise, provides a very sound basis for organization-wide commitment to the adult education agency.

The second approach of context analysis assumes the object of analysis to be adults in their various roles and contexts. This understanding is influenced by Havighurst's application of role concept as used in social science research on adult education. Havighurst and Orr (1956) view middle age as a developmental period determined by three major forces: (1) the expectations and values of our society; (2) the maturing and then the aging of our bodies; and (3) our own personal values or aspirations. These forces result in eleven categories of tasks, each a fascinating source for program ideas (1956; p. 9):

1. Setting adolescent children free and helping them to become happy and responsible adults.
2. Discovering new satisfactions in relations with one's spouse.
3. Working out an affectionate but independent relationship with aging parents.
4. Creating a beautiful and comfortable home.
5. Reaching the peak in one's work career.
6. Achieving mature social and civic responsibility.
7. Accepting and adjusting to the physiological changes of middle age.
8. Making an art of friendship.
9. Making a satisfying and creative use of leisure time.
10. Becoming or maintaining oneself as an active club or organiza-tion member.
11. Becoming or maintaining oneself as an active church member.

While these are individual needs, the cumulative need for im-proved performance in these developmental tasks becomes a social need and, thus, an even more appropriate object for adult educa-tion. One problem in responding with appropriate programs, how-ever, is that those who have the worst need may lack sufficient insight to interpret it as a felt educational need (Havighurst and Orr, 1956).

A comprehensive consolidation of research and information on adult development, abundant in implications for the practitioner, is Alan Knox's *Adult Development and Learning* (1977a). Knox pays particular attention to the context for development. Community differences, social change, attitudes toward adulthood, intergenerational relations, political power, social class, living arrangements, and contextual opportunities are all considered, and Knox finds substantial evidence that the opportunity system in a community affects adult participation in educational activities. The London, Wenkert, and Hagstrom study (1963) underscores this point with the following conclusions:

1. There is a strong relationship between organizational and adult participation.
2. Adult males who have high rates of participation in adult education are also likely to be engaged in a greater variety of informal leisure activities.
3. Frequent participation in cultural matters, social relations outside the immediate family or neighborhood or immediate work situation, and active engagement in sports tend to be highly related to participation in adult education.
4. Studying at home as part of the job most typically characterizes the professional and technical occupations and is an important predictor of participation.
5. The desire to change jobs is also an important indicator of the likelihood of participating in adult education.
6. Awareness of existing opportunities is a necessary condition for participating in adult education.

Although contextual factors greatly affect program development, most adult education program administrators seem to give little deliberate attention to them. These factors include travels within the parent organization; efforts by other providers in the service area; social, political, and economic conditions; influences on adult development (such as satisfying the developmental tasks) that affect the clientele; and links between client systems and resource systems. Administrators who analyze these contextual factors to generate new program ideas use various procedures: participating in groups in the parent organization and in the community service area; raising questions with group members about influences and trends; exploring conclusions with agency staff regarding implications for new program directions; and periodically scanning media (such as organizational newsletters, community newspapers, or radio call-in programs) to note emerging organizational or social issues that suggest new program ideas. If an agency has unique or distinctive resources (such as an outstanding faculty member, laboratory, or library collection), this may suggest an adult education program not likely to be provided by other agencies. The availability of grants from government agencies or private foundations tends to be a stimulus to new program directions, especially for higher education institutions. Another valuable administrative response is to collaborate with practitioners from other agencies on cooperative projects such as research on unmet adult education needs, marketing of the lifelong learning concept, or community-based educational counseling to increase program access to underserved adults. Administrators who recognize the potential influence of the opportunities, demands, and constraints in their environment can be alert to promising program directions and can help agency personnel take these factors into account in program development activities.

Needs Assessment

The term *needs assessment* implies many useful concepts. The most general meaning of the term is identification of a deficient state (Monette, 1977). The need may be general or specific, objective or subjective. In terms of insight or perception, there may be felt or unknown needs. In terms of the observer, there may be felt (self) or ascribed (other) needs. In terms of validity or objectivity, the needs may be wants or diagnosed deficiencies, descriptive or prescriptive. In terms of settings in which the needs may be satisfied, there are educational needs, system needs, housing needs, and the like. In terms of who is in need, they may be described as individual, organizational, or societal (Atwood and Ellis, 1973; Knowles, 1970; Valley and Hamilton, 1976).

Failure to clarify the definition and procedures used in

needs assessment may result in the selection or recognition of an entirely inappropriate program idea. Consider for example a manager who requests secretarial skills-improvement programs for the clerical personnel in the division. The trainer who conducts the programs may not be aware of the rationale of the manager, but might unconsciously assume that the manager had either diagnosed a performance gap that could be closed by training or was reporting a group need felt by the clerical staff. In reality, the manager may have been responding to a need felt by himself alone, and only in regard to one secretary. The manager may have tried to avoid embarrassing that secretary by reporting the need as a group need. A subsequent discussion with the secretary in an attempt to assess actual needs might reveal excellent work performance reports by all supervisors other than the manager in question; and it might further be determined that performance had slipped recently because the secretary did not like the new manager. In this case, transfer to a different work setting would accomplish what a training program could not.

Needs assessment often requires base lines: What specific performance is standard? What competencies have recently become required? To what extent do the potential participants measure up to these standards or competencies? Is there a difference of opinion between potential participants and observers of the participants? Is there a gap between performance and expectation based on standards and competencies? Do experts have an opinion as to the cause of the gap? Is the cause of the gap suggestive of remedy by means of adult education?

The assessment of social needs is even more subtle. Bradshaw (1974) has developed a taxonomy of social need to assist the practitioner in probing the phenomenon tentatively identified as a social need for its normative, felt, expressed, and comparative qualities. Given limited resources, the Bradshaw taxonomy would provide one way of assigning priorities to possible program responses.

In order to determine the quality of need expressed by society, organizations and groups, and even individuals, practitioners are increasingly turning to diagnostic procedures that sensitize the researcher to the possibility that an expression of need may be only a symptom of an educational problem. *Educational problem,* in turn, is defined by Atwood (1973, pp. 3–4) as "a human difficulty of thinking, feeling, and/or acting, the presence of which is predicted because of symptoms that indicate ignorance, misunderstanding, or inappropriate actions." McKinley (1973) distinguishes between social system needs and individual needs in presenting emerging views about the nature of diagnosis and diagnostic models in adult education. Whatever the procedures used, the most useful needs assessments typically combine several types and sources of information.

In practice, the most widespread needs assessment procedure in adult education consists of offering educational opportunities and then noting how many and what types of adults enroll. Within an agency, this occurs as practitioners consider enrollment trends over the years for each type of program and as new offerings are presented on a modest basis and a clientele analysis is conducted to estimate the potential market. This approach of offering a sample program to test the market has the advantage of allowing potential participants to respond not only to a phrase in a list of topics but to a specific program description, resource person, day, time, location, and price. Furthermore, the commitment of time, money, and attention provides a much firmer basis for predicting future enrollments by similar adults than merely indicating a topic on an interest inventory. The approach is disadvantageous, however, when information from a needs assessment is required to plan a sample program, especially when the agency would incur an unacceptably high loss of money or image by offering a program for which there was inadequate response.

The second most widespread needs assessment procedure is the interest inventory. For example, toward the end of an adult education program, participants sometimes complete a reaction or evaluation form that asks for topics or programs in which they would be interested in the future. Some agencies use this procedure as the main form of needs assessment, but it tends to result in more specified programs for the current clientele instead of programs to attract a broader clientele. Another example of an interest inventory—one directed especially toward professional association memberships and residents of smaller communities or neighborhoods—is a questionnaire composed of a list of topics; adults indicate the extent of their interest in learning more about each topic. Several studies have shown that the high-frequency topics are also the most familiar ones, and that when programs are actually offered, the highly popular topics do not necessarily receive the highest enrollments.

Another needs assessment procedure is to depend on experts familiar with a category of adults to estimate their educational needs. Examples include clergymen and social workers who are closely associated with less advantaged adults in their neighborhoods and instructors at a professional college who are closely associated with practitioners in their field. Some adult education planning committees are composed exclusively of these experts, who decide what potential participants need; the potential participants are not represented directly. These assessments provide valuable but insufficient information about the educational needs of adults for program development purposes.

One of the most effective adult education needs assessment procedures occurs in employment settings in conjunction with performance review. Periodically each employee describes actual performance along with desired changes and improvements. The employee's supervisor completes a parallel form that describes the employee's actual and desired performance. The employee and the supervisor then exchange performance review forms, discuss similarities and differences in perceptions and expectations, talk about recommended salary increase or promotion, and agree on specific growth goals for the employee. This procedure provides exceedingly valuable educational needs assessment for employee, supervisor, and adult education personnel to use for selecting and planning effective educational activities. The purpose of highly targeted educational activities is then to close the gap between current and desired competence. This procedure also illustrates major features of effective needs assessment procedures generally, including attention to both current and changed competence, identification of gaps to be closed by educational activities, information from potential participants to encourage commitment to change, and information from others to provide perspective and assistance.

Directions for the Future

A recent study by Hohman (1977) confirms the suspicion that the astonishing recent growth in continuing education has been the result of many practitioners having backed, fallen, or been pushed into the field. The Pennington and Green study (1976, p. 20) highlights some of the symptoms of this general lack of foresight: "This study brought to light some very important discrepancies between program planning models found within the literature and actual practice in diverse fields of continuing professional education. Planning . . . was superficial at best."

It is necessary for practitioners to have a rich variety of procedures with which to assess needs, generate and refine program ideas, plan future strategies and administrative arrangements, explore likely and desirable alternative futures, and influence the parent organization's priorities. Resulting commitments will then reflect resource allocations for the future and complementarity in relation to other agencies. As part of this process, the practitioner can look to other agencies' planning procedures, but it is the adoption of regular methods of data collection, analysis, discussion, and decision making that is significant. The *Michigan State University Task Force on Lifelong Education Report* is instructive in this regard (a summary can be found in Hesburgh, Miller, and Wharton, 1973), as is a University of Illinois study conducted by Farmer and Knox (1977).

Information about possible future directions tends to be most useful when it is included in a broader framework, in which possibilities can be related to preferences (Ziegler, 1970). During the past decade, some adult education practitioners have participated in "alternative futures workshops," which entail speculation about possible future directions for an agency, a target market, the field of adult education, or an aspect of the larger society. Each alternative is then analyzed in terms of likelihood, influences, consequences, and desirability. Workshop participants explore what they can do to increase the probability that the more desirable alternatives materialize and reduce the negative impact of the less desirable alternatives.

Effective practitioners realize that there are many sources of program ideas, and they have a strategy for drawing upon those sources that are appropriate. Less creative or less disciplined practitioners routinely draw upon only one or two sources, such as interest inventories completed by potential participants or descriptions of adult education programs conducted by other providers. This limited way of generating new program ideas may overlook information about client needs, agency purposes, potential resources, and relative priorities.

The purposes, traditions, and resources of an adult education agency and its parent organization provide a practitioner with a frame of reference regarding the types of adults about whom to collect information and the types of educational needs on which to focus. Familiarity with exemplary adult education needs assessment projects can suggest effective procedures for collection and analysis of data. Preliminary information about educational needs of adults in a target market can indicate how much and what type of additional information would be useful. Research on the needs assessment process has demonstrated the utility of multiple sources of needs assessment in order to cross-validate conclusions and to specify both current and desired levels and types of competence. Summary findings from similar needs assessment studies enable a practitioner to interpret local findings. Procedural comments about the costs and benefits of needs assessment studies provide a basis for choosing the scale and type of needs assessment effort warranted in a specific instance.

Practitioners who reflect on the traditions of their agency and of the general field of adult and continuing education—and who allow these traditions to guide but not dominate their thinking—can use the resulting information to generate new program ideas. An awareness of typical programs of one's own adult education agency and of other agencies in the field can contribute to useful differentiation and strengthening of distinctive agency emphases. Awareness of traditions also facilitates referral of new program ideas to other agencies if that alternative seems more appropriate. Study of an agency's traditions may also reveal past program ideas with potential for the future as well as information that could help develop the idea into a viable program. Such program ideas from the past may enable a practitioner to explore needs and resources effectively and, if the results are encouraging, to launch a program. One benefit of familiarity with scholarly analyses in the field is the perspective a practitioner gains on emerging trends and issues. Because the field of adult education tends to be very present oriented and responsive to client preferences, such a perspective can be useful in planning timely programs.

Analysis of the context of agency, parent organization, service area, and clientele also contributes to the generation of new program ideas, especially in combination with other sources, such as needs and traditions. Each adult education agency tends to have a distinctive set of purposes and resources as reflected in talent, facilities, organizational commitment, and financial support. A practitioner can use the results of a context analysis or resource inventory to supplement general impressions gained from working in the parent organization. Program ideas that relate to both high-priority societal and client needs and high-priority agency purposes and resources have special promise for outstanding success. With many agencies providing adult education programs in many service areas, attention to the distinctive mission of each agency provides a way of increasing complementarity among agencies and of increasing the total impact. Studies of adult education agencies as social systems can help practitioners understand ways in which agency functioning influences both generation of new program ideas and use of such ideas in other aspects of the program development process.

In addition to using concepts from the literature to enrich their own generation of new program ideas, practitioners can add to the literature their experiences regarding origins of adult education programs. These contributions may be in the form of articles about promising ideas or procedures to generate them. Practitioners can also conduct or cooperate with research or evaluation studies on origins of adult education program ideas. This is an especially promising area for research in light of the amount of wasted effort that goes into useless needs assessment projects.

University graduate programs with a major in adult and continuing education should be making greater contributions to the field regarding effective program development procedures, including origins. This can be done through noncredit workshops for practitioners as well as credit courses in the degree program. Professional associations can devote time at meetings and space in publications to help practitioners in the field increase their competence through exposure to concepts and practices that are central to agency effectiveness and vitality. Any effort to increase professional competence in the field will be especially useful if it enables practitioners to draw upon relevant knowledge in creative and disciplined ways to enhance daily practice.

Chapter Three

Objectives and Activities

Ronald Szczypkowski

Chapter Two described procedures for identifying adult education program ideas. This chapter focuses on two closely related components of the program development process—formulating relevant objectives and selecting activities designed to maximize the likelihood that the program objectives will be achieved.

Planning and implementing a successful educational program is the responsibility of the adult education program administrator. The educational program could be for a single adult learner, such as those offered by some public libraries under the adult services function; for a small special-interest group meeting for informal study; for a larger group, such as a series of adult education courses for hundreds or perhaps thousands of people attending a professional conference; or for mass audiences reached through radio or television.

General Perspective

Learning is an active process. Adult learning is individual learning and does not take place unless the adult participant does something (such as listen, read, ask questions, perform, sort, write, or think). Therefore, the fundamental focus of teaching-learning transactions should be on what happens to learners and not on the activities engaged in by teachers.

Learning results from interactions between an adult and his environment and occurs continuously throughout adult life. Much learning is incidental, and many learning projects are conducted entirely by the learner (Tough, 1978). Typically, adult education agencies and practitioners are concerned with adult learning activities that are *deliberate, systematic,* and *sustained.* Deliberate learning activities are engaged in for the main purpose of increasing proficiencies, often with an application in mind. Systematic learning activities reflect attention to needs, resources, objectives, activities, and evaluation. Sustained learning activities include a series of learning episodes on a topic. Adult education, then, consists of deliberate, systematic, and sustained learning activities in which adults beyond their full-time schooling engage on a part-time or short-term basis. In addition, many adults enter an adult education program intending to close a perceived gap in role performance. As a consequence, the need to acquire additional competence is frequently associated with a sense of immediacy.

Adults entering an educational program frequently possess considerable knowledge about most topics studied. Thus, people who assume facilitating or leadership roles should be aware of the potential teacher dimension in every student. Conversely, adult learners need to become aware of the student dimension of every teacher involved in an adult education program and be made to feel that their contributions play an important role in enriching the teaching-learning process.

Although generalizations about useful adult learning activities are frequently derived from very special contexts (such as small group process techniques from human relations training), the applicability of such generalizations to broader settings was the criterion used to select them for this chapter. Although many elements of general program development in adult education are discussed in this book, there are five generic processes present for each program cycle:

- assessment of learner needs,
- consideration of relevant resources and influences,
- preparation of specific and important objectives,
- selection and organization of learning activities to achieve intended program objectives, and
- evaluation of the educational program.

Although the focus for this chapter is clearly on the fourth—objectives and learning activities—the other processes are interrelated, and effective program planning thus requires sensitivity to all five processes simultaneously.

How useful to the intended audiences are existing adult education programs? Below are some illustrations from actual practice:

- A lay church committee plans a series of talks designed to enrich the quality of adult spirituality. At the first session, a guest specialist who has never met the group before begins by delivering a 45-minute lecture. Although some of the group found the lecture stimulating, most felt that the technical vocabulary and concepts were hard to follow, and they generally lost interest.
- A continuing professional education activity is conducted for ten program administrators in a university's continuing education office. Several resource people are invited to assist participants increase their proficiency in program development. At the first meeting, the resource people with backgrounds in marketing, funding, and program development talk about things they feel are important from their specialty area. During the first two hours, only two members of the continuing education office staff—the intended beneficiaries—ask questions concerning issues raised by the resource people.
- A public television station offers a series of educational programs designed to improve viewers' knowledge about the national economy. The director of the series uses sophisticated

approaches to attract audience attention and hires a well-known professor to communicate information to the viewers. The program receives wide publicity and becomes a core component of an adult education course. After initial enthusiasm, course participants complain that the program is boring, and class attendance falls off considerably.

- A library decides to expand its adult services to include direct guidance for self-directed adult learners. The librarian given the responsibility to provide the service spends her time developing reading lists in a number of subject areas and provides them to adult independent learners who inquire about a specific content area. Although publicity is not very extensive, fifty independent adult learners are attracted to the library during the first three months. After receiving the reading list, only two of the fifty return for further consultation and guidance.

The foregoing examples are instances of ineffective practices that commonly occur in adult education. To be sure, many adult education programs are of high quality—that is, they are very satisfying and useful to participants. Yet, the number of adults who encounter poor-quality part-time educational activities is likely to be high in a field that does not require much in the way of specialized educational preparation for practitioners. Unsatisfactory teaching of adults is sufficiently widespread to warrant attention by adult education administrators. Because participation in a learning activity could be an adult's "last gamble on education," administrators have a responsibility to provide effective learning experiences (Mezirow, Darkenwald, and Knox, 1975).

Administrator Concern for Objectives and Activities

Why should adult education administrators show concern for objective setting and the selection of learning activities? Are not these activities the teacher's domain? Some answers to these questions come from a brief consideration of adult education characteristics and trends. One distinctive characteristic of adult education is the great variety of providers. Practically every type of institution, organization, and special-interest group has some arrangement to assist adults to learn. In this pluralistic field, there are few restrictions on subject area, age of learner, method of learning, location of learning, qualifications of resource people, scheduling of learning, standards for judging success, and other factors that tend to be sharply defined in more formal preparatory education systems. Many distinctive features of adult education reflect the nature of the adult as a learner and the art of helping adults learn (Brunner and Associates, 1959; Kidd, 1973; Knowles, 1975; Knox, 1976, 1977a; Whipple, 1957).

In many other fields, service providers typically have formal preparatory professional education related to their role performance. This is not the case for much of adult education. People who facilitate adult learning often do so on a part-time basis, move in and out of the field, and have little or no preparation in the principles and practices of adult education. As a consequence, the adult education administrator is usually the only person who has sufficient professional commitment to the field to become acquainted with relevant literature and practice. Thus the administrator tends to be more involved in planning teaching-learning transactions than is usually the case for administrators in preparatory education.

Administrative involvement in teaching-learning transactions can occur indirectly, through in-service education of teachers and resource people, and directly, as program administrators help set objectives and select learning activities. Widespread reliance on part-time teachers and teams of resource personnel tends to blur the distinction between teacher and administrator roles found in preparatory education. For example, conference coordinators typically serve on planning committees that set objectives and select learning activities. The coordinator works with a number of resource people who have content expertise but little familiarity with adult learning and program development. Many successful programs reflect the program administrator's proficiency in planning effective learning activities. The increased extent and visibility of adult education programs increases the importance of program development proficiency by program administrators. Several decades ago, adult education programs were marginal and clamoring for the attention of the public (Clark,

1956; Johnstone and Rivera, 1965; Wann and Woodward, 1959). During the past decade, however, many people "discovered" adult education and now have expectations about its effectiveness.

Framework for Program Development

Obtaining agreement on important, clear, and realistic educational objectives and then selecting and organizing learning activities to achieve those objectives entail many specific tasks. Additional program development tasks are associated with origins and evaluation. Various combinations of adult participants, resource people, and program administrators perform program development tasks. A framework for considering these program development tasks is necessary so that important tasks are attended to and the contributions of participants, resource people, and administrators can be coordinated.

Attracting, retaining, and helping adult education participants entail various interrelated processes. Some of these processes, such as encouraging participation and reducing obstacles to participation, are discussed in detail in relation to needs assessment, marketing, and counseling services. However, these processes are relevant to objective setting because an understanding of the interests and circumstances of potential participants helps practitioners establish objectives that are attractive and realistic for a specific group of learners. Further, potential participants' awareness of the features and objectives of adult education opportunities helps crystalize and increase their motivation to participate.

Helping potential participants understand proficiency goals of the educational program is a major task of the adult educator (Miller, 1964). A clear idea of what is to be learned can be communicated in several ways: using audiovisual materials that portray the desired proficiency, providing opportunities for potential participants to acquire some proficiency in a sample of the program, and publicizing testimonials from past participants regarding the proficiencies they acquired. This information helps potential participants understand the fit between educational opportunities and their own aspirations. The most common way to communicate what is to be learned in adult education is through program descriptions in catalogues and brochures, and these program descriptions should therefore include a clear statement of proficiencies to be acquired by learners.

Another important process related to effective learning activities for adults is the provision of a supportive environment for change. Especially for adults without recent experience in formal educational activities, entering an adult education program can be accompanied by uncertainty and anxiety. It is difficult to predict which new participants are likely to be apprehensive about the prospects of embarassment and failure; teachers, counselors, and administrators should therefore provide a supportive environment for all adult learners in each educational activity, especially during the initial stages. A humanistic administrative approach to all aspects of an adult education delivery system will generally enhance the quality of the teaching and learning transaction (Rogers, 1969).

The most familiar process in the facilitation of adult learning is assisting participants to engage in learning activities in order to acquire desired proficiency. This is a dual process that includes both understanding the proficiency to be acquired and engaging in learning tasks in order to increase proficiency. For many learning activities, some demonstration or modeling of proficient performance can serve as a standard against which the adult learner can compare his current proficiency. Examples include physical performance (using a jeweler's saw without breaking the blade), social performance (leading a discussion group), and intellectual performance (documenting local historical events by use of primary and secondary sources). The adult learner can use these models to engage in systematic practice that builds on current proficiency and moves toward the desired proficiency. Practice is understood to be essential when learning to play a musical instrument. It is equally essential for adults who seek to increase their proficiency in interpersonal relations or comprehension and application of abstract concepts. The adult should also be helped to apply the increased proficiency in the educational setting or in adult life roles in family, work, and community. This application of new proficiency serves to increase persistence in learning activities and retention of increased proficiency.

Many program administrators use planning committees to

discuss and determine the general design of adult education programs, and effective adult education practitioners must be able to select, orient, and work with these planning committees. The main products of these committees are specific program objectives, a general program design, selection of resource people, and a marketing plan. Planning committees tend to be most effective when they represent the interests of program administrator, resource people, and potential participants. If these three role perspectives are not reflected in the composition of the planning committee, the program administrator can arrange for missing background information and viewpoints to be presented. For example, if the planning committee does not include potential participants, the coordinator can share the results of a needs assessment.

In practice there is great variety in the frameworks for program development within which adult education program administrators operate. Because most practitioners in the field have devised their own program development procedures, practices tend to be quite personal and intuitive. One widespread procedure is for the program administrator to select resource people to do the teaching. Both the program administrator and the resource person assume that the latter understands the educational needs of potential participants and the objectives of the program and is proficient in teaching adults, especially in the content area to be covered. The program administrator tries to rely on resource people who have been successful in the past, who tend to make adjustments in their plans as the program proceeds, and who are responsive to the interests of adult learners. Instructor responsiveness typically reflects a sense of participant expectations and of a satisfactory learning environment; a responsive instructor is seen as responsive in part because he takes the learners' expectations into consideration in organizing and presenting his material. The adjustments in his plan come partly from his knowledge of learners' expectations. If resource people are not responsive, attrition rates tend to be high, participants' evaluation forms tend to be negative, and program administrators tend to seek other resource people for future programs. Unfortunately, this natural selection process is often influenced by irrelevant conditions such as mandatory continuing education (which forces learners to accept whatever instruction is given) or appointment of instructional personnel by the parent organization, which has no major responsibility for the adult education program. Also, some resource people view their roles as presenters of information and assume that participants will deal with practice and application outside of the educational program.

Objective Setting

Mager (1962) has written that if you do not know where you are going, any road will take you there, but you are liable to end up someplace else and not even know it. There is no more crucial aspect of the program development process than objective setting, and no aspect is more misunderstood and misapplied.

For most adult education courses or workshops, the planners have at least some sense of the program goals and content, which usually emerge from the origins of the program or from assumed or formally assessed educational needs of potential participants. An experienced adult education instructor tends to modify emphases and content each time the course is taught, often with little deliberate attention to objectives or content. A conference planning committee may deliberate for many hours to select the concepts that appear to be most relevant for the participants (Leagans, Copeland, and Kaiser, 1971). Ideally, the objective setting process should be both explicit and useful.

Components of Objective Setting

Three important components of objective setting are (1) audiences, (2) form, and (3) selection procedures. Various audiences have expectations about the objectives of an adult education activity and are affected by the outcomes. The number of audiences varies with the complexity of the program. In a self-directed learning project the learner is the only audience; in a complex adult education program with multiple funding and sponsorship, multiple audiences may be interested in and affected by program objectives. Table 1 illustrates a multiple audience adult education program. Essentially, the program administrator in this example would be expected to obtain information from all the audiences under the program's jurisdiction and to report findings about program impact in forms tailored to the interests of each provider organization. An administrator who understands how these audiences are associated with objective setting should be able to orchestrate the process systematically.

The objective-setting process should provide the several audiences with a framework for relating philosophy and goals to specific objectives and action steps. This framework includes several levels of specification and is portrayed in Figure 1. Higher level statements typically have specific subordinate statements supporting them. For example, a single subobjective may have five or more specific action steps or tasks required for successful execution. Generally, a program has an overall statement of philosophy or mission coupled with a few broad purposes or goals. Audiences most interested in broad statements of missions, purposes, or goals typically include policymakers and decision makers associated with funding agencies, institutional sponsors, and advisory boards. The major audiences for statements at the levels of specific objectives, subobjectives, and action steps are program administrators, resource people, and adult learners.

Figure 1. Objective-Setting Schema

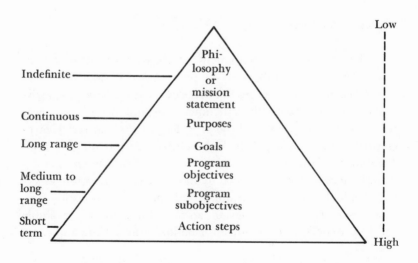

**Table 1. Examples of Multiple Audiences Related to
Adult Education Objective Setting as Seen from an
Adult Education Administrator's Perspective**

Audience	Interest in Program
Federal government	The U.S. Department of Labor identifies a need for 10,000 skilled people proficient as home health care aides; funds are provided to county governments for such adult education.
State government	The state licensing bureau is required to assess the degree to which such practitioners meet the state's standards for practice in the occupation.
County government	The county's Comprehensive Employment and Training Act (CETA) office wants to see that monies it has received can be used to train a sufficient number of home health care workers to meet the needs of the region; it provides grants to eligible adult education providers.
Parent organization	As recipient of the grant, the parent organization is concerned that this program fit its purposes and bring credit to the organization.
Adult education agency	The adult education office wants to: • retain a high percentage of learners recruited to the home health care aide program • have participants in the program satisfied so they will return for another adult education program • meet the funding agency's requirements so as to enhance the agency's ability to attract future funds
Resource person	The course instructor wants to: • have a significant portion of learners achieve proficiency required for licensing as a home health care aide • please the employer, thus retaining employment
Adult learner	An individual learner enrolls in the program to acquire proficiency as a home health care aide.
Ultimate beneficiary	An older adult living at home, but unable to care for herself, wants assistance from a health care aide to cope with the problems of everyday living.

The term *program objective* is being used in a specialized sense here. For purposes of accountability and on-going decision making, program objective describes outcomes that are expected to be assessed during or at a reasonable time after the completion of an educational program. All educational programs can generate multiple outcomes, both intended and unintended. The selection of one or more program objectives is a sampling of possible program effects. The program administrator chooses a limited number of program objectives to be the focus of planning efforts and to evaluate activities.

This restricted use of *program objectives* does not imply that other statements are not also made about the program, such as those commonly found in course descriptions in catalogues and the like. These other statements, however, rather than being called *program objectives,* are designated by one of the other terms inside the triangle of Figure 1.

Sometimes the time anticipated until the achievement of a program objective spans several years. In these instances it is advisable to develop a set of subobjectives as a guide to planning and monitoring the program. In some programs, no potential participants are involved during the initial stages of program development. Nevertheless, some statement of objectives is useful to identify expected outcomes; these objectives are referred to by such terms as *intermediate, process,* and *enabling* objectives. (These are included under "subobjectives" in Figure 1.)

Action steps are detailed tasks, typically resembling detailed lesson plans, and frequently expressed in terms of a time line or learner management matrix. They can be prepared by the learner in a self-directed learning project, jointly by learner and resource person, solely by the resource person, or jointly by the resource person and administrator. The detailed plans for a workshop, prepared by a planning committee, typically include both program objectives and action steps. The total set of action steps comprises the plan for achieving the program's objectives. Each action step should identify the nature of the task or activity to be performed, people responsible for carrying out the activity, resources available, and time or date for performing the task.

In practice, adult educators tend to state what they call "program objectives" in terms of activities that the instructor is expected to carry out or that the sponsoring agency is expected to accomplish. However, it is useful tor program planning, marketing, and evaluation to state objectives in terms that reflect expected or desired learner proficiency with regard to the subject matter of the educational activity. For example, a coordinator of a preretirement program might state the objectives of a series of life and career planning workshops describing knowledge, skills, and attitudes that potential participants are likely to acquire if they enroll.

Form

What form should a program objective take? Although various research suggests from three to ten elements contained in an objective statement, the following five elements are the most frequently suggested in educational program planning:

1. The conditions under which the proficiency of target group learners is expected to be demonstrated (for example, after exposure to a minimum number of hours of instruction or as a result of attending a workshop)
2. A description of the target learners (for example, adults enrolled in a first-year art class)
3. The proficiency to be demonstrated by a target group (for example, learner will replace a carburetor in any six-cyclinder American car)
4. The minimum level of proficiency (for example, 75 percent of the class will be able to demonstrate at least working-level proficiency specified in #3 above to the satisfaction of the course instructor)
5. A measurement instrument or method of assessing the outcome of the desired behavior (for example, as evidenced by a checklist completed by the course instructor)

Implicit in this approach to objective setting is a basic belief that all program objectives—including affective outcomes of instruction—are measurable. A measurable objective contains an operational definition of the performance or behavior expected of intended learners. Desired affective outcomes that cannot be measured directly require the identification of proxy behaviors that can be used to infer the existence of the desired traits. For example, evidence that could be used to make a case for the positive effects of a music appreciation course could come from one or more of the following sources:

• increased attendance at live classical music performances
• increased purchasing or borrowing of classical music records, tapes, or cassettes
• increased radio listening or television viewing of classical music programs
• statistically significant increases from pre- to post-music-appreciation attitude scales

A program objective statement must be congruent with the level and scope of the evaluation effort to be expended, and in this regard a rigorous, direct assessment of the desired learner changes in performance or attitude is preferred to subjective self-reports by participants on the worth of an educational program. However, what is often desirable may not be feasible, and therefore a realistic view of program objective setting is needed by adult education practitioners. In any case, the congruence between stated objectives and anticipated evaluation procedures should be established in advance in order to be reasonably sure that the evaluation information stated in the objective will be obtained. It makes little sense to prepare a set of elegant objectives and then not initiate the necessary procedures to determine whether the objectives were achieved.

To be sure, some educational programs permit their objectives to be stated in a form that describes expected summative outcomes in a real-life or simulated setting. For example, "At least 75 percent of the adults enrolled in the XYZ Learning Center's brush-up typing course for a minimum of twenty hours of instruction will increase their entry-level typing speed within established error tolerances by twenty words per minute as measured by a standard five-minute timing." The standards and the conditions stated in this objective should be derived from experience with similar groups previously enrolled in similar programs. In turn, the objective should be periodically revised to reflect up-dated results with learners. It is assumed that the example objective would be evaluated directly by the teacher or resource person in charge of the educational program and would take place between points B and D on the time continuum illustrated in Figure 2.

Figure 2. Educational Program Time Continuum

A	B	C	D	E	F	G
Antecedent conditions established	Program begins	Program in process	Program ends	Three months later	One year later	Some point in the future

Many continuing education programs require less than precise statements of objectives owing to such factors as the estimated effect of program length on desired mastery level, the resources available to collect and analyze evaluation data, and the anticipated willingness of participants to provide sensitive data. For example, planners of a one-day workshop may assume that in-depth practice for mastery will occur *after* one leaves the program (between points D and G in Figure 2); therefore, it may not be feasible to measure changed proficiency directly at the workshop. Under these circumstances, a two- or three-phase objective-setting strategy may be most useful for program administrators. An example of a two-phase objective-setting strategy follows:

Phase I—Objectives to be assessed during or immediately following the conclusion of a one-day workshop

Satisfaction: Psychiatric nurse practitioners attending a one-day professional workshop on transactional analysis techniques will indicate their overall satisfaction with the program as evidenced by a *mean* rating of five on a seven-point satisfaction scale.

Proficiency: At least 80 percent of the participants attending
                       the workshop will indicate that they have attained a
                       working level of proficiency with these techniques
                       on the Participant Reaction Form. Working-level
                       proficiency would be operationally defined by
                       a statement such as the following: "I think I
                       understood enough about these techniques to
                       begin to apply them in my practice or area of
                       responsibility."

Phase II—Objectives to be assessed by telephone or questionnaire three months after the completion of a short-term workshop

Performance: At least 60 percent of the participants attending
                       the one-day workshop on transactional analysis
                       techniques will report having used one or more
                       of these techniques in their practice during the
                       three-month period following the workshop.

Continued   Workshop participants who used one or more
Satisfaction: transactional analysis technique in the three-
                       month period following training will report a
                       mean satisfaction rate of four on a five-point
                       satisfaction scale.

The decision to employ follow-up evaluation procedures should
be anticipated in the original statement of relevant program objectives and is dependent upon the value of this information to the
administrators of the program. In the above example, the third
phase of an objective-setting strategy might involve direct assessment of the expected change in proficiency through an objective
examination, evidence from the ultimate beneficiary of increased
satisfaction of service obtained (client survey), and direct observation of practitioner behavior as part of a rigorous research study to
assess impacts of the training program.

    In sum, program administrators and resource people
should make realistic assessments of what can reasonably be
measured, given the time, resources, and other constraints of the
program. The congruence between desired learner outcomes and

the data available to assess the success of these outcomes is a crucial consideration of the program development process, once again highlighting the interrelatedness of learner expectations and program features. Some details of program objective selection follow.

The Process of Elimination. The origins of an adult education program typically yield an extensive and diffuse range of potential objectives. It is usually necessary to select a limited number of program objectives from this preliminary list. The first screen applied to the preliminary list is one of high *desirability:* Objectives that have the highest value and are most relevant for planners and learners should be emphasized. A second screen that should be applied is the degree of *harmony* among the statement of philosophy, program purposes, long-term goals, and selected program objectives. Objectives should reflect to a high degree the values stated or implied in the sponsoring agency's philosophy. It is essential that agency personnel have a clear sense of mission so that objectives that are most in harmony with that mission can be assigned high priority.

A third screen for selecting objectives is knowledge of the psychology of learning (Tyler, 1950). This screen, sometimes known as the *feasibility* screen, helps program planners to recognize realistic changes expected from a given learning process and to identify the objectives that are attainable in terms of relevant learner characteristics such as ability, time available, recency of previous learning, and handicaps. In addition, the feasibility screen plays a critical role in identifying conditions prerequisite to achieving desired objectives and eliminating objectives whose prerequisites cannot be reasonably satisfied with existing resources and time.

A fourth screen for selecting objectives is the *degree of application* the attainment of an objective has for potential participants. Adults frequently need to use tomorrow (if not before) what they learned today (Brunner, and others, 1959). A procedure that requires adult learners to spend time developing proficiencies with little likelihood of immediate and relevant application does not reflect sound adult education practices.

Unanticipated Outcomes. Most adult education programs produce unanticipated outcomes along with specified objectives. These unanticipated outcomes may be more valuable than the formally stated objectives, and resource people should develop procedures to identify them. One way to accomplish this is through periodic consensus building by participants and resource people. This consensus building is a discussion process involving students and instructors in which they reach agreement about what goals are being achieved even though the goals were not intentionally sought. Another approach that has gained popularity recently, especially for new program areas, is goal-free program development. With this approach, a general purpose but no specific program objective is set in advance; at the end of the program, participants and planners attempt to develop a set of program objectives for future participants as a result of the outcomes experienced by the initial participants.

Single and Multiple Resource People. In practice, the ways in which program administrators approach educational objective setting depend on whether a specific program entails one or more resource people. When there is only one resource person—for example, when an instructor from the parent organization teaches an evening or off-campus course for adults—the program administrator tends to select someone who seems to be effective and then to leave decisions regarding content and objectives to that person. In fact, when resource people are faculty members from educational institutions, there is sometimes resistance to the program administrator's participating in the objective-setting process. For many resource people who conduct their course or workshop independently, attention to objectives and especially learner outcomes tends to be implicit in the selection of topics and learning activities. In situations involving one resource person, while the program administrator often does not have much involvement in objective setting, he can encourage instructor response to the specific needs and interests of adult participants by sharing with the resource person information from past experience or needs assessment activities in an effort to convey a sense of participant background, interests, and expectations. Instructors can also be encouraged to establish direct contact with some potential participants. This contact will improve the instructor's understanding of client situations and aspirations and is especially effective when it takes place in the setting in which the potential participants will apply the knowledge they gain in the educational program. For example, visits to high-rise public housing units by authorities who have never visited such environments would help them to appreciate the situation of visiting public health nurses, literacy tutors, policemen, and others who work routinely in such places. Visits to work places in business and industry can be of value to those teaching group dynamics to foremen working in such locations.

When multiple resource people are involved in an educational program—as is typically found in a professional conference—the program administrator generally has substantive involvement in objective setting. In these instances, it is important that the administrator play a coordinating role, discussing program objectives and design with each resource person so that the contributions of all fit together into a coherent educational program.

When there are a few resource people from a single geographic area, it may be possible for them to meet to discuss the program plan and objectives. When this is not possible, the conference coordinator may be the only person who communicates with all resource people during the planning stage. For a program extending over a period of time or involving a large group, the resource people may not even see each other or all the participants at the event. In these instances, program administrators serve a crucial function in objective setting.

One way this function can be performed is to encourage resource people to consider the major program objectives. The administrator asks instructors to keep in mind what proficiencies their participants are supposed to have developed during the course. Calling attention to the proficiencies should remind the teachers of the key purposes their instruction is supposed to serve. Evaluation conclusions from previous programs can provide useful data for this purpose. The administrator might also include on the planning committee several potential program participants who can convey a sense of their background, circumstances, and expectations regarding the process and outcomes of the intended educational program directly to the resource people.

Selection and Organization of Learning Activities

The establishment of educational program objectives provides the basis for the selection and organization of learning activities to achieve those objectives. In preparatory education settings, it
is commonly accepted that the selection and organization of learning activities is the domain of the teacher or resource person. Unfortunately, this teacher-centered approach tends to be widespread
in adult education as well. Methods typically used to educate children and other "captured audiences," including university students,
constitute but a narrow range of the available learning opportunities for adults. Teachers of adults are often unaware of the rich
body of knowledge on processes that enhance adult learning, and it
is probably necessary for adult education program administrators
to help teachers gain access to this literature.

Many terms are used in the adult education literature to
label learning activities. Some of these terms describe general
formats for the total program, such as *conference, course,* or *lecture
series.* Other terms describe specific ways in which resource people
assist an adult to learn, such as *role playing, lecturette, drill, brainstorming,* and *coaching.* Verner (1964) refers to the former type of
activities as *methods* and the latter as *techniques.* Verner further
identifies as *devices* items such as *cassettes, television, audiovisual aids,*
and other mechanical instruments that facilitate the operation of
methods and techniques. Although these definitions make helpful
distinctions in adult education, especially in research studies, there
is little agreement among practitioners about what constitutes a
method, technique, or device (Johnson, 1970). Furthermore, what
Verner calls *techniques* and *devices* have been called *methods* and
materials in education courses for generations. The important point
is that practitioners *distinguish* among various methods and materials and select those that best fit each situation.

Selecting Learning Activities

A resource person can select from many learning activities,
depending on the educational objectives and the learner's characteristics. Shifting emphases should occur as part of the flow

through the beginning, middle, and end of a learning episode or series of episodes. This flow should reflect the desirability of modifying old habits and making a commitment to change at the outset, achieving change during the main part of the episode, and maintaining and applying the new proficiency at the culmination of the program (Knox, 1976).

Because few teachers of adults have formal preparation in adult education, program administrators often need to help select appropriate learning activities to achieve educational objectives. Criteria for selecting learning activities include:

- appropriateness of the activity for the objectives and content of the program
- suitability of the activity for the intended learner group
- effectiveness of the activity in relation to the stage of the adult education program
- satisfactory pacing and variety of learning activities for each session or learning episode
- compatibility with the resource person's teaching or facilitating style

Virtually hundreds of labels are used to describe learning activities in the literature. The inexperienced adult education administrator may try to keep up with the proliferation of these terms; the experienced administrator realizes that many of them are variations on generic learning formats or methods. The use of the term *lecturette* instead of *lecture* is one example of this transformation. The former term suggests a short talk by a qualified expert and is attractive to adult educators because it implies that only a limited time will be spent on a one-way communication of ideas in a group setting. Nevertheless, the structure imposed on the teaching-learning process is the same for the lecture as for the lecturette.

Learning formats that have been used extensively in adult education are presented in the following sections. For each term, the following data are provided: a definition from the *Dictionary of Education* (Good, 1973), a description of possible adult education uses, and suggestions for achieving maximum effectiveness in adult education practice. The guidelines for effective use are based in part on Tye (1966).

Brainstorming. "A popular nontechnical term for a specific technique to stimulate creative thinking in the development of new ideas; consists of individual or, more generally, a small-group activity in which a deliberate attempt is made to think uncritically but creatively about all possible approaches and solutions to a given problem; the group participating uses spontaneous and unrestrained discussion" (Good, 1973, p. 70).

This free-wheeling learning format appears to be an especially useful strategy for prompting adults to capitalize on their rich reservoir of experience and is an excellent way to get a new group of learners to participate actively. In addition, this format can be used to assist small groups of learners to identify a number of alternative courses of action before choosing a specific one. Furthermore, the technique of brainstorming is helpful in creating a convivial atmosphere for a new learning situation and has been found to stimulate the creative powers of adult learners.

In order to maximize the effectiveness of brainstorming in adult education settings, the following guidelines should be considered:

- There should be agreement on ground rules (such as unconditional acceptance for all suggestions at the outset).
- Only a minimum of clarifying questions should be permitted (for example, a clear understanding of the goal of the session should be kept in mind by the participants).
- One or more methods for recording responses should be chosen (flip chart, tape recorder, stenographer, or 3" × 5" cards).

Conference. A teaching and learning method that employs directed discussion of the topic rather than a lecture by the instructor.

Conferences are appropriate for large or small groups that are closely knit. The group discusses in depth a selected topic or problem or develops plans to promote a particular concept. Conferences are typically characterized by a predominance of talking and listening as opposed to doing. Usually the participants in attendance at a conference have a high interest in the area being discussed and their participation is voluntary.

For optimal effectiveness of a conference, the following factors should be kept in mind:

- Plan the conference well in advance; details such as facilities, meals, and other accommodations should be kept in mind from the outset.
- Ensure that those in attendance have the purpose of the conference firmly in mind.
- Arrange for the chairperson to open the session by setting the stage for the conference goals.
- Employ discussion techniques to prevent audience passivity.

Discussion. An activity in which learners, under teacher or student direction, exchange points of view concerning a topic, question, challenge, or problem in order to arrive at consensual agreement.

The discussion method is particularly effective for small groups with common interests in a defined problem area. By capitalizing on adult experiences, it clarifies problems and generates possible solutions. This method, as a supplement to other learning activities, can test new skills or be utilized as the generic method of learning and is used in some business and law schools. It is also a means for participants to explore and apply new learning.

Guides for optimal effectiveness of the discussion method are:

- Stress a flexible approach that allows participants to add or delete data as desired to provide more meaningful illustration of the problem area.
- Propose several pages of outline of the discussion topic and questions ahead of time for use during the discussion.

Forum. A form of adult education that utilizes a lecture or set of lectures and provides an opportunity for audience participation.

Forums are particularly effective in community settings because they provide an opportunity for people to express their views. A forum can be used as a major learning method or to supplement a film, panel, or other format.

For optimal effectiveness the following guidelines should be considered:

- An advance needs assessment of the audience is needed.
- A coordinator should facilitate balanced communication between audience and presenters.

Institute. "An arrangement for lectures and discussion sessions on a limited subject or theme, usually more intensive than a convention or conference" (Good, 1973, p. 303).

An institute typically lasts for several weeks, although it is sometimes offered for one to three days. It provides opportunities for special-interest groups to study, though not necessarily solve, a general problem area (such as career planning, teaching handicapped children, improving communication within the organization, the role of television in education, or preretirement planning). The institute format helps participants acquire practical skills in an area relevant to critical adult roles, especially the work role.

The following guidelines can help ensure successful implementation of an institute:

- A well-organized program format that includes efficient participant mobility between activities to facilitate flexible coverage of major topics
- Advance preparation to utilize multiple resources such as the library, field sites, and relevant resource materials
- Arrangements for individuals and small groups to be assisted and encouraged to set relevant objectives during the early stages of the institute

Lecture. "An instructional procedure by which the lecturer seeks to create interest, influence, stimulate, or mold opinion; to promote activity, to impart information; or to develop critical thinking, largely by the use of the verbal message, with a minimum of exchange; illustrations, maps, flow charts, graphs, and other visual aids may be displayed to supplement the spoken word" (Good, 1973, p. 334).

The major purposes of the lecture method are to assist a large group of learners to understand important relationships and to provide information that is not easily available from any other single source. The lecture format also can be used to identify critical issues as seen from an expert's point of view as well as to stimulate and motivate the participants to further study and research.

For maximum effectiveness, the following should be taken into consideration:

- The lecturer must develop a needs-sensing procedure for each audience.
- The sophistication of delivery must be geared to the sophistication of the audience.
- The lecturer must keep in mind that the attention span of the listeners declines after the first three to five minutes.

On-the-Job Training (OJT). The supervision and other supplemental instruction furnished to a learner employed as an apprentice or trainee in the regular duties of a position or job.

On-the-job training is the second most popular learning method in adult education, following formal class and lectures (Carp, Peterson, and Roelfs, 1974). This format is particularly effective for learners who do not have highly developed learning skills typically associated with higher levels of formal education.

On-the-job training can be an extremely effective technique if the supervisor and trainee consider the following:

- The supervisor should be a mentor to the trainee and should set the standards.
- A clear delineation of roles and responsibilities for both the supervisor and trainee should be established mutually at the outset.
- On-the-job training should be supplemented by other learning formats such as a programmed instruction manual.
- Feedback sessions between the supervisor and trainee should be held regularly and include specific recommendations for the trainee related to topics such as safety and scheduling.

Panel. A panel is a group of three to six people with expertise on an assigned topic who have a purposeful conversation with or without solicited audience participation; the panel is usually seated facing forward at a table in full view of the audience.

The panel format helps large groups of learners become familiar with various dimensions of a given topic, challenge, or problem. It is used increasingly by commercial and public television in their public affairs programming.

To gain maximum effectiveness from this format:

- The platform for panel members should be raised above the audience, and if the audience is large, microphones should be used.
- Members of the panel should coordinate individual presentations with the theme of the panel in advance.
- A panel should stress only limited aspects of the entire problem or topic.
- The moderator should facilitate a balanced flow of major ideas.

Programmed Instruction. Instruction utilizing a workbook or mechanical or electronic device designed to help learners attain a specified level of performance by (1) providing instruction in small steps, (2) asking one or more questions about each step in the instruction, (3) providing instant knowledge of whether each answer is right or wrong, and (4) enabling learners to progress at their own pace.

Programmed instruction appears to possess many features ideally suited for learning, including self-pacing and immediate feedback of learning results. Although this method is expensive, extensive use in large-scale educational situations has shown it to be cost-effective for federally supported adult basic education, military programs, and for private industry's educational programs.

Programmed instruction can be utilized to its optimal effectiveness with the following guidelines:

- Write and refine programmed materials carefully.
- Provide for learner-instructor interaction at stress points.
- Start instruction at the preparedness level of each individual learner.

Role Playing. An instructional technique involving a spontaneous portrayal (acting) of a situation, condition, or circumstance by selected or volunteer members of a learning group. Role playing is a method for developing insights into human relationships by acting out behavior in situations that are similar to real life.

Role playing, in particular, is highly productive for adults who have already undertaken one or more of their major roles in society. This method can be used to assist a small group of learners to increase awareness of self and others in specific role situations. Enlightening insights into contrasting attitudes and responses among the participants or among the people affected by the problem under study are important outcomes of this format. Situations can be devised that lead to the discovery of alternative solutions for emotion-laden problems.

In using this technique successfully, the following guidelines should be considered:

- Choose situations for role playing that resemble real-life experiences of the participants.
- Use resources that foster unconditional acceptance of roles as played.
- Be sure the leader is able to offset possible negative consequences that might result from spontaneous behavior of the participants.
- Begin with the more extroverted people in the group so that the role-playing format is initiated in a nonthreatening and minimally defensive atmosphere.

Seminar. An activity in which a group of learners, engaged in systematic research or advanced study, meets under the general direction of one or more staff members for a discussion of problems of mutual interest.

The seminar format provides an opportunity for in-depth study of a single subject or topic and supplies the participants with a wide range of viewpoints that reflect long-term analysis by the group of a common topic. The seminar helps learners to refine their problem-solving skills as well as serving to enlarge their individual perspectives. It is particularly appropriate for personal and social relations areas.

In utilizing this format, the following guidelines should be considered:

- A recognized authority with excellent process skills should guide a detailed and systematic discussion of the topic.
- A wide range of relevant source materials should be available to the participants for preparatory efforts.

Sensitivity Training. An activity in which a group and a trainer meet to examine self-consciously their immediate feelings and perceptions about themselves and each other in order to gain skill in communication, leadership, behavioral flexibility, or social sensitivity.

Sensitivity training can be used to loosen attitudinal blocks and lessen resistance to change. It is useful to help participants deal with highly charged issues as well as to serve as a stimulant to creativity.

In order for this format to be utilized effectively, the following should be kept in mind:

- Training groups should be led by competent professionals who are highly proficient in this technique.
- Members should be allowed to withdraw from the sensitive training experience if they feel it is a hindrance to their mental stability.
- Training should be of a sufficient length—one to two weeks, depending on the objectives set—in order to bring about change.

Short Course. "A form of class or correspondence course for adults, less extended and formalized than regular courses offered by colleges or universities" (Good, 1973, p. 151).

A short course, sometimes referred to as a mini-course, is well suited for a group of learners desiring to explore a particular subject area or requiring intensive training in a specific aspect that would normally be only superficially covered in a more general course.

To utilize the short course format most effectively, the following should be considered:

- Objectives to be covered should be clear, limited, and well defined from the outset.
- Materials utilized during the short course should be carefully selected in advance on the basis of the established objectives.
- Participants and instructor should be genuinely motivated and to a much greater degree than in longer programs.

Symposium. "An instructional technique in which two to five people qualified to speak with authority on different aspects of the same topic or on closely related topics present a series of related speeches" (Good, 1973, p. 579).

A symposium can eliminate some of the shortcomings of the panel. Speakers present formal speeches on a number of aspects of a given problem or topic; their views are then coordinated to ensure comprehensive coverage and logical sequencing to fit major dimensions of the problem area.

To gain maximum effectiveness from the symposium, the following should be considered:

- Speakers' topics should be coordinated.
- Different positions regarding the topic should be selected in advance so that proper sequencing can be established.
- Thoughtful sequential positioning of the various aspects should be used to add dimensions of valence and coherence that may not be explicit in a single aspect.

Workshop. "An instructional method in which persons with common interests and problems meet with appropriate specialists to acquire necessary information and develop solutions through group study; usually residential and of several days' duration" (Good, 1973, p. 652).

The functions of the workshop format are similar to those of the institute. Workshop participants are provided with an opportunity to learn what they are uniquely interested in learning instead of what the leader conceives as important. The format compels each participant to search for meaning in a climate that maximizes group support for individual efforts. The workshop provides an opportunity for learners to develop and practice new skills in a nonthreatening setting.

To ensure optimal effectiveness in presenting a workshop, the following suggestions should be considered:

- A needs assessment should be carried out in advance of the workshop.
- A framework should be provided to permit participants to move at will among large groups, small groups, and self-directed study.
- Large group sessions should have both a chairman and a recorder. Methods should be selected to ensure effective and continuous communication among participants.
- Six to ten people interested in similar aspects of a general theme should meet in small group sessions.
- Flexible resource people should be chosen who are sensitive and aware of individual needs.
- Assistance should be offered to individuals or small groups to set relevant objectives during the early stages of the workshop.

Adult Education Settings

Most formal teaching-learning transactions in schools and colleges take place in a single setting—the structured classroom for a group of students. Systematic adult learning, in contrast, occurs in a variety of settings including: individual, temporary group, organization, and community. Within each of these settings, the main responsibility for planning and directing learning activities can vary between learners and those who facilitate learning. One schema for describing this relationship was developed by Knox (1976) and is presented in Table 2.

Organizing Learning Activities

In addition to selection of learning activities, program development includes organization of activities to form an effective learning sequence. A useful guide for creating an effective learning sequence was developed by Miller (1964, pp. 37–50):

> *Step one:* Select activities that attempt to increase the motivation of participants to engage in systematic learning.

Table 2. Classification of Continuing Education Learning-Teaching Activities

Locus of responsibility for planning and directing learning activities

Setting	Category	Learner	Learner (with facilitator's help)	Facilitator (with learner's help)	Facilitator
Individual	Inter-personal	group visits	nondirective counseling	supervisory coaching	psychoevaluative demonstration
	Mediated print	self-directed reading on topic	library readers advisory service	correspondence course	how-to-do-it book
	Electronic	select related films, television programs	film forum	television course with materials, phoning	television course, no materials
Temporary group	Small	study-discussion	brainstorming, seminar, workshop	case study, role play	lecture discussion, process demonstration
	Large	problem clinic, buzz groups	listening panel, lecture from problems presented	lecture questions, interview resource person	lecture, forum, panel, symposium
Organization	Small	informal staff study groups	staff meeting series on organizational problems	training sessions for work teams	discuss management consultant's recommendations
	Large	organizational self-study	educational community development, organizational conference	action research	members react to proposal for organizational change
Community	Small	community problems discussion group	action seminar	demonstration project	technical briefing of community leaders on issue
	Large	field trips to other segments of community	result demonstration	community survey	lecture series on community problems

Step two: Select activities that help learners to grasp the inadequacy of their present behavior in relationship to an identifiable problem or role.

Step three: Select activities that help learners to visualize the desired behavior to be acquired in relation to the problem or role; that is, develop standards of acceptable performance.

Step four: Select activities that provide opportunities for learners to practice the desired behavior.

Step five: Select activities that reinforce the desired behavior.

Step six: Select activities that build upon each other in a logical and sequential order.

Effective program developers are aware that various design criteria exist for different learning situations. For example, one way to enhance a workshop or course is to encourage participants to feel comfortable with one another by using name tags and arranging for social interaction through refreshment breaks. Another is to allow sufficient time for input of new ideas and consideration of their applicability to achieve objectives. For a larger program, such as a conference sponsored by a professional association, some appropriate program design guidelines include covering major areas of relevant subject matter, continuity without needless overlap among separate parts of the program, and sequencing so that early parts of the conference provide building blocks for subsequent sessions. There are also several ways to improve the effectiveness of organizational and community development programs: focus preliminary efforts on diagnosing problems, identifying resources, and understanding aspirations of individuals or agency representatives; build support for the efforts and attempt to reduce defensiveness of participants, by focusing on the common goal; and attempt to achieve consensus and participation of the group regarding tasks to be achieved and procedures to be followed.

The most crucial aspect of learning-activity organization occurs during the implementation stage, when planning activities reach fruition in the teaching-learning transaction. The capability of resource people to be responsive and effective during the course or workshop depends in part on their preparation during the planning stage. This capability is illustrated by the extent of individualization, which is based on preparation of instructional materials and subgroup activities (Cross, Valley, and Associates, 1974). However, instructional effectiveness also depends on the style and proficiency of resource people during program sessions and the extent to which the program design allows and encourages them to take advantage of those aspects of teaching they do best.

Teachers of adults vary in their teaching style (Rogers, 1971; Solomon, Bezdek, and Rosenberg, 1963), and they have available a variety of instructional methods and materials that can enrich their performance during the program (Burton, 1958; Gage, 1963; Travers, 1973). In addition to having a thorough understanding of the content of the adult education program—so that it can be conveyed clearly and persuasively through example, explanation, and demonstration—effective teachers of adults tend to be proficient in interpersonal relations and group processes. Fortunately, there is an extensive professional literature available in this area, covering sensitivity training (Bradford, Gibb, and Benne, 1964), workshop procedures (Kelley, 1951), staff development and human relations training (Nylen and Associates, 1967), discussion leadership (Gray, 1964), case study (Stenzel and Feeney, 1970), and teaching older adults (Hiemstra, 1975; Jacobs, Mason, and Kauffman, 1970). In addition, several pamphlets are available that help acquaint inexperienced teachers with characteristics of adults as learners and with effective teaching procedures (Bock, 1979; Davis and McCallon, 1974; Dickinson, 1973; Lloyd, 1972; Los Angeles City Schools, 1977; Texas A & M, 1977; Ulmer, 1969).

It is important for program administrators to select resource people to accomplish instructional tasks at which they are proficient, to encourage them to use instructional procedures that fit program objectives and their own teaching style, and to give attention to the likely impact of the educational program on subsequent performance by participants as well as participant satisfaction with the process of the program. (Procedures to assess learner achievement and satisfaction as well as program impact are presented in Chapter Four.) In practice, the program administrator's role in relation to learning activities is similar to that for objectives. The resource person's role in helping adults learn tends to be quite personal and dependent on teaching style and repertoire of instructional methods. The program administrator influences learning activities when decisions are made on the general program design and on specific resource people. In the case of a course composed of ten weekly sessions taught by one instructor, the main influence of the program administrator on the learning activities occurs in the selection and orientation of the instructor. For an educational program that entails multiple resource people, the program administrator is more likely to have greater influence on the type and sequences of learning activities.

Program administrators and planning committees tend to leave many of the decisions regarding the selection and sequencing of learning activities to chance. A general topic or theme is often chosen, and a list of desirable resource people is prepared. If there are to be multiple resource people, their sequence in the program depends somewhat on their availability. Unless they are invited to perform a specific role—such as keynote speaker, panel member, or discussion leader—the individual resource people usually select whatever instructional materials and methods they prefer. Under these conditions, the program administrator can contribute little to either the range or sequence of learning activities. If a program administrator has proficiency in designing effective learning activities for adults, it is a shame to waste that capability. Effective practitioners develop many subtle ways to question possible learning activities and effective sequencing. It is most effective to raise these issues early in the planning process, before commitments are made to resource people. Administrators can also raise questions that are useful for program evaluation, and the evaluation conclusions can be used in turn to strengthen the remainder of the educational program or to revise it before it is repeated.

Future Directions

As more people become aware of adult education, greater attention and precision is needed in stating educational objectives and in selecting appropriate learning activities. The performance of those who conduct adult education programs tends to lag behind available knowledge. With the emergence of new and challenging communication and learning devices—such as two-way television, visual telephones, and home computers—adult educators are in an enviable position to take advantage of new opportunities. However, increasingly sophisticated hardware tends to confound rather than improve instructional procedures unless deliberate attention is given to software—the information mediated by the hardware.

Many adult education resource people and program administrators are unfamiliar with professional literature and practice beyond their personal experience, and greater dissemination of organized knowledge about objective setting and learning activities has become a major need in the field. Because so many resource people are employed on a part-time and short-term basis, program administrators are in the best position to disseminate and urge the use of such knowledge. Program administrators who wish to assume this responsibility must (1) be committed to the importance of the effort, (2) be familiar with concepts such as those contained in this chapter and in Chapters Two and Four, and (3) be effective in staff development activities such as described in Chapter Seven.

A number of future directions relate to discrepancies between current and ideal practice in the field of adult education. Some of these issues are listed in the following sections, along with suggestions on how thoughtful program administrators can incorporate successful objective setting and organization of learning activities into their practice.

1. How can practitioners effectively use information from program origins and needs assessment setting objectives? Resource people and planning committees vary greatly in the amount of information they have at their disposal about program origins and educational needs. Some have little information and proceed mainly on assumptions. Some are overwhelmed by the amount of relevant information and have difficulty identifying high-priority objectives. Effective adult education program administrators are able to relate needs and objectives while taking into account agency purposes and resources. Indications that an educational need exists—based on information from potential participants, opinions of experts, and successful programs elsewhere—tend to be more persuasive than indications from any one of these sources taken separately. Effective practitioners summarize the most

salient information about origins and needs and use their conclusions in setting objectives with resource people and planning
committees.

Objective setting is often satisfactory at the level of individual courses and workshops. In the future, there should be more
attention to the objectives of the aggregate of courses and workshops that an agency provides. Summary information about the
match between client needs and agency purposes, derived from the
objectives of individual courses and workshops, can contribute to
priority setting for the whole agency adult education program. In
addition, most agencies need to give greater attention to policy and
mission statements so that the total program reflects desirable priorities and directions instead of simply the collection of courses and
workshops that happen to occur.

2. What planning procedures are most effective for objective setting? Program administrators all too often work out their
own personal approaches to program development based exclusively on their experience, with little consideration for or familiarity with the effectiveness of procedures used by others. Ideally,
people with expertise in a content area can help identify important
aspects of the topic, and potential participants can usually indicate
the relevance of the topic to them. Effective program administrators are able to bring together information from both sources.
Most importantly, effective practitioners use public, explicit procedures for objective setting that allow various relevant viewpoints
to be represented.

3. How can the interests of potential participants be reflected in program objectives and learning activities? Effective
practitioners are able to give appropriate attention to learner
concerns in the program development process by including representative potential participants on planning committees and by
ensuring that detailed information about educational needs and
preferences of potential participants is available during program
planning. Guidelines for collecting and summarizing information
about client needs for the benefit of program planners would be
very helpful. In addition, attention should be given to procedures
that can be used during the educational program to enable participants to help select the objectives and learning activities that fit

their preferences and learning styles. Examples are nominal group process, agenda building for a session, and concurrent sessions on a topic that use contrasting formats.

4. How can program administrators effectively use program development concepts in the selection and orientation of resource people? Practitioners who understand how to use program development procedures can use the underlying concepts to decide which available resource person is most likely to plan and conduct an adult education program effectively. As expectations regarding the resource person's performance are discussed, consideration can be given to various approaches to objective setting and selection and organization of learning activities. In programs with more than one resource person, the program administrator can sometimes choose program objectives and design directly and then select resource people who can implement the program. The important task for the practitioner is to select resource people whose performance fits program purposes and clientele.

5. How can resource people be encouraged to give more attention to practice and application in adult education programs (where appropriate)? Sometimes adult education participants just want information from the program; usually, however, they want more opportunity to do something with the new ideas than the typical program provides. Effective program administrators are able to help resource people include opportunities for participants to discuss and practice new ideas and procedures in small group or simulated activities and to explore how they will apply what they learn after the program. One way to do so is to arrange for an inexperienced resource person to team teach with one who is very effective in using methods that enable participants to practice new ideas and techniques. Another is to arrange for resource people to spend time, during the planning process, with potential participants in the settings in which they intend to apply what they learn.

6. How can concepts about objectives and activities be useful for program evaluation? Most of this chapter has emphasized planning and conducting effective educational programs for adults. However, these same concepts can be used as standards against which to judge the effectiveness of an adult education activity in the process of program evaluation. Such an evaluation study

would compare current practice with these standards to identify areas needing improvement. Effective practitioners are able to reflect major program development concepts in the criteria for program evaluation and to use the findings for program improvement. Attention to achievable and measurable objectives is essential in both planning and evaluation. Attention should also be given to ways in which evaluation findings can be used to modify program objectives and learning activities to improve the total program.

7. How can program development be useful for staff development? One technique is to identify areas of program development that diverge from ideal practice and to use these as the content for staff development activities, especially for teachers of adults. A second technique is to apply major program development concepts and procedures to the design of staff development activities. For example, staff development activities for those who help adults learn should have clear and achievable objectives that reflect participant needs and agency purposes, should provide participants with opportunities to try out interactive instructional methods, and should exemplify use of program evaluation procedures that could be adapted for use by participants.

Chapter Four

Program Evaluation

Arden D. Grotelueschen

During the past decade, the emphasis on program evaluation in educational practice and writing has increased greatly. This change is particularly important to educational administrators, who increasingly are being held accountable for their programs. Adult and continuing education administrators have also been affected by this increased emphasis, but unlike other administrators, they have had a great deal of practical experience in program evaluation. This experience is mainly due to the voluntary nature of adult and continuing education programs, the practical nature of early writings in adult education evaluation (Byrn, 1959; Tyler, 1950), and the influence of research on adult education clientele (Knox, 1965a).

Because of this experience, effective adult education administrators are convinced of the merit of program evaluation. They also are convinced that new approaches and conceptions of program evaluation are needed. Circumstances and conditions have changed in education and in society, and administrators are aware that what worked in the past may well be inappropriate today. They certainly agree that the concepts that guided effective educational practice in the past must now be reexamined. This chapter presents current concepts of educational program evaluation and links those concepts to practical aspects of the adult education administrator's responsibility through a comprehensive discussion of the interactive aspects of program evaluation.

Evaluation Defined

The definition of evaluation depends largely upon one's general philosophy of education and on how one intends to use the acquired evaluation information (Tyler, 1969). In other words, evaluation means different things to different people, particularly as it is practiced. For example, it is a process of:

- documenting the congruence of learner outcomes and program objectives (Tyler, 1950)
- comparing performance data with a commonly accepted standard (Popham, 1969; Provus, 1969; Rivlin, 1971)
- specifying, obtaining, and providing relevant information for judging decision alternatives (Alkin, 1967; Stufflebeam, 1969)
- comparing actual effects of a program with a variety of demonstrated needs (Scriven, 1972)
- judging program merit against the value positions of relevant audiences (McDonald, 1974; Owens, 1973; Rippey, 1973; Stake, 1974a)
- judging a program critically, using expert knowledge (Eisner, 1976)
- describing and interpreting the wider context in which a program functions (Parlett and Hamilton, 1976)

These and other approaches to program evaluation have been compared and summarized in several sources (House, 1978; Stake,

1974b; Stufflebeam, 1977; Taylor, 1976; and Worthen and Sanders, 1973).

Some common elements run through these definitions—elements to which the adult and continuing education administrator needs to be particularly sensitive. Most definitions call for a thorough description of an educational program. Trivial as this may seem, experience demonstrates that describing any educational program is a difficult task and is often left incomplete. Selecting variables that describe an adult education program is often difficult until the evaluator assesses not only the purposes of the evaluation and the needs and preferences of the audience but also the nature of the program and the context in which it operates. Additionally, selecting isolated variables for program description may be seriously misleading: Variables purporting to give critical information about a program, such as levels of achievement, can rarely be ascertained, and evaluators need to avoid limiting themselves to this type of descriptive variable. Therefore, it is often advisable to consider the totality of program variables, including general program descriptors (such as type of agency, relation to parent organization, staff characteristics, type and extent of collaboration, participant characteristics, financial support, and governance structure), explicitly stated program goals or objectives (initial and restated goals), program states (how the program is perceived at varying times), and the central concerns for and about the program (procedural concerns expressed during program operation).

Intimately associated with evaluation is the need to gather or make value judgments about educational programs. Evaluation is determining value or merit; thus it is more than mere data gathering, although values are reflected by the indicators used—standardized test scores, verbal testimony of program participants, or the criticism of a program observer. The objectivity or subjectivity of the information obtained depends on how the information is gathered rather than to the inherent value of the information.

Ascertaining the value of something is consistent with the notion of a process—the *activity* of evaluating—and the notion of a *product*—the result of evaluating, a value judgment about something (Taylor, 1961). Therefore, the adult education administrator can both *do* an evaluation and *have* an evaluation. By continuously making and holding judgments of educational value, adult education administrators participate informally not only in the process but also the product of evaluation. Not so evident, though, is the extent to which the process or product follows certain principles of systematic evaluative inquiry—the focus of formal program evaluation.

Most definitions of evaluation suggest the rationale of providing relevant information to those who seek to increase their understanding about educational programs. This understanding may then serve as a basis for making decisions. But the decisions take the form of ideas or opinions as much as actions and are not always entirely rational. The decisions are rarely made by one individual but usually by several people exerting their influence on programming (Gooler and Grotelueschen, 1971). Evaluation often provides information that equalizes or neutralizes these diverse influences so that accommodations can be made among those involved in decision making. In essence, evaluation from this point of view is a democratic activity (McDonald, 1974).

In an adult education setting with a variety of people making many kinds of decisions, the evaluator provides information that helps others understand the educational choices available within the context of a sociopolitical institutional system (Belasco and Trice, 1969; Roth, 1964). Examples of this are apparent when one considers that administrators must organize the program format and operation; instructors must ascertain the value and use of materials and instructional methods for adult learners; participants must assess the suitability of the program for their own needs; and program sponsors must decide whether continued support is merited. All those involved with a program's operation—from sponsors to consumers—may use the information gained from evaluation to increase understanding and aid decision making.

Purposes and Goal of Evaluation

There are many reasons why an administrator of adult education might conduct a program evaluation: to account for funds or resources and monitor compliance with legal regulations and guidelines; to document major program accomplishments and examine the expedience of program goals; to identify potential participant needs and establish program emphases; to ascertain collaboration opportunities and evaluate coordination efforts with other institutions and agencies; and to identify program weaknesses and assess progress toward stated goals. These reasons are clearly less philosophical than the evaluation definitions presented earlier, and they may be influenced by specific circumstances, may be internal or external to the program, and may be affected by the general context in which the program functions. Most of these reasons for evaluation fall into one or more of the following three categories: past activities or outcomes; current program activities; and possible future actions (Grotelueschen and others, 1974).

In the first instance, when evaluation is conducted on past program activities or outcomes, it is usually being conducted for the purpose of justification or accountability. Activities and programs currently being conducted or being planned can also be evaluated for justification reasons, of course, but most evaluations for accountability are done on activities or programs that have been completed. Scriven (1967) calls this *summative evaluation*. Most accountability evaluations are initiated from sources external to the program, although they may also stem from the concern of program personnel. External initiation usually occurs at a different program level (such as state or federal) but can also occur within offices with explicit evaluation responsibilities (such as the Government Accounting Office). Typical questions asked by external sources include: Would an alternative program have been more cost effective? Do program elements tend to be more satisfactory than alternative elements? Have the program goals been appropriate for the target audience? Was the program delivered to whom it was intended and in the intended way? Will subsequent program efforts be better than what has been done?

When program evaluation focuses on current efforts, it is typically conducted for the purpose of program improvement (Cronbach, 1963). Evaluation conducted for this reason seeks to obtain information about a program during its implementation

stage for the purpose of remedying any shortcomings. This, according to Scriven (1967), is *formative evaluation*. Improvement is,
of course, the stated principle behind most evaluations and has
received the emphasis of adult education evaluators (see Knox,
1969). Specific questions addressed include: What procedures
might be undertaken to improve the instruction being offered?
How might program content be strengthened? How might planning activities be improved to enhance broader participation?

A third reason for conducting an evaluation is to assist in
planning a future educational program (Grotelueschen and Gooler,
1972). As Moynihan (1970) has noted, this is "evaluation in advance" and seeks to ascertain the worth of potential program goals,
alternative means for reaching potential goals, and possible consequences of each alternative. It is typically more comprehensive
than a needs assessment, in that it addresses means-ends alternatives and ascertains their merit. However, its procedures are similar
to those of needs assessments, clientele analyses, and feasibility
studies. Questions that might be addressed include: What agencies
may be interested in program collaboration? Are the proposed
procedures likely to produce the desired consequences? Are we
overlooking any important potential program goals? Can the intended outcomes be obtained efficiently?

There may be additional reasons for conducting an evaluation beyond the three broad reasons that have been presented
here. There are also combinations of reasons for conducting an
evaluation. Furthermore, today's reason may be seen in a different
light tomorrow. Information gathered for improving a program,
for example, may assist the practitioner in planning future programs. Thus an evaluation may be valuable beyond its immediate
and intended purpose, by enlightening choices among alternatives
not directly experienced or studied.

Whatever its specific rationale, the basic goal of an evaluation is to determine the worth of what is being evaluated. This
point has both theoretical and practical significance: theoretically,
it distinguishes program evaluation from other forms of inquiry
such as educational research; practically, any information on program merit contributes to the evaluation process, aiding an administrator deliberating between alternatives.

Educational Research and Evaluation

As educational program evaluation has increased in significance, it has been compared with educational research, with similarities and differences noted by various writers (Cronbach and Suppes, 1969; Glass and Worthen, 1972; Guba, 1969; Hemphill, 1969; Simon, 1969; Stake, 1969; Stanley, 1969; Wardrop, 1969; Worthen and Sanders, 1973). The basic similarity between educational research and evaluation is, of course, that they deal with educational phenomena. They also use similar techniques of investigation—such as questionnaires, interviews, participant observation, and rating scales—and similar procedures for collecting data—such as sampling.

The differences between evaluation and research relate to how they are initiated, conducted, and used. In general, program evaluation is not concerned with knowledge for its own sake but with knowledge for action. It is less concerned with making generalizations than with making decisions in a specific setting. Additionally, evaluation is usually guided by the concerns of the audiences interested in a program rather than by those of the evaluator. Table 1 compares educational program evaluation with educational research. Some useful evaluations may also have characteristics of research, making these comparisons somewhat overstated; nevertheless, the differences presented should at least help practitioners to avoid a situation in which they need an evaluation but are actually getting research.

Various meanings of evaluation have been presented. Most approaches to evaluation have been concerned with description, judgment, and the facilitation of understanding and decision making. Evaluation is further defined by its purposes, goals, and relationship to educational research. The next section presents some defining characteristics of an educational program, which will assist in providing a conceptual framework for specifying adult education evaluation questions.

Program Defined

Before proceeding to a discussion of how evaluations are planned and conducted, it is important to think first about just what

Table 1. Comparison of Evaluation and Educational Research

Evaluation	*Research*
Investigates what happens (descriptive)	Investigates why it happens (explanatory)
Deals directly with program worth	Avoids judgments of program's worth
Focus is determined by issues of a particular situation	Focus is determined independently from a special situation
Client initiates study	Researcher initiates study
Client is primary audience	Researchers are the primary audience
Contributes to agency functioning	Contributes to academic guild functioning
Naturalistic and practice-inquiry	Inquiry guided by discipline
Results are specific to designated setting	Results generalizable to other settings
Primary objective is to service client	Primary objective is to add to body of knowledge
Time constrained	Unbounded by time limitations
Assesses educational and social utility directly	Assesses educational and social utility indirectly

a program is, because programs are the subject of evaluations. To adult education practitioners, this may seem redundant, because their area of expertise is the administration, development, and implementation of programs. But a close-working familiarity with educational programs does not necessarily guarantee a complete understanding of them, and at times some amount of distance and perspective is desirable.

In defining the term *program,* it is useful as a starting point to note that a program differs somewhat from the traditional notion of curriculum, though certainly it is also related to it. From a casual sampling of definitions (Axford, 1970; Boyle and Jahns, 1970; London, 1960; Thomas, 1964), the notion of an adult education program primarily connotes short-term learning experiences that are responsive to learner needs and are implemented outside of the traditional educational delivery system. Additionally, these definitions emphasize the characteristics of flexibility, variability, and all-inclusiveness of programs. However, we must not conclude that programs are always nonformal, highly flexible, variable, or all inclusive. Rather, we need to recognize that educational programs for adults vary along several continua from very informal to highly structured, from very general to highly specialized, and from specific single programs to programs that consist of a number of offerings.

At the more structured end of the continuum, program characteristics approximate traditional curriculum characteristics in several ways. The clarity provided by this formality and structure makes it easier to analyze what is involved in a program than if we began with programs at the unstructured end of the continuum. It is therefore appropriate to begin with curriculum theory, acquiring an understanding of what is involved in more formal programs, in an effort not to miss some important element due to the lack of clarity in the less formal programs.

Program Elements

Schwab (1973) offers a conceptual approach to defining the elements of a curriculum, of which he claims there are four: the student, the teacher, the subject matter, and the milieu. These are the "commonplaces of educational curricula." For the adult educator, who thinks in terms of programs, these elements might be thought of as program elements: the participant, the instructor, the topic area, and the context. Each element has equal status and each is indispensable to both the curriculum and the program.

To translate Schwab's curriculum elements even further into the terms of adult and continuing education, students are generally regarded as "adult participants." These participants have a variety of life roles (such as family member, citizen, worker, organization member, user of leisure) that have potential for contributing to or detracting from their learning capacity and background. And all of these elements, in turn, potentially interact with other program elements to form a personal program for the participants.

Teachers—also called *mentors, resource people,* and *instructors*—also have various inherent and acquired characteristics that influence their ability to deal effectively with various teaching situations. Their personality, experience, knowledge, teaching style, professional orientation, willingness to learn and change, self-confidence, flexibility, and private goals are specific aspects that interact with other program elements and that demand attention in analyzing a curriculum.

Subject matter, or *program topics,* refers to the substantive aspects of what is being learned and taught. It is the body of organized knowledge about something that is useful in attaining new understanding, attitudes, values, or skills. Subject matter can be either integrated and holistic or differentiated and fragmented; and depending upon the participant's or the instructor's outlook and the nature of the subject matter, it will be relevant or irrelevant.

The milieu—the context or general setting—is the social, psychological, and physical environment of the teaching-learning transaction. In the words of Parlett and Hamilton (1976, p. 145), "The learning milieu represents a network or nexus of cultural, social, institutional, and psychological variables." More specifically, it includes the participant's family or social group; the community; the meeting place; the institution or agency that provides the program; the image of adult and continuing education; numerous administrative, occupational, and financial constraints; social and ethnic structures; and prevailing legal and ethical standards.

These basic program elements highlight the essential aspects of a program which, in interaction with one another, provide an analytic platform for considering evaluation issues. This analytic approach alone is not sufficient, however; it must be contrasted with a more concrete approach that attends to actual characteristics (Chin, 1969). The following section discusses programs using this latter approach, in an attempt to gain some balance and to maximize our coverage of the facets of programs in planning an evaluation activity.

Program Perspectives

A major responsibility of the adult educator is planning and conducting educational programs. Attention to these processes constitutes a concrete approach to understanding the characteristics to which the adult educator gives specific attention: goals, designs, implementation, and outcomes.

Goals are important to the program developer for a number

of reasons. First, program goals explicitly designate what should be pursued or attained in an educational program; that is, they are statements of program intention. Second, goals express the values of the people involved in the program; as such they are judgment data (Stake, 1970). Third, goals are priority statements; even though broadly stated, they imply that something is more important than something else.

The relationship between program goals and program evaluation has raised a number of issues (Atkin, 1963; Eisner, 1967; Stanford Evaluation Consortium, 1976). In general these issues relate to three viewpoints about the contribution of program goals to evaluation. One familiar view stresses that evaluation's main function is to ascertain whether a program is accomplishing its goals (Tyler, 1950). When Tyler introduced this notion into educational theory, he did not call for a specification of program stimuli and learner responses in advance. He was merely interested in various types of outcomes and examples of what learners might do if they developed in a manner consistent with what a program planner wanted. Cronbach (1978, p. 413) cautions us about this approach to evaluation as it is commonly practiced.

> Even a well-specified list of goals is necessarily incomplete as a source of questions. It does not give attention to unwanted outcomes. A properly Devilish evaluator will direct attention to side effects and opportunity costs as well as goals. To ask whether a program "has achieved its goals" implies a quantitative target. Such levels are meaningful in industrial training; for the trainee moving onto the production line, minimum standards of safety, speed, and freedom from spoilage may be defined. In educational contexts, however, increments of progress are welcome no matter where the student is on the scale. No breaking point represents minimal adequacy. To ask planners to set a quantitative target calls for gamesmanship; if they promise too little they lose customers, and if they claim too much they lay the program open to a charge of "failure." Pressure to state quantitative targets leads to evasions (will show gains in self-confidence) or arbitrary and ill-considered specifics (will gain twelve months in reading level on a standardized test). At the time the study is planned, the only reasonable question is, "What outcomes should we attend to?" Whether the level reached is satisfactory is to be judged after the assessment, through a process of political negotiation.

A second view asserts that program goals have a limited role in evaluating a program. Scriven (1972) has referred to this approach as "goal-free" evaluation, which to him means that a program's final appraisal should focus on importance and value, not on intention. A third view emphasizes the importance of evaluating the goals themselves (Scriven, 1967). These issues are far from being settled in evaluation studies, and all three are practiced in evaluations. Thus, it is important for adult educators to consider just what they have in mind regarding program goals when they start thinking about evaluation.

Another important characteristic—the design component of program planning, implementing, or revising—serves as the program blueprint. It is a concrete plan that links what is generally valued with what is specifically desired. It is the result of a goals-to-means-to-ends deliberation within the framework of specific institutional constraints. It is a flexible rationale for action, which responds as new insights are gained, opportunities arise, or circumstances change.

The rationale behind a program design is not always explicitly formulated. In fact, in some instances the program design itself must be inferred from the state of affairs. Program developers and implementers often do not conceive of their efforts in segmented parts and are reluctant to specify them in categories, partly because specified program parts are more open to criticism than a more holistically described program (Freeman, 1977). Furthermore, many professionals justify their actions by relying on intuitive "know-how." Whether program design is explicit or implicit, it can be an important focus of evaluation. Questions about various aspects of program design can be asked, and some questions, asked during the planning phase, are crucial because it is often easier to make adjustments at the drawing board than to have to revise plans after implementation has begun.

Implementation is putting the goals and designs to work. It is the process by which the program is conducted and involves a variety of teaching-learning-administering transactions, aimed at fulfilling the desired expectations of a target audience. As a focus of evaluation, implementation includes both the substance and the quality of what occurs in the pursuit of program goals.

The final program perspective under consideration, outcomes, has traditionally received the most attention from program personnel during evaluations. The emphasis is usually on immediate intended learner accomplishments, but these can be illusionary (Caulley and Grotelueschen, 1978). Not only are unintended, long-term, and latent outcomes emphasized less but also outcomes associated with nonlearners (such as instructors or institutions) are often overlooked. Because of this it is important to distinguish between two types of outcomes. *First-order outcomes* refer to accomplishments that are attained by those instructors, participants, and program administrators who are involved in the program and who share its direct experience. For example, physicians attending a continuing medical education program might have an increased awareness of the importance of quality patient care and have some new knowledge of how to improve patient care in their medical practice. *Second-order outcomes* are once-removed effects of the program and refer to the impact on people or institutions due to their first-order program accomplishments. For example, the changes in patient care resulting from a physician's participation in a continuing medical education program would be a second-order outcome. Clearly both of these outcomes are important for the adult and continuing educator. While the extent to which second-order outcomes can be assessed is controversial, it is useful for the program administrator to consider them carefully.

We have defined an evaluation and an educational program from several vantage points. Consideration will now be given to a conceptual framework for specifying adult education evaluation questions.

A Classification Scheme

Three general dimensions of the program evaluation process have been presented: evaluation purposes, program elements, and program characteristics. When taken together, these three dimensions afford us a classification scheme that can specify evaluation questions in adult education and clarify relationships among those questions. Most importantly, this scheme can assist the adult education administrator in thinking through evaluation situations.

The categories contained within each of these dimensions are by no means mutually exclusive. In fact, it is important that overlap be recognized because this recognition can have significant impact upon evaluation considerations. The classification will aid the adult education administrator to make this recognition. Overlap among the evaluation purposes implies that data gathered for one evaluation purpose may prove valuable for another evaluation purpose. Overlap among program elements illustrates that sometimes the same questions can be related to different elements, leading potentially to both confusion and reality, for which the administrator should be prepared. Further overlap among the program characteristics, although perhaps less common, indicates the importance of identifying the process in which one is engaged and of preventing the contamination of one with another—for example, by letting one's feelings about implementation obscure certain desirable participant goals.

It is helpful at the outset to ask just what the program evaluation is all about. That is, we must ask and answer the question "What is the purpose of the evaluation?" This question asks us to make a choice among the three evaluation purposes presented earlier, namely, for justification, for improvement, and for planning. The answer in each case may include one or a combination of these purposes. The designated purposes of the evaluation, then, help us consider combinations of program elements and program characteristics that are important to us and help us frame questions for those important combinations. This first stage is presented in Figure 1.

Assuming that we have chosen to do an evaluation for justification of a program, our next task is to consider the questions which would fit the variety of combinations of program elements and characteristics that constitute a program. Figure 2 shows a sampling of questions across the entire framework of possible questions that might be important.

Tables 2, 3, and 4 present the classification scheme in its entirety. Each illustration provides, respectively, justification, improvement, and planning questions for program evaluation. Sixteen question cells are contained in each table, relating to what one is evaluating (element) and at what programmatic stage one is

Figure 1. Identifying the Evaluation Purpose

Is The Evaluation Purpose . . .

Past Oriented	Present Oriented	Future Oriented
To justify the program	To improve the program	To plan the program

Four Program Perspectives to Review

	Goals	Designs	Implemen- tation	Outcomes
Participants				
Instructors				
Topics				
Contexts				

Four Program Elements to Review

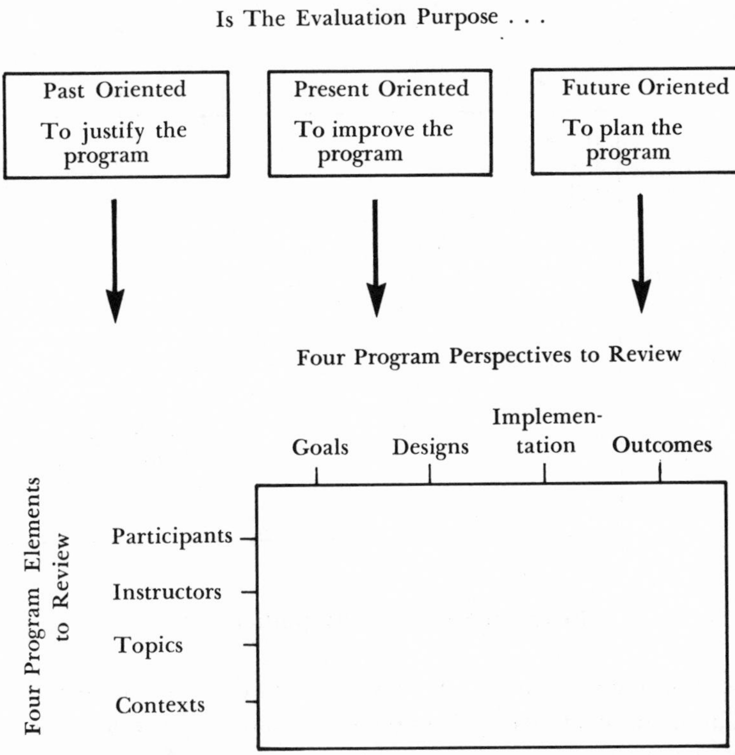

evaluating (perspective) within a purpose classification. The questions presented here are not necessarily important in their own right but serve to help the adult educator think comprehensively and systematically about the kinds of questions or issues useful in an evaluation situation.

Although knowing about program evaluation is necessary, it is not a sufficient condition for conducting an effective evaluation. Experience with the process of program evaluation is also important (Grotelueschen, Gooler and Knox, 1976; Knox and others, 1974). The next section discusses the program evaluation ingredients that one might attend to while engaging in the practical evaluation process.

**Figure 2. Justification Evaluation Questions for
Program Element and Perspective Categories**

Program Perspectives

	Goals	Designs	Implementation	Outcomes
Participants	Are the educational goals appropriate for these participants?			
Instructors		Did the instructors follow the program design?		
Topics			Was the topic dealt with as intended?	
Contexts				Was the impact of outcomes on the agency appropriate?

Program Elements

Program Evaluation Ingredients

There are a variety of ways in which one can conduct an evaluation, depending largely upon one's philosophy of evaluation. If, for example, a person's view of evaluation is similar to Tyler's (documenting the congruence of learner outcomes and program objectives), the evaluation task simply involves gathering participant outcome data and relating them to program objectives. If an evaluator is partial to Scriven's goal-free approach, in contrast, documentation of congruence between learner outcomes and program objectives is of little or no concern.

Whatever the approach, the adult educator should gauge its compatibility with naturalistic and democratic process criteria. Often evaluation approaches used by practitioners are not natural parts of the program development and implementation process but instead become cumbersome techniques imposed upon the democratic process. Effective administrators use naturalistic evaluations—built in to the various program processes—as they continuously "take the pulse" of their program.

Table 2. Evaluation Justification Questions

		Program Perspectives		
Program Elements	Goals	Designs	Implementation	Outcomes
Participants	Are the educational goals appropriate for these participants?	Is the program emphasis appropriate for the target population?	Was the time allocated to participant discussion sufficient?	Were the attained learner outcomes the most desired by the program sponsor?
Instructors	Are the primary purposes of instruction implicitly incompatible with program purposes?	Did the instructors follow the program design?	Was the method of instruction most suitable for the content being taught?	Were the unintended outcomes of instruction desirable?
Topics	Is this the best topic for achieving program goals?	Are the best topics selected, given the constraints of time and resources?	Was the topic dealt with as intended?	How was this topic useful to program participants?
Contexts	Were the attained goals educationally important?	Does the design optimize available resources?	Was the implementation of this program timely?	Was the impact of outcomes on the agency appropriate?

Table 3. Evaluation Improvement Questions

| | | *Program Perspectives* | | |
	Goals	*Designs*	*Implementation*	*Outcomes*
Participants	How could program goals more realistically correspond to learner goals?	Do learners have adequate opportunity to address their practical concerns?	Does the mode of instruction facilitate active learner involvement?	How might greater learner achievement be attained?
Instructors	Would a revision of some of the instructors' goals make them more compatible with one another?	Would the proposed method of instruction be compatible with the learning styles of the target group?	Are instructors capable of using the chosen method of instruction?	What emphasis in technique would increase the likelihood of noncognitive instructional outcomes?
Topics	Are there alternative topics which would better facilitate achieving stated program goals?	Does the explicit ordering of the topics facilitate learning?	Given the topic area, is there a better means for implementing it?	Would it be useful to go into greater topic depth?
Contexts	Does our current knowledge of the context suggest a change of goals?	Is the format of the program consistent with the setting of the instruction?	Does the selection of participants comply with equal opportunity regulations?	How might greater impact on the learners' institutional setting be attained?

Program Elements (row labels: Participants, Instructors, Topics, Contexts)

Table 4. Evaluation Planning Questions

Program Elements	Program Perspectives			
	Goals	Designs	Implementation	Outcomes
Participants	Have expectations been achieved by different potential learners?	Has feedback concerning the design been obtained from potential learners?	Is the sequencing of program components appropriate for the intended learners?	Can the intended learner outcomes be attained?
Instructors	How might an appropriate array of instructional goals be attained?	Have alternative designs of instruction been considered?	Is the proposed method of instruction consistent with the intended goals?	Are the instructor's desired outcomes attainable?
Topics	Is the topic relevant to the proposed goals?	Is the intended scope of topic coverage appropriate?	What is the best method of instruction for this topic?	Will exposure to this topic be beneficial to participants?
Contexts	Are the proposed program goals consistent with the image of the sponsoring agency?	Does the design reflect an awareness of setting differences of program offerings?	Is the pacing of instruction consistent with the philosophy of the program?	What kind of impact will the anticipated goals have on the sponsoring institution?

Evaluations are not always democratic; they may be bureaucratic or autocratic (McDonald, 1974). Consequently, in a democratic society, some evaluation approaches may be politically incompatible with institutional and societal norms. Conversely, in a nondemocratic society, the democratic approach to evaluation may be inappropriate. This latter point is of particular significance for persons conducting evaluations of international programs.

Conducting an evaluation requires a certain degree of planning. As Brophy, Grotelueschen, and Gooler (1976, p. 1) have stated: "A plan for evaluation may be viewed as a blueprint which provides information about the intended activities (and implicit philosophy) of an evaluation task to the client before implementation. The client then has an opportunity to see if he approves of the evaluation's intended actions and may state his concerns if he feels this is necessary." In short, a plan can focus on the intentions of both evaluator and client before the evaluation begins. This type of evaluation is what Stake (1974a, p. 14) has described as the "responsive approach" to evaluation. He calls an evaluation responsive if "it orients more directly to program activities than to program intents; responds to audience requirements for information; and if the different value perspectives present are referred to in reporting the success and failure of the program." More important, perhaps, is the fact that regardless of whether or not adult education practitioners are convinced of the value of the responsive method, the existence of a plan will nonetheless help them avoid a common problem: answering questions that no one is asking. Considering evaluation ingredients (things that go into planning and conducting an evaluation) enables an adult education administrator to respond more effectively to both the information needs of programs and the usefulness of the evaluation effort and to carry out evaluation responsibilities, enhancing not only the program's effectiveness but also its accountability.

The major program evaluation ingredients exemplify one approach to evaluation planning. This approach involves the identification of the evaluation purposes, the audiences of the evaluation, the relevant issues to be addressed, and the resources that are either available or needed to conduct the evaluation. Attention to these ingredients by the adult education evaluator will assist in defining the scope, focus, priorities, and balance of an evaluation. By focusing on the kind of evidence to be sought and the data-gathering, analysis, and reporting techniques to be used, alternative evaluation designs tailored to a program's purposes, audiences, issues, and resources can be identified. The eight ingredients of evaluations are described in the following sections. Much of the content presented is taken from Grotelueschen and others (1974). For an alternative approach to designing educational evaluations, see Cronbach (1978).

Purpose: Why Evaluate?

Evaluation of adult education programs is usually conducted by program personnel or by external evaluators in response to concerns expressed by people within the program or from outside agencies. It may respond to a current concern or to mandated responsibility. Evaluation may focus on past activities or outcomes, current activities, or what might be done in the future. Formal evaluation activities represent a small but important component of an adult educator's major responsibilities.

While specific evaluation purposes may vary, the general goal of evaluation is to ascertain the worth of something. In the course of an evaluation, an evaluator may help clarify program issues, decide what data to gather, and determine how to report information. The evaluation report may include the judgments of various people related to the program in addition to descriptions of the educational program being evaluated. However, the final conclusions about the worth of a program may be left to the person or group that requests or desires the evaluation. The role of the evaluator is to obtain and communicate information that will guide decision making, reduce uncertainty, and assist clients and audiences to consider issues related to their program. The evaluation should help the decision maker by reflecting the many-sided reality of the program. To oversimplify the issues or underestimate their complexity may mislead decision making, not facilitate it.

Though evaluation sometimes uses social and behavioral science techniques, one must remember that evaluation is concerned not with knowledge for its own sake but with knowledge for action.

It is less concerned with making generalizations than with making decisions in a specific setting. The evaluation activity is usually guided by the concerns of audiences who have an interest in the program rather than by the concerns of the evaluator. Evaluation may thus serve the purposes of program planning, policymaking, program improvement, or program justification or accountability. Evaluation activities may also entail documenting the history and impact of a program.

Audiences: Who Is the Evaluation For?

People who request an adult education evaluation have a special interest in the program that is evaluated; however, the results of an evaluation may also be interesting or necessary to others who did not request the evaluation. Those audiences most typically served by program evaluation are program funders, people involved in conducting the program (for example, teachers and administrators), program participants, and various supporters and opponents of the program. Other interested groups may include community groups, content specialists, and legislators.

Each potential audience of an evaluation should be considered, especially the people or groups who request or desire the evaluation. In identifying the primary audience of the evaluation, the evaluator should decide on the legitimacy and urgency of the claims of each potential audience. Some audiences want to have their accountability demands heard; given limited resources, the evaluator should assign priorities among these demands. The evaluator should consider the costs of failing to serve some audiences but should also recognize that usually not all can be served and that the most vocal group may not have the greatest legitimacy. In general, the evaluator focuses on only one audience while attempting to accommodate others as much as possible.

Different audiences have different concerns about the program, so selecting the primary audience for a specific evaluation effort in effect determines the main questions to be addressed by the evaluation. The range of concerns and interests in primary audiences will suggest secondary audiences that might also be interested in the evaluation. The evaluator should collect and con-

sider information about various potential audiences. This information might include the legitimacy of their claims on the program
for evaluation, their expectations of the evaluation and of the program, the criteria by which they will judge the success of the program, the indicators of program performance they prefer, their
standards of program success, and the forms of reporting they will
find most useful.

Issues: What Questions Should the Evaluation Address?

A classification scheme was presented earlier as a framework
for specifying program evaluation questions in adult education.
These questions can be viewed as issues around which an evaluation activity might be organized. The evaluator proceeds by engaging in discussion with the audiences to be addressed by the
evaluation—especially with those who request the evaluation or
who are members of other primary audiences—and by drawing
upon his past experience with other adult education evaluations and conceptions of how evaluation questions might be classified. In this process the evaluator should identify the concerns
and problems of the primary audiences with respect to the program and the questions they are asking about it in order to make
the evaluation effort useful and responsive. Sometimes evaluations
address questions of interest to no one in particular, which can
mislead audiences by focusing attention on relatively arbitrary indicators of program success or on indicators important only to the
evaluator. As evaluators choose issues, they should relate them
closely to the needs and interests of the audiences to be addressed.

Discussions among evaluators and clients usually culminate
in agreement about the appropriate range of issues to be addressed in an evaluation. If all selected issues cannot be adequately
addressed with available resources—and they rarely can be—
priorities are assigned. These priorities may change over time, as
may the interests of audiences. Nonetheless, identification of important issues provides guidelines as to the kinds of data that
should be sought. The adult education evaluator should periodically reconsider the issues to be addressed, for issues may change
or lose importance as the evaluation progresses, and it may be
necessary to revise the focus or scope of the evaluation.

One general issue of evaluation is accountability, and the evaluation enables program staff to respond with appropriate data to a variety of accountability demands. Evaluation in adult education is also likely to address some specific issues, including evidence on various possible program outcomes; program processes and costs; the extent to which needs were addressed and ignored and goals were fulfilled and unfulfilled; whether program promises were kept or broken; and comparisons with competitors or alternatives.

Resources: What Resources Are Available for the Evaluation?

Before embarking on an evaluation, the evaluator should decide what resources are likely to be available for the evaluation and its anticipated benefit. Making this determination in advance helps set broad parameters for the scope of the evaluation. As the evaluation design is developed, costs can be estimated and decisions can be made about the deployment of limited resources.

An evaluation plan should include cost estimates in terms of dollar outlay (for supplies), time expenditures (for interviews, meetings, and so forth), and expertise needed (such as program personnel). The plan should also indicate how the evaluation will be managed and who will be responsible for each aspect of the evaluation.

Estimates of the cost of acquiring information should take into account hidden costs such as time lost to the program by evaluating; tradeoffs and alternative uses of funds; and human costs such as invasion of privacy, dangers of evoking negative reactions, sparking controversy, or generating pressure on program personnel. Although existing information, regularly collected by an adult education program, should be used in the evaluation, some new information is often required and may be costly to acquire because it is not part of regularly budgeted program documentation. All of these hidden costs can be compared with the costs of not evaluating.

It is not easy to decide in advance the percentage of program resources to be expended on evaluation. Every dollar and hour spent on evaluation takes away from other aspects of the program, but evaluation may also be an investment in the future of the program. The value of the investment will vary with the urgency of accountability demands on the program and the value of reporting program performance. A reasonable cost for an evaluation can be decided by estimating the significance of issues and the likely impact of the evaluation. Various evaluation needs and legitimacies will entail different expenditures of resources, but some form and effort of evaluation is possible within any budget.

Evidence: What Evidence Should Be Collected?

Evidence is any information that contributes to the consideration of a particular issue being addressed by an evaluation. Judgments of the effectiveness of an adult education program should be made on the basis of evidence. Evaluation efforts are usefully organized around selected issues; once issues are selected, a search for evidence may begin.

Evidence may take many forms, including descriptions of program personnel; adult participants; program processes, content, and goals; program costs; and the social milieu within which the program operates. In addition, descriptions of program activities and outcomes might be prepared; statements about the value of the program might be collected from various people; speculations about causes and effects of program success or failure might be made. Various kinds of evidence will be appropriate for different issues and audiences.

The quality of evidence can be assessed by considering the relevance of the data to issues and audiences (determining what and who are counted as evidence); the balance and scope of the evidence; the validity of measures—that is, the extent to which they measure what they are supposed to measure; the reliability of measures—that is, the extent to which measures are accurate and consistent; the degree to which claimed outcomes actually result from the program rather than from other factors; the degree to which side effects and other anticipated and unanticipated outcomes have been identified; and the degree to which the evaluator is credible.

A useful rule of thumb for specific evaluation efforts is to collect as many data as are needed to address the issue in question while avoiding using data simply because they are available. Not all data are relevant in addressing the issues at hand; this does not deny the importance of continuing general documentation, however. The evaluator should not take too narrow a view of need, because new evaluation issues may emerge during the course of an evaluation, or priorities may change, modifying earlier plans. Ultimately, selection of evidence depends upon its descriptive or judgmental value, its utility to decision makers, and its cost.

Data Gathering: How Is the Evidence to Be Collected?

After deciding on the evidence to be collected, the evaluator should decide how much information to collect and from which data sources. Data sources are people or things—including program participants and personnel, existing documents, and related evaluation studies—that provide evidence about the program. Both the kinds of data sources and the quantity of each should be considered before beginning the sampling procedures. Proper consideration must be given to ethical questions raised in data gathering. Considerations of treatment and interpretation of data and constraints imposed by limitations of resources must also be made.

Various data-gathering strategies might be considered. For example, regarding the relative contribution of formal and informal collection efforts, should one simply ask adult education program participants to express their feelings about the program? Or would it be better to construct a more formal instrument to obtain attitudinal data? Some thought should be given to the appropriateness of various data-gathering techniques, such as observations, questionnaire rating scales, historical data, and interviews. Some data-gathering methods intrude more on program operation than others. Excellent sources on various data-gathering techniques include Hyman, Wright, and Shelton (1975) on the use of existing data; Anastasi (1976) on standardized tests; McCall and Simmons (1969) on making observations; Jacobs (1974) and Berdie and Anderson (1974) on constructing questionnaires; and Gordon (1975) on conducting interviews.

Existing instruments or procedures may sometimes be applicable to a particular evaluation need, although in other instances the evaluator may wish to develop new instruments or procedures. In either case, the instrument should provide information relevant to the evaluation questions being asked.

Some data-gathering techniques may be useful in collecting information about the standards for each aspect of an adult education program. Because adults and interest groups differ in the criteria they use to define an acceptable level of performance or outcome, the evaluator will find it useful to become acquainted with the varying levels expected by his primary audience. In addition to knowing how well the desired objectives were attained, the evaluator will need to know how important achieving the goal was to his primary audience. Attaining high level proficiency in a skill that is considered to be inconsequential is not a valued outcome.

The evaluator must also consider the timing of information collection, explanations of data collection to affected people, and appropriate means of coding and storing information. If these issues are not dealt with before beginning data collection, the evaluator may be faced with insufficient, misleading, or inappropriate information. Once these issues have been considered, appropriate instruments and procedures can be selected or constructed, and data can be gathered.

Analysis: How Is the Evidence to Be Analyzed?

Once evidence has been gathered, it must be analyzed to ascertain what it says about the program. It is important, of course, that analyses be of appropriate quality and scope in relation to the data—sophisticated analyses performed on inadequate or inappropriate data may lead to false implications or conclusions. It is also important that the analysis relate to audience concerns. Good data analysis will provide descriptions of the program being evaluated, highlighting those aspects relevant to particular issues or audiences. An analysis may describe a program during a given time period; it may also document change in a program over time. Comparisons might be made, for example, between current program inputs, processes, or outcomes and previous program aspects or comparable aspects of other programs. Data analysis is seldom conducted to make predictions about future programs. Some analyses are conducted in an effort to determine why certain outcomes occurred, although cause-and-effect relationships are difficult to ascertain, especially given the naturalistic nature of program evaluation. Some analyses are conducted with a very specific question or point in mind, for example: Does the program have an effect? To what extent were program objectives met? How well does this program compare with that program? Other data analyses are performed in an effort to reveal unanticipated problems.

There are many ways to analyze evaluation data, the choice of analytical technique depending on the nature of information to be analyzed, the purpose of the analysis, and the resources available for the analysis. In some instances, particular quantitative statistical techniques may be appropriate; percentages, averages, or correlations might well suit the purposes of the analysis. In other cases, qualitative analytic techniques such as content analysis, critical reviews, narrative portrayals, or expert opinion should be chosen. Kerlinger (1973) is an excellent general analysis source. Two very good quantitative resources are Minium (1978) and Hopkins and Glass (1978). Guba (1978) and Becker and Geer (1960) are excellent qualitative analysis references. In general, the type of data analysis conducted is directly linked to the concerns of audiences, the type and quality of evidence, and the audiences' ability to understand summary information.

Reporting: How Should Evaluation Findings Be Reported?

People have different abilities and experiences that influence the way they receive and use evaluation reports, and the adult education evaluator should take these differences into account in reporting evaluation information. Reporting standard scores from an achievement test, for example, may be meaningful to some audiences, while information may need to be presented in a different form for other audiences. Technical or statistical information may not be meaningful or comprehensible to some groups; nontechnical, nonstatistical descriptions of program functioning can be useful forms of evaluation data, and may sometimes be most appropriate.

It is important to understand the criteria, standards, and indicators that various audiences have in mind as they consider a program and to prepare findings for dissemination that address those concerns in a language that the audience will understand. Audiences are more likely to understand a program and to use evaluation findings if their members are associated with the evaluation effort and the program, if they are committed to program evaluation and improvement, and if they receive honest and understandable evaluation findings when they need them. The evaluator might consider various reporting procedures such as case history, graphics, scenarios, question-answer reports, and testimonials. The criterion for selection of the appropriate procedure is simple: use the procedure that best communicates findings on the particular issue to the specific audience.

If the evaluator is asked to draw specific implications or recommendations from the findings, the evaluator's own background and preferences should be understood by the audience as it considers the implications or recommendations made. In other cases, the audience may prefer to draw its own conclusions. The evaluator should determine in advance the audience expectations with regard to drawing conclusions.

These program evaluation ingredients incorporate the major evaluation tasks to be accomplished. No one ingredient is necessarily more important than another, although some might be more important at various phases of the evaluation process. At the early phases, for instance, the purpose, audience, and issue ingredients will be very important to the evaluator; in the latter phases of evaluation, analysis and reporting will become more important. Also note that information relating to each of the evaluation ingredients may be collected either continuously during program operation (for example, general program improvement purposes) or only when relevant evaluation efforts are mandated or commissioned. No ingredient, however, is important by itself. The issues addressed by an evaluation are frequently the ones raised by the audiences of the evaluation; further, the type of evidence sought should be consistent with what is acceptable to the audience, the issue raised, and the purpose of the evaluation. Because the ingredients are interrelated, the evaluator is advised to use them in an iterative manner, moving back and forth among the ingredients, making accommodations and adaptations as the evaluation proceeds.

Some Practical Applications

The preceding sections have provided general concepts to help adult and continuing education administrators develop a common conceptual framework for program evaluation. In addition, practitioners need to consider the practical and concrete tasks that are a part of program evaluation. Four practical evaluation examples follow. Each describes an adult education program followed by an evaluation plan. Although the plans are not comprehensive and vary according to purpose, focus, and instrumentation, each focuses on a specific issue and illustrates an evaluation process and a data-gathering technique. The examples —continuing medical education, adult religious education, adult basic education, and executive development—demonstrate the adaptability of evaluation approaches to different sponsoring agencies, clienteles, and modes of instruction. The reader should observe the relationship between these examples and the conceptual material presented in earlier sections.

Continuing Medical Education

A workshop program, sponsored by a national medical society, is designed to improve academic skills of faculty members in family practice residency programs. Though the participants are physicians, they lack specialized preparation for teaching residents or administering academic programs. A workshop structure helps them develop a systematic approach to conducting residency programs by role playing various positions such as instructor, administrator, evaluator, and researcher. The workshop is designed and conducted by three staff members from a university residency program with assistance from guest lecturers and discussants. Activities are conducted during fifteen sessions over four consecutive days. At each session, instructional material is presented through lectures, followed by a question session and small group role playing. The workshop is situated at a remote conference center that has access to a local family practice residency center.

The Education Committee of the Family Medicine Society, as the primary audience for this evaluation plan, is concerned not only that the workshop is an effective system for disseminating information about faculty competencies but also that the techniques, content, and other aspects will work in future workshops. Their main purposes for evaluation are to *justify* this workshop as a future offering and, if necessary, to *improve* aspects of it. The evaluation specifically addresses some of the program elements and characteristics discussed earlier, including the implementation of instruction, the outcomes for participants, and the context of the program.

Various techniques may be used to gather information about the main concerns of the evaluation audience, but the effort must take into account both the available financial resources and the evaluator's expertise. Furthermore, the information gathered must be seen as important by the evaluation audience. Taking all these factors into consideration, the effectiveness of the program can be evaluated using an instrument like the following questionnaire. This instrument would be administered to participants, but the information might be verified by obtaining similar data from an observer or an instructor, thereby increasing the credibility of the information.

Workshop Effectiveness Questionnaire

Directions: As part of our effort to evaluate the effectiveness of this workshop, we would appreciate your completing this questionnaire. You need not indicate your name.

Participant Expectations

1. Participants in workshops have specific individual purposes for attending a workshop. Please recall, if you will, your major objective(s) for attending this workshop.

2. What specific aspects of the workshop experience, if any, contributed to your achieving your personal objective(s)?

_____

3. What aspects of the experience, if any, detracted from your achieving your objective(s)?

_____

4. In general, was your personal objective(s) accomplished?

5	4	3	2	1
Very much	Quite well	Somewhat	Hardly	Not at all

Instructional Staff

5. Indicate the extent to which the instructional staff was *enthusiastic* about the topics they presented.

5	4	3	2	1
Very much	Quite well	Somewhat	Hardly	Not at all

6. Indicate the extent to which the staff was properly *prepared*.

5	4	3	2	1
Very much	Quite well	Somewhat	Hardly	Not at all

7. Indicate the degree to which the staff was *helpful and friendly*.

5	4	3	2	1
Very much	Quite well	Somewhat	Hardly	Not at all

8. In general, how would you rate the instructional staff?

5	4	3	2	1
Superior	Good	Average	Fair	Poor

Comment: _____

Agency Support

9. Did the agency that conducted this workshop provide adequate planning for an effective learning experience?

Yes ( )   Undecided ( )   No ( )

Comment: _____

10. Was adequate support provided by the agency?

   Yes ( )   Undecided ( )   No ( )

   Comment: _____

11. How important does this workshop seem to be to the agency that conducts it?

5	4	3	2	1
Very	Quite	Somewhat	Hardly	Not at all

   Comment: _____

12. How important is your attendance at this workshop to the organization/institution that employs you?

5	4	3	2	1
Very	Quite	Somewhat	Hardly	Not at all

   Comment: _____

Workshop Benefits

13. In your own words, briefly indicate the one or two major personal benefits you have gained as a result of participation in this workshop.

   _____

   _____

   _____

14. Can you envision any benefits accruing to your organization or institution? If so, please describe.

   _____

   _____

15. Was your involvement worth the time and effort?

   Yes ( )   Undecided ( )   No ( )

The following recommendation form deals with whether aspects of the workshop may be improved for future workshop use. It focuses on implementation aspects of a workshop presentation and would be administered to workshop instructors.

Instructor Recommendations for Improving Workshop

As you reflect on the instruction you provided, please make recommendations that might improve your involvement in future workshops.

1. What one or two changes might be considered by you to improve your involvement in this workshop?

   _____

   _____

2. What components/features would you especially want to retain in the content of your presentation in future workshops?

   _____

   _____

3. What one or two factors (such as experience of participant, increased presentation time, workshop facilities) should not be changed for you to maintain the quality of your presentation?

   _____

   _____

4. How might the organization and administration of the workshop be improved so that your involvement would have greater impact?

   _____

   _____

The data obtained from these instruments would be analyzed and summarized in a written report to the Education Planning Committee. (This example was adapted in part from Reineke and Welch, 1977.)

Adult Religious Education

A consortium of Lutheran churches in a midwestern community are interested in sponsoring a program called Lutherans in Theological Encounter (LITE). This program would provide an opportunity for Lutherans and members of other denominations grow in their knowledge of their faith and to apply that faith to the contemporary world. The program will feature short courses (six ninety-minute sessions) that will meet weekly during the fall of the year in the educational facilities of a centrally located church. In order to ascertain the goal expectations and topic interests of potential participants, the LITE Planning Committee will conduct a survey. The planning information it gains will assist the committee in establishing specific goals in the design of the LITE program.

The following questionnaire is an instrument to be sent to a random sample of adult members in each of the consortium congregations. Using these data, the LITE Planning Committee can gain an increased understanding of what participants expect from an adult Christian education program.

My Religious Education Goals

One of the issues facing adult religious education has to do with its goals or aims. Below we have listed a number of the more commonly claimed goals, intentions, or aims of adult religious education. We, as a planning committee for the development of an adult religious education program, would like you to react to each statement by indicating the personal importance you attach to each goal. You need not indicate your name.

Goal	*Great importance*	*Medium importance*	*Little importance*	*No importance*
1. To provide experiences for people to maintain or develop good moral character	( )	( )	( )	( )
2. To train lay leaders for the church	( )	( )	( )	( )

Goal	Great importance	Medium importance	Little importance	No importance
3. To encourage people to examine critically their religious beliefs	( )	( )	( )	( )
4. To facilitate the thorough learning of the history of our church	( )	( )	( )	( )
5. To provide facilities and opportunities for religious fellowship	( )	( )	( )	( )
6. To provide indoctrination in religious fellowship	( )	( )	( )	( )
7. To encourage religious meaning as a way of life	( )	( )	( )	( )
8. To increase church attendance	( )	( )	( )	( )
9. To encourage the growth of organized religion in the world	( )	( )	( )	( )
10. To provide enrichment and enjoyment through religious experiences	( )	( )	( )	( )

A sample of adults within each congregation of the consortium might also be asked to complete a similar questionnaire to reflect their preferences for specific topic areas.

Religious Topic Preference Scale

On a scale of 1 to 5, circle the numeral that best describes your interest in the following topic areas.

Topic Area	Low Interest	Some Interest	High Interest		
1. Books of the Bible, textual study	1	2	3	4	5
2. Doctrines of the church, confessional study	1	2	3	4	5
3. Ethical issues	1	2	3	4	5
4. Social issues	1	2	3	4	5
5. Personal/spiritual sharing	1	2	3	4	5
6. Evangelism	1	2	3	4	5
7. Basic religious/philosophical questions	1	2	3	4	5
8. Other _____	1	2	3	4	5

The data obtained from these instruments together with the judgments of the committee would be summarized and used in planning and designing the LITE program.

Adult Basic Education

A local adult basic education program, supported in part by Federal Elementary and Secondary Education Act Title III funds, is situated in an Adult Education Center—a renovated elementary school building. About half of the 200 participants attend full time. The reading level for many participants is equivalent to the sixth grade. Some of the participants are unable to read when they enter the program; others are able to pass the GED after a few weeks of instruction. Individualized and group instruction opportunities are provided in reading, arithmetic, social studies, and consumer and health education. In addition, auxiliary services such as transportation and complete daycare allow participants to study while carrying out family responsibilities.

The illustrative evaluation plan for this program focuses on the learning atmosphere of the center, which has become increasingly important since sixteen- and seventeen-year-olds have been allowed to enroll in the program. Most of the participants range from late adolescence to middle age, but the social and learning attitudes of the youth differ greatly from those in their twenties and thirties and, according to the center director and several teachers, are apparently causing tension among the participants.

Sensitive issues such as student tension must be addressed if improvements are to be made. Data-gathering techniques range from formal and somewhat obtrusive types to those that try to be as unobtrusive as possible. (For a detailed discussion of unobtrusive measures see Webb and others, 1966.) An unobtrusive technique would be more successful in evaluating conflict and tension in learning situations than the use of direct questioning. The following questionnaire demonstrates a somewhat obtrusive technique, consisting of several types of questions to which participants would respond either in written or oral form.

Satisfaction with Program Context

Please indicate the extent of your general satisfaction with the adult basic education context or setting.

	Highly Satisfied	*Quite Satisfied*	*Hardly Satisfied*	*Not Satisfied*
1. Are you satisfied:				
with the kinds of people it is serving?	( )	( )	( )	( )
with the learning atmosphere?	( )	( )	( )	( )
with the type of social interaction?	( )	( )	( )	( )
with the level of communication among learners?	( )	( )	( )	( )
with the maturity of the learners?	( )	( )	( )	( )
with the commitment to learning?	( )	( )	( )	( )

2. I am:

_____Male	_____Beginning (1–3)	_____16–18 years old
_____Female	_____Intermediate (4–6)	_____19–25 years old
	_____Advanced (7–8)	_____26–35 years old
_____Full time	_____GED	_____36–50 years old
_____Part time		_____Over 50 years old

These questions would not, of course, indicate how the program might be improved. The responses would only assist in ascertaining whether the atmosphere of the learning context is really an issue.

An unobtrusive evaluation approach also looks for improvement by reading the "natural indicators" of the program. For example, are graffiti directed to any group? Do various age groups selectively exclude members of other age groups in the cafeteria? Is involvement purposefully avoided in free-choice situations such as classroom projects? Has the identification with and care of the physical setting decreased? These and other questions might be discussed with the staff.

The responses to both types of evaluation efforts and the conclusions drawn from these data-gathering efforts serve as the basis for staff discussion. Whether or not actions are taken to improve aspects of the setting depends on the seriousness of the problem and the likelihood that constructive action can be taken.

Executive Development

The Executive Development Program has been offered annually for twenty-five years by the college of business administration of a major university. Designed for middle to senior level managers in business, industry, and government organizations, the program is an intensive six-week summer course of instruction held on the university campus. Lecture, case analysis, role playing, and small group discussion comprise the instruction, which focuses on four topic areas: business environment, human resource management, information systems and decision making, and business administration policy. Course instructors include regular university faculty members as well as visiting faculty.

There are many issues that might be addressed in the evaluation of such a program. Dominant issues perceived by the program administrators include the quality of instructional content and of presentation by faculty members as well as the quality of weekly program units. These issues are important because program administrators not only decide whether to invite back instructors for subsequent programs but also make decisions about the scheduling and sequencing of sessions in an effort to maintain quality. The following Session Evaluation Form, given to participants after each session, might be useful to program administrators.

Session Evaluation Form

This scale contains statements about session content and preparation. For each statement, draw a circle around the letter that represents *your own reaction* to this session.

SA if you strongly agree with the statement
A if you agree but not strongly
N if you are neutral or undecided
D if you disagree but not strongly
SD if you strongly disagree with the statement

Remember, the only correct answer is the one that actually represents your own reaction to this session.

1. The information provided by the
   presenter was new to me.   SA   A   N   D   SD

2. To me the topic was presented in an
   organized manner.   SA   A   N   D   SD

3. What I learned in this session will make
   me more competent in my work.   SA   A   N   D   SD

4. The presenter was enthusiastic about
   the topic.   SA   A   N   D   SD

5. The session content was too theoretical
    for me.   SA   A   N   D   SD

6. The presentation was difficult for me
    to understand.   SA   A   N   D   SD

Comments:

_____

_____

_____

_____

The following Weekly Rating Form addresses the issue of session structure and sequencing and would be administered to participants on a weekly basis.

Weekly Rating Form
Executive Development Program

The following general questions are being asked so that you can provide feedback to the program planners about this past week's sessions. Space has also been provided for your comments.

1. In general, do you think the topics were sufficiently well covered?

    Yes ( )   Undecided ( )   No ( )

    Comment: _____

2. Was the sequencing of sessions conducive to effective learning?

    Yes ( )   Undecided ( )   No ( )

    Comment: _____

3. Does the program schedule appear to be sufficiently structured, but flexible enough to be responsive to your concerns?

    Yes ( )   Undecided ( )   No ( )

    Comment: _____

4. How would you describe the pace of session activities?

    Too fast ( )   About right ( )   Too slow ( )

    Comment: _____

5. In general, how do you rate this week's program schedule and sessions?

5	4	3	2	1
Well above average	Above average	Average	Below average	Well below average

6. If you have further comments at this time about any aspect of the program, please express them below.

    _____

    _____

The data from these instruments would be summarized and analyzed by the program administration staff, and they might also help decide whether to involve certain instructors in future programs and how to improve the organization of program sessions. Depending on the audience of an evaluation, different program elements or components might be emphasized. Rarely, however, can all concerns be addressed. Nor can all types of evidence be gathered, for priority choices have to be made. These choices reflect the importance placed on the evaluation endeavor and the resources available for it.

Internal and External Evaluations

Several types of evaluation purposes have been discussed that not only frame the evaluation approach but also relate almost directly to the evaluator's role. That is, an evaluation to justify program worth is likely to be conducted by an external evaluator. Evaluations to improve a program or to plan future programs are likely to be conducted by an internal evaluator. Clearly, then, issues of involvement, conflict of interest, and bias enter into the picture.

In an internally conducted evaluation, the evaluator is typically a member of the program or project staff, is an advocate of the program, is personally involved in it, and consequently is likely to look at it positively, particularly at those components where he has shared some responsibility. Furthermore, the internal evaluator's perspective is likely to be narrower than an outsider's perspective. That is, the value basis for the evaluation is likely to be derived from the program context rather than from a broader, more general context. The internal evaluator is also less likely to be inclined toward any radical change in the program than to have a commitment to maintaining a steady state of affairs.

The external evaluator's role also contains bias, but of a different kind. This type of evaluator may be biased either positively or negatively by the commissioning process—especially if that process shows a lack of independence between the commissioner and evaluator. Relevancy bias may occur if the value orientation of the external evaluator is not in concert with the orientation and commitment of program personnel. There are many more aspects of both bias and the evaluator's role. (For a more extensive discussion of them, see Scriven, 1976.)

Table 5 outlines other dimensions of the evaluator's role that can be compared and contrasted. The earlier contributions of Craig Gjerde in making these distinctions is acknowledged. Adult educators who are thinking about doing an evaluation may find this outline a useful step toward increased insight and understanding of the evaluation process. In considering each of the characteristics, however, keep in mind that the contrasts may be somewhat exaggerated for purposes of illustration. In practice, often a combination of both internal and external evaluation roles leads to greater satisfaction with the process, because the best features of each process can be utilized.

Meta-Evaluation

This chapter has stressed that the evaluator's approach should be responsive. Being responsive, however, is not necessarily being accountable. Accountability requires that the evaluators and their evaluations be evaluated. This important concept, referred to by Scriven (1969) as "meta-evaluation," is receiving increased atten-

Table 5. Emphases of Internal and External Evaluator Roles

Emphasis	Internal	External
Aim	To help the program succeed; to improve program functioning	To legitimize the worth of the program; to justify program
Orientation	Micro-; attention to program component processes and internal relationships; responsiveness to program activities and issues	Macro-; attention to general program outcomes and external relationships; concerned with intents and effectiveness
Concern	Means and relations to ends; questions how things are being conducted	Ends; questions why things are being conducted
Bias	Program advocate; ego involved with program	Assume neutral stance, but commissioning process may implicitly reflect advocate or adversary bias
Commissioner	Program administrator or director	Central program monitor or sponsor; outside official
Involvement	Continuous; on site	Occasional; at end of project
Audience	Program director and staff	Program sponsor or funding agency
Criterion	Usefulness	Validity; objectivity
Reporting	Verbal; written memos; nontechnical	Written; narrative; technical
Role	Program facilitator	Program auditor
Impact	Dependent on commitment of program administrator and staff; incremental	Dependent on authority and clout of commissioner; substantial or not at all
Data	Mostly qualitative and judgmental	Mostly quantitative (if not a site visit procedure) and descriptive

tion. Journals such as *Evaluation Network,* symposia of annual professional association meetings such as the American Educational Research Association, and commissioned meta-evaluations by government agencies and private foundations as reflected in House (1979) have recently increased the visibility of meta-evaluation.

Aside from Scriven's input (1969, 1976), the most significant report on this topic has been prepared by Stufflebeam (1975), who analyzes background problems of meta-evaluation and suggests criteria for developing a meta-evaluation methodology. These criteria are applied to the objects of evaluation—goals, designs, processes, and results. According to Stufflebeam "meta-evaluation should assess the importance of evaluation objectives, the appropriateness of evaluation designs, the adequacy of implementation of the designs, and the quality and importance of evaluation results" (1975, p. 70). He creates, then, a scheme that is compatible with the concept that evaluation be applied to program components (goals, designs, implementation, and outcomes). Stufflebeam further argues that the criteria of technical adequacy, usefulness, and efficiency should be used to judge the merit of evaluations. That is, evaluations should produce technically sound information (internally and externally valid, reliable, objective) that is useful to some audience (relevant, important, adequate in scope, credible, timely, pervasive) and that is worth more to the audience than it costs. The article on meta-evaluation by Cook and Gruder (1978) and the preliminary statement by the Joint Committee on Standards for Educational Evaluation (1978) are important recent additions to the literature.

Knowing about meta-evaluation is important for adult education administrators because if their program is externally evaluated, they may seek to have a meta-evaluation conducted. If a formalized meta-evaluation is not feasible, however, there are several procedures that might be used by the adult education administrator in the spirit of meta-evaluation. They might (1) have program personnel provide written feedback on a preliminary evaluation report to the evaluator, (2) have representatives of the program—such as board members, trustees, and elected officials who are not directly involved—react to an evaluation report, and (3) ask an evaluation specialist who is knowledgeable about adult education to critique a draft of the evaluation report. All of these will, of course, be most successfully implemented if they are agreed upon during the initial commissioning of the evaluation.

Evaluation Issues

As continuing education administrators go about the task of evaluation, they confront a variety of issues, the significance of which depends on the importance placed on evaluation, the extent to which evaluation is an integral part of program development, and relevant contextual factors associated with a program. Many issues are likely to be unique to a specific setting, time, and circumstance. The following paragraphs suggest a range of selected issues that administrators and evaluators might confront. The importance of specific issues in a particular instance depends on local circumstances and personal perspectives.

1. How can adult education program evaluation be conducted on a scale that is cost effective? Costs include staff time and program disruption as well as salary and expense for personnel directly engaged in evaluation. The issue of evaluation cost effectiveness is contrasted with program cost effectiveness; the latter is discussed by Levin (1975).

2. How much impact do adult education programs have? Especially for purposes of accountability, practitioners and policy makers want to know to what extent participation in an adult education program is beneficial to the individual and to society. Evidence of these second-order outcomes is sometimes difficult to obtain.

3. How can program evaluation be conducted with minimal disruption of the adult education program? Unobtrusive measures are one way; brief and interesting instruments can also help.

4. How can the audiences for evaluation conclusions and reports be encouraged to use the findings for program improvement and justification? Too many evaluation reports go unused.

5. Who evaluates the evaluator and evaluation reports?

6. Are the evaluation observations valid? Evaluation procedures "see" programs in various ways. The way we validate these observations is of utmost importance, because the value we ascribe to something is influenced by how we see it. For example, we see educational accomplishment in the adult basic education student through performance on a standardized reading test. We see educational value in the satisfaction indices of a questionnaire administered to business executives attending a conference. We see educational value in the personal testimony of participants in a book-based discussion group. But serious issue can be taken with any view, because assessing the validity of observations is a continu-

ous challenge: Not only are the observations themselves judgmental, but we must judge those judgments.

7. On what does the evaluation focus? The focus of evaluation has traditionally been concerned with the outcomes of educational effort. More attention might be given to the evaluation of educational processes. When results are unsatisfactory, they provide a basis for improvements. Also more attention might be given to describing incentives and barriers to the participation of adults. For example, the description of program inaccessibility due to physical, financial, social, or educational reasons would, in particular, illuminate program value.

8. Who ascribes program value? It is assumed by some evaluators that it is their own task to describe the value of a program by collecting the value judgments of others but not make judgments themselves. Other evaluators believe that they should themselves determine the value of the program. Still others feel that the evaluation audience (to whom the reports are submitted) is the ultimate judge of program worth. This issue is relevant for both those who gather program information and those who receive it. The issue, simply put, is, "Who judges the worth of the program?"

9. Is the utilitarian value of information also just? Educational evaluation information is used to legitimize the actions of the program administrator. In doing so, it has utilitarian value. At issue is whether using evaluation information in this way is in fact valid and fair. It is not valid if the information is not true. It is not fair if the decisions based on the information unjustly assign value. This "justice-as-fairness" issue in program evaluation has been raised by House (1976), who claims that what is judged to be good may not be right or just.

10. If it is desirable to portray program merit based on multiple indicators, how are these indicators aggregated and how should weights be assigned to them? Furthermore, how much should information be compressed into a single index, if at all? Educational programs are complex endeavors that yield multiple effects. Their evaluations are also complex, and whether this complexity should be simplified or maintained is a fundamental issue in reporting evaluation conclusions. Attaining a balance between mes-

sages that are brief and simple and messages that are comprehensive and complex is exceedingly difficult. This issue is further complicated when consideration is given to the background and sophistication of the evaluation audience.

11. Is the evaluation information gathered to justify past decisions or to make decisions rationally and increase understanding? If it is done to justify decisions (even if not admittedly), its motive is usually political. Evidence is gathered to support a political decision already made but not necessarily revealed. The evaluation outcomes are not only dictated a priori but the processes are also directly influenced. For example, if the decision were made to terminate support for a federal program in adult education, an evaluator might be selected who was biased against the program from the beginning. If the motives are more educational, the decision maker will want to learn more about the program and its effects prior to making a decision.

12. To what extent does the revelation of program worth expose value positions and thereby create value conflict? Knowing more is not necessarily understanding better. With the shift of many adult values away from tradition, an evaluation effort might have an unsettling effect on a program. At issue is whether a lack of value consensus explicitly obtained from an evaluation has more of a negative effect on the program than it has utility for decision making.

13. When evaluators are required to judge irrational data on programs against rationally based standards, which should they consider inappropriate—the data or the standards? To disregard the data would assume human behavior to be fully rational. To disregard the standards denies rationality as a vital element in human processes. Clearly, the evaluator is faced with a dilemma.

14. Which are more useful and meaningful in program evaluation—qualitative or quantitative indicators? Usually this issue generates more heat than light. Nevertheless, enlightened thought is welcome. Qualitative indicators emphasize holistic and tacit understanding demonstrated by illustrations and case studies. Quantitative indicators emphasize the rigorous analysis of key indicators of worth.

In summary, this chapter has presented a conceptual framework of evaluation purposes, program elements, and program components that should assist the practitioner in thinking through what he is about in an evaluation task.

Chapter Five

♦♦♦♦♦♦♦♦♦♦♦♦♦♦♦♦♦♦♦♦♦♦♦♦
♦♦♦♦♦♦♦♦♦♦♦♦♦♦♦♦♦♦♦♦♦♦♦♦

Participation

♦♦♦♦♦♦♦♦♦♦♦♦♦♦♦♦♦♦♦♦♦♦♦♦
♦♦♦♦♦♦♦♦♦♦♦♦♦♦♦♦♦♦♦♦♦♦♦♦

Linda K. Bock

Decisions to participate and persist in adult education activities reflect multiple influences on the adult, including the marketing and counseling practices of adult education agencies. This chapter discusses the concepts relating to the process by which adults find out about and decide to participate in part-time educational activities, and concepts relating to adult education marketing and counseling to attract and retain adult participants. These concepts are generalizations based on research or experience that can help practitioners deal effectively with practical decisions. The chapter also contains descriptions of current practice and suggestions for future directions. Particular attention is given to reaching underserved adults.

A unique strength of adult education is its flexibility to meet the diverse needs and interests found in a highly dynamic society. During the middle 1970s, more than thirty million adults participated annually in major adult education activities, and some eighty million adults between the ages of eighteen and sixty—or three fourths of all American adults—expressed interest in continued learning of some kind (Cross, Valley, and Associates, 1974). Between 1969 and 1972, the number of participants increased three times as fast as the eligible population; women participants increased by 29 percent, contrasted with 14 percent for men (Okes, 1976). Yet there are millions of potential participants who are not presently involved in educational programs, and only a small percentage of the twenty-five million United States adults with less than an eighth-grade education participate in basic remedial education.

Influences on Participation

One basic concept for marketing and counseling is that many factors influence participation in educative activity. Participation research suggests the intricate pattern of these factors among various subpopulations. Sex, age, social class, previous education, self-concept, level of aspiration, and reference groups are among the major factors. An administrator's recruiting of adults can be greatly enhanced by an understanding of adult information seeking and the decision to participate in an educational activity.

A person's familiarity with educational opportunities is related to his previous education: Adults with higher levels of formal education are more likely to be aware of local educational opportunities (Johnstone and Rivera, 1965). But the source of the information is sometimes as important as the information itself. Adults seek information from people they trust, and personal contact tends to be especially important in recruiting adult basic education (ABE) participants (Seaman, 1971; Snyder, 1971; Walden, 1975). Thus, type and source of information about educational opportunities are both influential.

When adults decide to engage in a new activity, they typically move through various stages. The entire practice adoption process is a useful concept for practitioners. Innovators and opinion leaders, who are among the first to engage in a new activity, tend to obtain information from the mass media to a greater extent than those who adopt the practice later. Systematic efforts to encourage adults to use new knowledge typically entail a linkage process in which people who are familiar with both the resource system and the client system help clients alternate between clarification of their action problems and use of relevant knowledge resources (Knox, 1977a). The adoption process typically consists of five stages.

1. *Awareness* entails obtaining initial information from one or more sources. During this stage, nonpersonal sources of information (mass media) usually provide the initial exposure to a new idea or program. In contrast with white-collar adults, who typically obtain information about adult education programs from nonpersonal sources, such as newspapers, magazines, pamphlets, radio, and television, blue-collar adults' typical sources of information are personal (neighbors, friends, and acquaintances). Blue-collar adults are thus at a disadvantage, because their acquaintances are likely to have a low participation rate in adult education and are likely to have little knowledge about opportunities and programs (London, Wenkert, and Hagstrom, 1963; Parker and Paisley, 1966).

2. *Interest* is reflected in seeking additional information about the program. Among undereducated adults, personal sources are more effective than nonpersonal sources (Snyder, 1971). Among non-college-bound young adults, somewhat older significant others are an important source of information (Knox, 1970).

3. *Evaluation* consists of weighing the advantages and disadvantages of participation. Personal sources are more influential than nonpersonal mass media. People who influence evaluation tend to be friends rather than relatives, professional counselors, or teachers. Conversations with these influential people provide information and emotional support for the decision and tend to reaffirm rather than change previous attitudes (Booth and Knox, 1967). Personal influence and contact are also important in scientists' decisions to participate in professional conferences. People who influence decisions to participate in continuing

professional education programs have good communication skills, extensive interpersonal resources, and high professional status. (People with these characteristics would be valuable on a program planning committee; Booth, 1967.)

4. *Trial* consists of trying the idea on a small scale in a tentative manner. This is the stage where many undereducated participants drop out, and it calls for counseling for adult education participants and for assurance that the first class session will be a positive experience.

5. *Adoption* consists of deciding to continue in the educational activity. (Sometimes after a practice is adopted it is rejected, and this stage is sometimes termed *disadoption.*)

Decisions by adults to participate in part-time educational activities are influenced by an interplay of various personal and situational facilitators and barriers. Although specific reasons for participation vary with people and activities, a number of variables have been identified, which at desirable levels encourage adult education participation and at undesirable levels discourage participation. The decision to participate reflects the greater influence of the encouraging forces than of the discouraging forces. Administrators can use a diagnosis of positive and negative influences in a specific instance to try to tip the balance in favor of participation (Knox, 1977a; Miller, 1967). Examples of positive influences include personal factors (such as being interested in a topic, having a goal that would be promoted by increased proficiency, having a high educational level, and having a strong need for achievement) as well as situational factors (such as experiencing a major role change that requires adjustment, being aware of opportunities to participate, having significant others provide encouragement, and receiving financial assistance).

Another important personal influence is life-style, which is associated with socioeconomic status. One component of life-style that is most highly and positively associated with extent of adult education participation is level of formal education. Only 10 percent of all adults who did not complete high school participate each year in adult education programs while 50 percent of adults who completed at least a masters degree do so. Other aspects of life-style that are positively associated with participation include occupational prestige, income, communication ability, extent of reading, and amount of participation in voluntary associations or cultural activities (Booth, 1967; Johnstone and Rivera, 1965; Knox, 1968b; Knox, 1970; London, Wenkert, and Hagstrom, 1963).

Another personal influence is an adult's anticipated benefits from participation in educational activities. Examples of perceived benefits include interest in the topic, enjoyment of the learning activity or of other participants, and satisfaction of applying new learning to achieve work, family, or community goals (Boshier, 1973; Burgess, 1971; Knox, 1974; Tough, 1968). Personal needs for achievement or affiliation can also encourage participation, especially if the program format is designed to ensure these outcomes (Miller, 1967; Parker and Paisley, 1966). Placing a high valuation on education is positively associated with participation. For example, even though a higher proportion of blue-collar than white-collar adults believes that education is only for children, within socioeconomic strata the sense of educational efficacy is still associated with extent of participation (Anderson and Niemi, 1969; Knox, 1977a).

Participation rates decline only a small amount during most of adulthood within any given level of formal educational attainment. There are few differences in participation rates for men and women, although there are life-cycle fluctuations, such as lower rates for mothers of young children and higher rates for older women compared with their male counterparts at the same functional or chronological stages (Johnstone and Rivera, 1965; Knox, 1977a).

Less advantaged adults, especially the unemployed, tend to possess the characteristics associated with low participation rate. When a low sense of educational efficacy is combined with low self-confidence, it is not surprising that participation rates are so much lower for the unemployed disadvantaged than for middle-class adults (Anderson and Niemi, 1969; London, Wenkert, and Hagstrom, 1963; Parker and Paisley, 1966).

Costs and competing time demands are socially acceptable excuses for nonparticipation and are widely reported. However, it is clear that other influences affect the willingness of adults to spend some of their time and money on adult education, since some high-cost programs are much in demand, and adult education participants tend to participate broadly in a variety of social activities (Cross, Valley, and Associates, 1974; Kurland and Comly, 1975; London, Wenkert, and Hagstrom, 1963). A major situational influence on participation in adult education activities is adult life-role changes in family, work, and community. Major increases and changes in the knowledge base that affect performance in some occupational fields are also closely related to participation (Knox, 1974, 1977a, 1979b). Public concern about quality control in some occupations is having a similar effect. Another major situational facilitator is encouragement by significant others to obtain further education. The belief of friends, relatives, and work supervisors that participation in adult education is desirable helps to offset some uncertainty and may provide useful information about opportunities (Knox, 1968a, 1970).

Increasing public awareness of and regard for adult education is helping to offset one long-standing barrier to participation—unfamiliarity with available opportunities. Over the years, most of the adult education programs in which adults, responding to surveys, said they would enroll if they were available, were in fact available (Knox, 1968a). In addition, adult education providers have been able to increase participation by increasing accessibility and responsiveness to the interests of clienteles. This has included provision of relevant programs at a price that adults in the target market are willing to pay, offered at times and locations that are convenient. It also includes provision of programs, materials, and encouragement that makes participation attractive (Knox, 1974). Counseling services can also facilitate participation by providing information about childcare, sources of financial assistance, and help with study skills.

To summarize, then, the reasons why adults participate in part-time educational programs vary among people and among activities. A range of personal and situational reasons influence the decision to participate. Some of the important reasons for participating in an educational activity are related to the benefits an individual receives for participating, such as interest in the subject matter or enjoyment of the method of learning, the setting, or the interaction with other people (Boshier, 1977; Houle, 1961). Other reasons for participation relate to the benefits derived as one applies the outcome of the learning activity to achieve other purposes. For example, a professional might use increased proficiency to achieve a career change or to serve others more effectively.

Administrators who understand the wide range of influences on adult participation in part-time and short-term educational programs can apply this concept to improve their understanding of the specific target markets of adults whom they seek to reach and serve. Marketing and counseling are two specific ways to enhance attraction and retention of participants.

Marketing

Effective marketing, which includes analysis, planning, implementation, and control, has become as important for adult education agencies as it has for other nonprofit organizations. This is understandable because marketing is inherent in all organizations: All organizations offer some product or service to some type of consumer and use marketing to regulate demand. In adult education, the service is part-time or short-term education and the clients are typically adults.

Marketing Concepts

The central concept underlying marketing is exchange: marketing offers something of value (in our case, education) to someone (adults) in exchange for value (participation and money). Adult education practitioners are interested in marketing concepts because they want to be able to do a better job of informing the public about adult education programs and encouraging participation in them.

The essence of modern marketing is that an organization exists to serve its clients. This "client needs" orientation aims at creating client satisfaction as the key to satisfying organizational goals. Resources must be attracted, employees must be stimulated, clients must be found. Enhancement of incentives to encourage participation is crucial to stimulation of these exchanges. Marketing is thus concerned with managing exchanges between the agency and its public effectively and efficiently.

Marketing can render two specific benefits to adult education practitioners. One is increased satisfaction of clients through increased attention to desires of potential participants. The second is improved efficiency in recruitment activities. Marketing emphasizes planning and managing activities related to development, pricing, publicity, and provision of educational programs for adults.

Kotler (1974) defines a target market as a distinct group of people with resources they want to exchange for distinct benefits. Marketing is a voluntary exchange relationship between an organization and its various publics. A marketing orientation entails developing specific strategies, such as analyzing an agency's opportunities, establishing objectives, segmenting the target public and then choosing key segments of it, synchronizing the implementation of strategies, formulating an overall marketing plan, implementing the plan, and evaluating the results continuously. A marketing orientation defines high-priority target publics, looks outward toward the needs of these publics, and relies heavily on designing the agency's services in terms of the client needs and desires and on using effective pricing, communication, and distribution to inform, motivate, and serve (Kotler, 1974). Effective marketing thus optimizes the match between client needs and program offerings.

The marketing process also includes market research, which can be regarded as needs assessment. There are various ways in which practitioners can market the services of an adult education agency. Findings from needs assessments and other forms of market research, along with generalizations about adult development, help practitioners understand the needs of target clients. These findings can also help identify the most likely channels of communication to use in reaching potential clients, including use of mass media (mailing brochures, newspaper articles, and announcements on radio and television) and encouragement of word-of-mouth dissemination by current and former participants and by others who know about adult education opportunities (Knox and Farmer, 1977).

Marketing Audit. A marketing audit includes three activities: (1) evaluating the marketing environment of the agency, including its publics, clients, competitors, and the larger society; (2) evaluating the marketing system within the organization, specifically the agency's objectives, programs, and organization; and (3) evaluating the major marketing activities of the agency, specifically its programs, pricing, and distribution (where the programs are held, personal contact, advertising, publicity, and promotion). An adult education administrator who reviews findings from all three parts of a marketing audit should have an improved understanding of the marketing problems and opportunities that face the agency.

Marketing Mix. The challenge of adult education marketing is to provide the right program at the right place, time and price to the right clientele and to communicate information about this activity to that market segment effectively. This is known as the "marketing mix" and in the adult education literature is sometimes referred to as the "four P's"—product (service), place, price, and promotion. These activities are subsumed in effective program development. The following are major questions to raise in a review of the marketing mix of an adult education agency.

1. Regarding the product or service, what are the main types of programs (conferences, self-study materials, extramural activities, short courses, adult basic education programs, vocational courses)?
2. Regarding price, what are the standards for deciding costs to clients (covering costs, matching competition, subsidizing certain groups)? Also, what would be the response of important clienteles to alternative price levels?
3. Regarding distribution, can improvements be made in the physical locations and arrangements?
4. Regarding personal contact, are there enough people involved in client contact to achieve the objectives?
5. Regarding advertising and publicity, is enough being done in the best media channels, and is the advertising reaching the right people?

Marketing Techniques. All providers of adult education programs engage in some forms of marketing to encourage potential clients to participate. Marketing services range from general public information efforts designed to increase the visibility of the program to active efforts to obtain referrals of new learners from other agencies and to recruit participants through mass media and person-to-person contact. Direct-mail brochures are relied upon as the most cost-effective method of reaching the greatest number of people. Studies of reasons for attendance in adult education programs indicate that mass media such as brochures promote awareness and interest in the educational program but that personal contact with friends or others familiar with the program is also usually influential in the decision to attend (Booth and Knox, 1967; Parker and Paisley, 1966). Most agencies make little effort to establish personal contact with potential participants. Promotion strategies using mass media techniques usually attract more of the same rather than attracting a broader range of participants.

Adult education administrators who serve a well-educated target public, as is the case for continuing professional education programs, have found that brochure mailings effectively attract participants who are accustomed to reading to obtain information for such decisions. However, administrators who seek to attract undereducated adults, as they do for adult basic education programs, cannot rely on printed media. However, undereducated adults are active television viewers (although they tend not to use the information for instrumental purposes). Therefore, marketing for programs such as adult basic education can include television public service announcements, appearances on talk shows, and coverage by local television news reporters of important program events such as the presentation of awards or the holding of an open house. Those who respond positively to such media tend to be the most upwardly mobile. Some participants will be attracted by recruitment methods that make limited use of reading, such as posters, fliers, billboards, and marquees placed in shopping centers, banks, post offices, factories, grocery stores, community action facilities, housing projects, laundromats, and churches. Fliers can be distributed in grocery bags, by school children to parents, in employees' pay envelopes, at PTA meetings, inside church bulletins, inserted in newspapers, in housing project offices, and in doctors' offices (Walden, 1975).

Publics. A responsive agency takes into account the needs and preferences of all of its publics. In addition to obtaining support from clients, marketing procedures can be used to develop support from other important publics of the agency. A public is a distinct group of people with potential or actual interest in and impact on an organization (Kotler, 1974). The publics of an adult education agency, in addition to the clients, include people within the agency, such as faculty and staff; people who support the agency, such as alumni and foundations who lend time, money, and encouragement; people who indirectly benefit from the agency's offerings, such as the general public; and people who regulate the agency by establishing rules of conduct. Administrators should consider the information that is significant to each of these publics and how the agency can be responsive to each and should reflect these considerations in the marketing strategies. For example, some educational institutions have made special efforts to encourage additional faculty members to conduct educational programs for adults. These efforts include improving the incentives for teaching adults, using newsletters and meetings to provide information about effective teaching of adults, and arranging for faculty members with limited experience teaching adults to do so with others who are experienced and effective in the field (Bock, 1979; Stern, 1961).

In summary, a number of marketing concepts from the professional literature can help practitioners attract participants, staff, and resources.

1. Marketing is a voluntary exchange of something of value between an agency and its various markets and publics.
2. The marketing audit is used to assess the marketing environment, system, and activities in order to strengthen the total marketing effort.
3. The marketing mix indicates to the agency how product (service), place, price, and promotion should be considered to market a specific course or workshop effectively.
4. Various marketing techniques are available from which to select those most likely to reach adults in a target market for a specific program.
5. In addition to reaching potential participants, marketing procedures can be used to develop support from other important

publics of the agency, including those who teach in programs and those who may support, regulate, and benefit from agency activities.

Marketing Practices

The concepts discussed above will now be applied to specific marketing practices that can be used by adult education administrators to strengthen their agencies.

Typical Practice. Typical marketing practices can be illustrated by the continuing education and extension division of a hypothetical Midwest state university. Marketing is equated with the attraction of participants to extension programs. Little systematic attention is given to increasing support for the outreach function among faculty members and the general public. There is no person, place, or publication from which one can obtain an overview of the thousands of current continuing education and extension activities. Marketing consists mainly of distributing catalogues of evening and off-campus courses for adults each academic term and mailing brochures for conferences and institutes. News releases are prepared for activities that are especially noteworthy or that need additional promotion to boost enrollments. When budgets, facilities, or staff time are strained to accommodate current enrollments, there seems to be little incentive to increase the marketing effort, which would compound the problem. As a result of these practices, the faculty and public image of the extension program is largely shaped by the outreach activities that are publicized, so few harder-to-reach adults are attracted to programs.

Another example of typical marketing practice is the adult education program of a Jewish community center in a middle-sized eastern city. The target market of participants is quite well defined, and a monthly newsletter is sent to all families associated with the center. The newsletter contains listings of forthcoming adult education activities along with human interest notes about topics, resource people, and participants. Information about mail registration and the name and phone number of the adult education coordinator is also included.

Many labor unions publicize their labor education programs for apprentices, shop stewards, and business managers, mainly through notices that are mailed and posted. Marketing of the adult education offerings of a museum in a western state tends to rely on announcements in the newsletter sent to members, supplemented by posters and by community calendar and public service announcements in newspapers, radio, and television. For major activities, a news release with a picture is sent to the newspapers.

The marketing practices of the education and training department of many employers (business, industry, government, and military) reflect a major advantage they have in encouraging participation by employees, especially blue-collar workers (Miller, 1967). The training department of a large company in a southeastern state provides in-plant educational programs for employees and provides tuition reimbursement for courses taken at local schools and colleges. The in-plant programs are especially effective in reaching blue-collar workers, who tend not to respond to mass media marketing of other adult education programs. The key ingredient is supervision: supervisors identify employees who could benefit from training and provide some thorough on-the-job training. Supervisors also recommend that workers participate in programs partly conducted on company time by the training department, where the expenses are charged to the operating unit. In this case, the supervisor helps provide marketing, counseling, and evaluation services.

Exemplary Practice. Some adult education marketing efforts appear to be more effective than others. The effectiveness of some agencies reflects their comprehensive marketing effort to multiple publics. For example, a midwestern public community college has a marketing program aimed at four publics: (1) past participants receive catalogues and brochures; (2) the general public (potential participants) are the target of newspaper listings of courses and news releases on human interest stories; (3) faculty understanding and support is promoted by attendance at divisional faculty meetings and by a "Continuing Education Notes" section of the faculty and staff newsletter; and (4) the commitment of policy makers to the continuing education and community services function of the college is strengthened through oral and written reports to the community college policy board and the state coordinating board. The director of adult education periodically reviews and revises this comprehensive marketing effort with members of the staff and the advisory committee.

Some years ago a private organization in an eastern city pioneered the use of livingroom learning groups for undereducated adults. Former participants in adult basic education programs served as recruiters in each neighborhood to encourage harder-to-reach adults to participate in informal sessions held in a familiar location such as a participant's livingroom. The recruiters were able to combine familiarity with the program with an ability to relate to neighborhood residents. Participation in the livingroom sessions helped to increase aspiration, awareness of educational and occupational opportunities, and self-confidence. This informal learning experience helped participants enter adult basic education and vocational education programs that many would not have entered directly (Snyder, 1971).

Effective marketing is also illustrated by a public school adult education program in the Great Lakes region. Along with other school systems in the area, the agency uses a symbol and slogan that encourages adults to recognize that they can increase their proficiency and achieve some of their objectives through participation in adult education. The symbol helps increase the visibility of adult education programs and is used on brochures and in advertisements. These promotional activities are concentrated during the several months before each registration period. In addition to extensive use of mass media and printed items carrying the slogan "Night Life that Pays", advisory committee members provide advice about program direction and also disseminate information about program offerings among their friends and neighbors. Current participants are also encouraged to tell their friends about the program around registration time. During the registration period, demonstrations by some instructors and their adult students portray more vividly what a course is like than would a typical written description. In addition, administrators, counselors, and some teachers meet with interested community groups to describe adult education offerings and to answer questions.

Another example of good marketing is a national professional association, which has discovered that one way to maximize enrollments with a given marketing budget is to send three mailings to members for the major continuing professional education programs they provide or cosponsor with universities. The first mailing is an announcement of topics, dates, and locations well in advance of the programs. The second is the detailed brochure several months beforehand. The third is a reminder flyer sent several weeks before the programs begin, especially if preregistrations are below expectations. If enrollments are at an acceptable level, the third mailing may be considered an unnecessary cost. For some specialized topics, mailings would be concentrated on those members who declared relevant interest on their annual membership renewal.

Sometimes adult education marketing and counseling services are closely coordinated (as will be discussed in more detail later in this chapter). For example, on many military bases, both functions are performed by the same staff. On one southern base, counselors identify and contact personnel who are in need of adult basic education or high school equivalency courses. Letters are sent to all new personnel as they report to the base. In addition to providing assistance to base personnel interested in further education, counselors seek to establish working relationships with commanding officers so that they appreciate the value of education and provide support and encouragement to personnel.

Counseling

Encouraging participation in adult education entails attention to both attraction and persistence. We have seen how marketing focuses primarily on the attraction component. Retention rates and satisfaction surveys are widely used measures of persistence. Although these measures are not very refined, they are important because if people do not remain in a program they cannot learn from it.

Counseling Concepts

There are numerous individual and program factors that may contribute to dropping out of adult education programs. Among the individual factors are the following:

1. Some students accomplish their goals before the end of the course and see no need to continue to the end.
2. Some students have low academic aptitudes and cannot keep up with the work.
3. Some students encounter problems in their personal lives that prevent continued attendance.
4. Some adults have never "learned how to learn."

Some program factors that influence persistence are: (1) poor teaching, (2) inadequate counseling, (3) inappropriate materials, (4) dissatisfaction with administrative policies and procedures, (5) inconvenient locations, (6) rigid scheduling of classes, (7) large classes, and (8) misunderstanding (or lack of understanding) of what the course offers. Sainty (1971) has characterized dropouts as less intelligent, younger, with less formal education, and from a lower socioeconomic class than those who remain in educational programs. People who do not normally participate actively in the organized life of their community are also more likely to withdraw from adult education activities (Verner and Davis, 1964). Less advantaged adults are also more dependent upon personal contact in making decisions about entering educational programs. The counseling component of adult education must address all of the individual and program factors leading to dropping out as well as the particular needs of the target publics.

There are several approaches to encouraging persistence and discouraging withdrawal. If recruitment activities state the new competencies that participants should acquire, there is more likely to be a good fit between the adults' expectations and the actual program. Dropouts are more likely than persisters to believe that adult basic education programs will help them solve many of their personal, vocational, and educational problems. When participants have expectations that a program is a panacea for all their problems, they become disillusioned and drop out (Seaman, 1971).

Another way to increase persistence is to provide counseling for problems that interfere with learning. The counseling available currently in many programs is inadequate (Seaman, 1971). Participants need someone to turn to when problems or concerns develop. For example, expectations may far exceed learning abilities, or progress may be far less than desired. When help or advice is needed, a competent person should be available to assist or to provide referral (Ironside and Jacobs, 1977). Effective counseling can encourage persistence by giving attention to both the reasons for withdrawal and the ways in which an agency can overcome—or help the participant overcome—those reasons.

Grabowski (1976) claims that counseling adults is the most impoverished but developing aspect of adult education because of the lack of a commitment by adult educators, of adequate literature, and of clear-cut role distinctions. One of the few research studies on counseling of adults revealed that there is more progress along educational, occupational, and social dimensions among counseled participants than among noncounseled participants (Grabowski, 1976).

The essence of counseling is the relationship between the counselor and the client. The counselor must try to understand the problems adult clients may be facing, especially in relation to how the clients perceive their environment: feelings of lack of confidence in ability to learn (prevalent among adult basic education participants), lack of efficient reading and study habits (true of many people returning to formal education after an absence as well as people who have never developed effective study habits), and past negative associations with learning, to name a few (Porter, 1970b).

The initial purpose of counseling services is to assist adult learners to explore their personal aspirations and available opportunities and to plan their educational development accordingly. The counseling function entails many tasks. Counselors give information about educational and career opportunities, assess client aptitudes and interests, assist with educational and career planning, and help clients cope with related problems. They may advocate client rights before sponsors of educational programs, and they also refer clients to other agencies for assistance that they themselves do not provide, including medical, psychiatric, legal, child care, family, housing, recreation, and further educational services. Professional counselors, adult education administrators and teachers, practitioners in related agencies, and paraprofessional aides can all make some contribution to each of these counseling functions, although the contributions of professional counselors tend to be most crucial for the assessment, planning, and problem-solving functions (Knox and Farmer, 1977). In urban areas (and some rural regions) there are often directories of such services and opportunities (Knox and Farmer, 1977).

Adult counseling requires distinct and special training, and a recurrent theme in the literature on educational counseling for adults is the problem of inadequate preparation of counselors. Three very important competencies are a knowledge of the decision-making process, an understanding of adult development, and an awareness of one's own age bias (Schlossberg, 1976).

The counseling function is sometimes performed by relatively untrained adults called paraprofessionals or counselor aides. The counselor aide may serve full or part time in a counseling capacity by giving information, assisting with planning, and providing other support services to the adult learner. Many counselor aides have an educational and cultural background that is similar to the adult clients served, which can facilitate rapport and trust. Family members and friends may perform a similar function. The use of counselor aides should be encouraged, although it is very clear that the effectiveness of paraprofessional aides depends in part on the quality and quantity of supervision they receive. Finally, in any setting, the utilization of counseling services related to adult learning tends to increase when the services are provided near the clients' homes or jobs and in forms that fit their typical information-seeking patterns (Knox and Farmer, 1977).

In summary, there are a number of major counseling concepts from the professional literature that can help practitioners strengthen the counseling function in an agency:

1. Personal contact is a powerful way to encourage participation and persistence in educational programs by adults, especially less advantaged adults.
2. Encouraging persistence entails attention both to individual and program reasons for withdrawal and to the various ways in which agency personnel can encourage persistence.
3. The essence of counseling is the relationship between the counselor and client, which enables the client to deal with planning, problems, feelings, and decisions.

4. The counseling function relates to most aspects of the agency.
5. The counseling function entails multiple tasks to help adults plan and participate effectively in educational programs, including provision of information, assistance with planning, help with problem solving, advocacy, and referrals.
6. The counseling function is performed by people in various roles, including professional counselors, adult education administrators and teachers, practitioners in related agencies, and paraprofessional aides.

Counseling Practices

The adult education counseling function is performed by professional counselors, teachers, administrators, and paraprofessionals. Only a few adult and continuing education agencies employ professional counselors for adult learners. The most visible examples occur in conjunction with the evening credit course programs of urban university continuing education divisions. For some other types of adult education agencies, counseling personnel are based elsewhere in the parent organization but frequently assist adult learners. This is the case in community college counseling divisions, where counselor work schedules include evening hours, and in personnel departments of larger companies and government agencies. In most agencies providing adult education, the counseling function is handled by administrators and teachers.

Typical Practice. An example of adult education counseling is a large manufacturing company based in the South. Counseling personnel exist in both the education and personnel departments. Counseling personnel help employees with assessment and career planning, especially for management development programs and for training specialists in fields such as engineering, sales, and finance. Supervisors and training specialists also provide counseling. Educational programs may be selected from inside and outside the company. In recent years, many large companies and government agencies have expanded their attention to career development to include analysis of past performance and exploration of personal development plans (Bell, 1975).

Typical counseling practice in a small agency is illustrated by the director of religious education in a large urban church in the Midwest. Church members frequently ask the director about current or potential adult education programs conducted by the church. When a member inquires about an activity beyond the scope of church offerings, the director uses her experience as a member of the metropolitan adult education directors round table to refer the member to relevant programs by other providers.

Much of the counseling of adult learners at a public school adult education program in the Northwest is provided by the director's secretary and by individual teachers at registration time. The secretary has been with the program for more than a decade and uses her familiarity with many aspects of the program to respond to questions received by phone and mail and in person. At registration, each adult education teacher works several hours at the registration desk helping adults decide on the courses that best fit their background, interests, and schedules.

Another example of counseling adult learners can be found in public libraries. In the early 1970s, nine public library systems in various parts of the nation established a learners' advisory service for adult independent learners. In each location, library personnel helped adults diagnose learning needs and develop learning plans. Librarians also established information support services to assist with the selection of relevant resources. The libraries that participated in this demonstration project experienced mixed success (Mavor, Toro, and DeProspo, 1976). An urban public library system in the Southwest continued and expanded the service. Although there was resistance from some librarians, strong administrative commitment shared by some younger librarians and paraprofessional staff has sustained the service at several branches and at the readers' service desk of the main library.

The main services provided by this program are preparation for exams such as the General Education Development Equivalency Examination (GED) and College Level Examination Program (CLEP), provision of book lists, and the operation of a learning exchange referral service. In addition to an extensive file on CLEP, and copies of diagnostic tests related to the GED, the library has a set of video tapes that adults can use in preparation for the GED high school equivalency examination. The GED videotapes and exams have also been used by library personnel in nearby correctional institutions. Dozens of book lists and annotated bibliographies have been prepared on topics such as small business administration and solar energy; the extent of use depends mainly on the initiative of library personnel. During 1977, a learning exchange file was created that lists more than 100 providers of adult education. Most are organizations with extensive course offerings, but some providers are individuals who are willing to teach or tutor. Although this service has been little publicized, it has been used by about fifty adults each month.

Exemplary Practice. Some adult education counseling efforts are quite comprehensive and illustrate exemplary practice given sufficient commitment and resources. About a decade ago, a community college fifty miles from a metropolitan area pioneered an educational and career guidance center for women. After a few years, the center was broadened to serve men as well. Counseling personnel help adults assess their abilities and interests, explore educational and occupational opportunities, and decide on appropriate steps. Both individual and small group counseling and guidance sessions are provided. Resource materials are available, and personnel help adults locate self-help groups and community agency services. Most of all, help is provided with planning and problem-solving procedures.

Another exemplary approach is illustrated by community-based educational counseling provided by the extension division of a state university in the north central area. Paraprofessional counselors reside and work half-time in four regions of the state. Ten hours a week are devoted to counseling and ten hours to publicity, follow-up, and administrative tasks. The counselors' purpose is to encourage adults to continue their education by matching their aspiration with educational resources and by gaining access to various educational programs for adults. The size of the regions served is matched with the number of counselors in order to maintain quality and continuity of service. Some communities are served once a month, others twice a month. As a result, about 6,000 adults receive an average of four counseling sessions. Almost half decide to participate in an educational program within one year after the first contact (Thompson and Jensen, 1977).

One especially effective adult education counseling service is actually part of a marketing effort. The parent organization is a large private urban university in the Northeast. Continuing education marketing materials, such as catalogues and brochures, refer to the continuing education counseling office as the place to begin. This image of a single, convenient door to the institution for the adult part-time student is reinforced by human-interest newspaper articles about local citizens who have benefited from the counseling service and by television commercials that highlight testimonials by former students. This marketing emphasis is designed to encourage new registrants, who may be apprehensive about their ability to continue their education, by letting them know that supportive counselors are available to listen; to help clarify career and academic goals; to describe relevant educational resources in the continuing education division, university, and community; to help with planning and referrals; and to anticipate and help with major adjustments.

Three full-time professional counselors serve about 5,000 adults each year. In addition, six adult students with a variety of experiences outside of educational institutions and of academic backgrounds work part time as peer counselors in an innovative telephone service. The peer counselors answer questions regarding practical problems of adult students in areas such as transportation, study locations, and library use. The counseling staff works mainly with adults pursuing a degree part time through the continuing education division, many of whom take some courses in the resident instruction program. Over the years that an adult pursues a degree part time, the counselor's continuity and ability to establish rapport with the student are important. The adult student expects the counselor to be familiar with the academic programs, to provide some career counseling, and sometimes to serve as an advocate for the adult student in relation to faculty members and administrators in the resident instruction program.

The director of the counseling office at this university gives attention to a variety of tasks in addition to counseling adults, including serving on policy committees; working with the adult student advisory council and the adult student alumni association; and increasing financial assistance for students through Basic Educational Opportunity Grants, grants-in-aid, and scholarships provided by women's groups, adult student alumni associations, and a "phone-a-thon." The director also speaks with various groups about the program and hopes to give more attention to job placement of adult students.

Coordination of Marketing and Counseling

Effective marketing and counseling activities are highly interrelated as well as related to other aspects of the adult education agency. When the parent organization is marketing or counseling oriented, the adult education agency tends to receive encouragement and support for the same orientation. Therefore, a crucial ingredient in strengthening the marketing and counseling functions is the leadership role of the agency administrator in coordinating marketing and counseling.

The organization and effectiveness of marketing and counseling services vary greatly among adult education agencies. Administrative understanding and commitment to marketing and counseling services can enhance or restrict their effectiveness. For example, adult education programs for specialized publics—such as adult basic education, university and community college programs for women, and employer training programs for unemployed youth—have typically included more formal marketing and counseling services than have other adult education programs. Attention to marketing and counseling can occur at many points. It occurs when provision is made for counseling and marketing as part of the planning for a new program area, especially one that is designed to attract a hard-to-reach target public. Administrative support is especially important in the allocation of resources in the form of personnel salaries, facilities, and expense funds for marketing and counseling services.

An important administrative function is staffing, which includes both selecting competent personnel and staff development. Staff development of personnel who counsel adult students is especially important, both because most counselors lack formal preparation in counseling adult students and because of the variety of personnel who perform the counseling function.

The provision and location of facilities for counseling and marketing personnel is an important administrative decision.

Facilities should be open at times that are convenient for clients and should be visible as well as readily accessible. For example, some community-oriented agencies have provided facilities in storefronts and shopping centers.

The function of marketing is to increase public awareness and agency visibility and to encourage potential participants to enroll in appropriate programs. A marketing specialist can help to plan and coordinate marketing activities and to prepare marketing materials such as brochures and news releases. However, marketing personnel can also function elsewhere in the parent organization—or outside of it, as in the case of contractual arrangements with advertising agencies. Voluntary advisory committees on marketing can also be useful. The advantage of internal personnel lies in the continuity and familiarity with agency purposes and procedures. External marketing personnel have the advantage of broader perspectives in the field.

Counseling personnel can also be based inside the agency, in the parent organization, or in the community. The use of counselors from within the parent organization, as is usually the case with universities, can increase resources but can also restrict responsiveness to the adult clientele. The counseling function of most agencies can be strengthened by establishing relationships with other agencies—for example referrals and participation in educational brokering organizations and learning exchanges. Collaborative relationships can improve the service to adult participants, but they require an investment of time and administrative support from each of the cooperating agencies if they are to function effectively.

In the process of assisting clients, counselors should acquire valuable insights about client needs, and these insights should be shared with program administrators for use in developing and conducting responsive programs. Communication between counselors and administrators should be encouraged, so that counselors' observations and insights can become integral parts of establishing program directions and needs assessment.

Some activities serve both marketing and counseling purposes, thus illustrating a "ready-made" coordination of the two activities. Consider for example community-based educational brokering centers. The need for these agencies, which combine marketing and counseling services, is well documented. Many adults need specific information about educational and career opportunities at convenient locations (Carp, Peterson, and Roelfs, 1974; Knox, 1968a). Half of the respondents in a recent national study said that they would have participated in adult education if they had known where to sign up for specific courses and training opportunities (Carp, Peterson, and Roelfs, 1974). One third said that they did not know about the existence of adult education programs in their communities. Disadvantaged adults were particularly poorly informed about adult education opportunities. Adult education agencies provide information about their own programs and sometimes about the educational programs of other providers. However, the types of adults who are underrepresented in current adult education programs are also unlikely to seek information from a provider about the range of learning opportunities. Examples of underrepresented adults include illiterate adults, women reentering the labor market, men and women in midcareer shifts, and retired people.

In response to these needs, there is now a small but growing number of community and regional educational brokering centers that provide information about educational and career opportunities for adults. There are many kinds of brokering agencies and services, from community-based counseling and advocacy agencies located in storefronts to community colleges without faculty or campus (Heffernan, Macy, and Vickers, 1976). They offer counseling, instructional, referral, and advocacy services in varying combinations. They provide adults with a wide range of educational and career alternatives and help them choose those most appropriate to their individual needs. Community-based brokering agencies are neutral toward the choices made; they do not recruit students for particular educational institutions. The people in brokering agencies who do the referral, counseling, or advocacy usually have no responsibility for teaching, grading, and awarding of credits and degrees. But in a few cases, such as the Regional Learning Service in Central New York State, the agency is able to have the adult learner's experience evaluated accredited.

Brokering centers reach out to people of all ages and educational backgrounds who want to earn a high school diploma or college degree, change careers, clarify goals, or simply gain more knowledge. The centers provide learning consultants to help clients select their goals and plan appropriate educational programs and to help clients locate other people with similar interests. The learning consultants are selected not on the basis of their academic background and credentials but on the basis of their personal qualities, and they themselves undergo an educational program that focuses in large part on developing their informational skills (Schlossberg, 1974).

Future Directions

Efforts to increase the effectiveness of marketing and counseling services can benefit from attention to both current practices and concepts from the literature. Current practices reflect an agency's purposes and resources. An administrator who assesses an agency's marketing or counseling services can discover strengths to be built upon, weaknesses to be avoided, constraints to be considered, and goals to be achieved. Conclusions regarding each of these aspects contribute to planning and improvement. An administrator who understands the basic concepts of adult education marketing and counseling can use the experience and insights of others to reflect on local purposes and procedures.

Most experienced adult education practitioners have an intuitive knowledge of basic marketing concepts. The fundamental marketing concept is that there should be a mutually satisfactory exchange between the agency and its publics. Because most adult education agencies depend upon sufficient satisfied customers who participate voluntarily, successful adult education practitioners have long demonstrated their client orientation. Attention to sound marketing procedures can increase the numbers and types of adults who participate. Experienced practitioners realize that effective marketing depends on educational programs that benefit the clientele so that satisfied participants enroll in additional activities and encourage their friends to do so. Announcements of upcoming events at the conclusion of programs can greatly aid this process.

A more detailed understanding of marketing concepts and

procedures enables an adult education administrator, working with others, to plan and implement a marketing strategy that will attract the types of adults who are underserved in relation to agency purposes. For example, an administrator who decides to broaden the agency clientele by attracting more adults with lower levels of formal education can engage in the following tasks.

1. Reading about adult development can increase understanding of developmental trends and variability associated with the roles and life-styles of men and women with low levels of formal education. This reading would alert the administrator to (a) multiple personal and situational influences on participation in adult education; (b) the extent to which lack of reading and limited organizational participation by adults in the target market discourage entry to many middle-class-oriented adult education programs; and (c) the benefits of encouragement by "significant others" in the decision to participate.

2. Reading about adult information seeking can help identify information sources, such as conversations with local opinion leaders, likely to be used by the target public with limited formal education. Needs assessments can identify the marketing mix—attractive topics, convenient locations and schedules, inexpensive and informal programs with an emphasis on discussion.

3. Marketing procedures can be selected that are likely to benefit both the agency and the potential participants. If it is important to maintain enrollments by more highly educated adults who are relatively easy to attract with mass media procedures (as is the case for most agencies), the administrator may devote a major portion of the marketing budget and time to direct-mail brochures and free public service announcements. The remainder of the marketing budget can be devoted to a targeted effort to attract adults with less formal education, emphasizing interpersonal marketing procedures. For example, the administrator may seek the assistance of advisory committees comprised of people likely to encourage potential participants to enroll and well-supervised recruiters who can relate to potential participants and provide accurate information about the program. Human interest testimonials by satisfied participants, based on program evaluation, can increase public awareness of adult education benefits and reinforce in-

formation that potential participants obtain from interpersonal sources.

4. The specific marketing strategy should be implemented with attention to educational needs of adults in the specific target market and to the purposes and resources of the agency. Information about similar marketing efforts in comparable agencies can be used to evaluate the local situation as a part of program evaluation regarding marketing services.

5. It is assumed that part of the marketing effort is devoted to publics other than clients, such as teachers and policy makers. If the agency is to function well, administrators should understand and be supportive of efforts by program staff to broaden the clientele and attract more underserved adults.

The counseling function is also familiar to most experienced adult education administrators, even though few have professional counselors on their staff. Analysis of current counseling services is a useful starting point for strengthening the counseling function and can be part of a broader agency program evaluation. Counseling service analysis serves a purpose similar to that served by needs assessment and market research for planning marketing services.

An underlying question is whether more or different types of counseling services are needed. To answer this question, it is helpful to have an overview of both current and desirable counseling services. Concepts from the literature can contribute to the administrator's idea of desirable counseling services, and major discrepancies from current practices provide a focus for administrative leadership. Because adult education agencies do not have full-time professional counseling staffs, but rely instead on administrators, teachers, paraprofessionals, and staff from other organizations, as well as a scattering of professional counselors, the effective director must give detailed attention to counselor competencies and tasks. Understanding the concepts of adult education counseling can facilitate this process.

For example, participants with low levels of formal education often enter adult education programs with very unrealistic expectations. This creates a quandary for counselors, teachers, and administrators, because the adult's unrealistic expectations may actually have overcome the obstacles to entering the educational program. To shatter the illusion as an unrealistic dream would be likely to cause the adult to drop out. However, to confirm the expectation as readily achievable would be dishonest and would ultimately cause resentment when the adult discovered that the expectations were unrealistic. Effective practitioners in adult basic education programs have discovered a relatively effective approach to this situation. It consists of helping the client identify an achievable short-term educational goal that will lead in the direction of the unrealistic expectation. If the client is able to achieve the short-term goal—and a series of subsequent short-term goals— perhaps with resulting increased proficiency, confidence, and experience, the initial expectation may become less unrealistic. However, even if major progress toward the client's expectation does not occur, experience with the adult education program and with the expectations and progress of other participants usually serves to place the original expectations in perspective and to suggest alternative goals that are both desirable and achievable.

The leadership that the adult education administrator provides regarding marketing and counseling services entails more than attention to each separate function, especially when an agency seeks to broaden its range of clientele and to attract and retain more hard-to-reach adults. Effective marketing and counseling services reinforce each other, and a single activity—such as a highly publicized registration period—sometimes serves both purposes. Efforts to strengthen marketing and counseling services also entail attention to agency purposes and resource allocation. Also, directors with an understanding of adult development and information seeking can use these insights in the orientation and supervision of staff members who perform marketing and counseling functions so that their efforts are responsive to adult needs.

Administrators can help to increase awareness of opportunities, for example, by providing a local directory of adult education activities or establishing an adult education clearinghouse to handle phone calls and letters. Administrators can also arrange to reduce problems related to location, scheduling, transportation, and child care. Other arrangements relate mainly to instructional personnel, such as attention to the first encounter not only at registration but also during the first instructional session. Staff selection and orientation can contribute to an increased proportion of participants who leave an initial meeting with the feeling that they were welcome and that they learned something of value.

Administrative leadership also includes attention to the functions performed by the agency and by other organizations. For example, a marketing specialist might be hired or marketing services might be contracted for from an advertising agency. A professional counselor might be hired or an agency might depend on counseling personnel who work elsewhere in the parent organization or in other agencies such as the employment service or community-based educational brokering center. The use of counseling personnel employed directly by the agency has the advantages of maintaining continuity and facilitating interaction with other agency staff. The use of contracted personnel has the advantages of specialization and ease of personnel changes. Consideration of marketing and counseling services in relation to agency goals also helps staff members choose the program areas and services that the agency will emphasize and recognize those better provided by other agencies.

Finally, administrative support and direction is especially important for research and evaluation projects, which produce findings of benefit to local staff and to colleagues throughout the field. Promising topics for study include reasons for nonparticipation, ways to increase persistence, and relations among marketing, counseling, and program development.

Chapter Six

Resources

Dennis A. Dahl

Adult education agencies vary considerably in their procedures for acquiring resources. This chapter describes the financial and nonfinancial resources generally involved in agency-sponsored adult education programs; the major influences on acquisition of these resources; procedures for acquiring, using, and evaluating resources; examples of current practices of resource acquisition and use; and a brief look at future directions of resource planning, acquisition, and evaluation.

Since the early 1970s, part-time students enrolled in postsecondary education programs have outnumbered their full-time counterparts, but most grant and need-based aid programs are heavily oriented toward full-time students. In the resident instruction programs of a majority of public higher education institutions, differential tuition rates still place a higher burden on part-time than on full-time students (Pitchell, 1974). In addition to financial obstacles, many aspects of higher education present barriers to part-time students. An increase in the number of opportunities for adults to enter higher education on a part-time basis is needed in terms of daytime and evening courses, summer courses, special short-term programs, and both degree and certificate programs as appropriate for adults throughout their working careers (Carnegie Commission on Higher Education, 1971).

Although some studies of part-time adult education participants (nontraditional learners) have produced results regarding financial resource practices in adult education programs (Cross, Valley and Associates, 1974), additional definitive studies are needed on comparative costs per program and per student in nontraditional and traditional postsecondary education. In addition, further analysis of the equity of alternative fee structures for nontraditional programs is needed before a clear case can be made for improving the resource base for adult education programs (Commission on Nontraditional Study, 1973). Because resource arrangements for adult education programs are complex and vary greatly with the characteristics of the providing agency, no clear pattern of resource availability and utilization exists. Differing agency purposes contribute to this lack of a discernible pattern. For example, there are enormous differences in financial practices among providing agencies such as university extension divisions, public school adult education departments, company training departments, and groups within large professional associations that conduct educational programs for members. This variable nature of resource acquisition and utilization in the field is not a new development (Kidd, 1962). However, vastly differing agency purposes do not necessarily result in different resource utilization practices. When differing agency purposes are recognized, there are far more similiarities than differences in the resource-related practices of adult education programs.

It should be noted that most information transmitted through adult education texts and journals deals with college- and school-sponsored programs, although estimated enrollments in adult education programs have consistently shown that programs sponsored by colleges and universities, community colleges, and public schools constitute only about one third of the total adult education enrollments nationally. Generalizations about adult education programs based on sources from this unrepresentative sample of agencies would of course be misleading; therefore, this chapter will include sources and examples of current practice from as wide a range of agencies as possible.

Types of Resources

There are two general categories of resources: financial resources involve provision of some form of money directly for program support; nonfinancial resources include contributions to programs that are not cash supported but do result in cost reduction in programs.

Financial Resources

The financial resources generally utilized in adult education programs fall into the following broad categories: (1) participant fees and tuition; (2) parent organization subsidy; (3) federal grants; (4) private foundation grants; (5) state and local tax support; (6) employer financial support; and (7) auxiliary enterprise income.

In educational institutions (for example, a university extension division), differences in financial resources between part-time adult education programs and full-time resident instruction programs reflect scale and emphasis rather than actual sources. Adult education programs in educational institutions generally obtain a much larger share of program expenses from student fees and tuition than do the preparatory education or resident instruction programs (Knowles, 1969; Kidd, 1962; Commission on Nontraditional Study, 1973; Trow, 1975; Bell, 1960; Pitchell, 1974; Carnegie Commission on Higher Education, 1971; Luke, 1969; Fischer, 1976; Bowen, 1973). However, despite the common assumption that most adult education programs are nearly self-supporting through student fees, a recent survey of a large sample of these programs shows that although student fees are still the largest single income source in adult education programs, they account for only 39 percent of the total program resources (Commission on Nontraditional Study, 1973). The proportion of total program costs paid by participant fees varies greatly, especially among agencies in noneducational parent organizations. For example, employees seldom pay fees for educational programs provided or required by their employers in business and industry. Rather, educational expenses are typically incurred by the education and training department and in many instances charged back to the operating department of the employee who receives the education. Many large firms reimburse all or part of the direct instructional fees that employees pay for work-related educational programs attended at external schools and colleges. Religious institutions seldom charge members for religious education programs; they also use inexpensive materials and volunteer leadership to keep costs low. Libraries, museums, and labor unions also tend to absorb the costs of educational programs. Professional and trade associations and proprietary schools, in contrast, typically budget each adult education activity to recover full costs.

Parent organization subsidy remains an important financial resource in most adult education agencies. The form of subsidy depends upon the nature of the parent organization but is normally seen as general support provided by the organization based upon its permanent, recurring financial base. This subsidy is not always clearly identified. In public institutions, federal, state, and local tax support comprise the base; in business- and labor-sponsored programs, the parent organization subsidy can also be seen as employer support aside from support for adult education programs conducted by the employers for employees. Employers may provide programs at the place of business for their employees or they may pay tuition to cover the costs of instruction for courses taken by their employees at some other institution.

Private foundation grants are becoming an increasingly important source of income for adult education programs as agency personnel gain experience in "grantsmanship." Broadly based national interest in innovative adult education approaches—such as the Open University, external degrees, and Adult Performance Level high school curricula for adults—have encouraged aggressive preparation of grant proposals to private foundations (Bowen, 1973; Luke, 1969; Wiles, 1977; Zelan and Gardner, 1975).

Auxiliary enterprise income is an occasional and minor source of income for adult education and refers to a program's income from the sale of educationally related materials—such as course syllabi, conference proceedings or other printed materials, and audio and video tapes—and from space rental. Although similar auxiliary enterprise income is produced in preparatory education programs, these funds can be even more important in adult education programs because of their flexible utility and the absence of major institutional subsidy.

Major changes in financial resources for adult education programs will depend upon future educational policies of local, state, and national government agencies and on the education priorities of private business and industry groups (Knowles, 1969; Trow, 1975; Wiles, 1977). Student fees will continue to be a significant financial resource for adult education programs in the absence of major policy changes by the majority of adult education parent organizations. It is ironic, however, that noneducational organizations, such as religious institutions, labor unions, and employers, typically expect adult participants to pay little or none of the instructional costs, whereas educational institutions, such as public schools, community colleges, and universities, expect adult participants to pay most or all of the instructional costs that are not covered by state or federal appropriations for adult basic education, vocational education, or cooperative extension.

Nonfinancial Resources

The most common nonfinancial resources used in adult education programs are facilities, equipment, and materials. These items, when contributed, can be as significant as direct financial subsidy, because they all constitute major expenses if purchased or rented on the open market.

Long-range planning for educational facilities for an agency's adult programs may include new construction or major renovation of an existing building. Detailed guides are available for planning and constructing buildings, presenting the basic parameters necessary for functional educational facilities (National Council on Schoolhouse Construction, 1964; Castaldi, 1969). Some sources describe specific methods of space planning for college buildings, along with guidelines for major renovations or conversions of existing structures (Bareither and Schillinger, 1968). Some of these sources take into account the physical and psychological needs of adult learners as individuals with distinctive learning environment needs (Alford, 1968; Knowles, 1969; Becker, 1960; Peters, 1969; Hunsaker and Pierce, 1959). Assigning an estimated cost to learning activity space provided without charge has become increasingly important in recent years because it can be used as in-kind matching for external grant projects.

In addition to office space, some agencies offer adult programs special facilities and materials, including conference rooms and equipment, classrooms, learning laboratories that operate both during the day and in the evening, continuing education centers for residential conferences and institutes, and meeting rooms in county or regional offices of a local cooperative extension service. The remaining facilities and equipment used by adult educational agencies are either provided without charge by the parent organization or a cosponsor or are rented by the agency. The policies regarding agency use of facilities and equipment typically are not formal policies but informal arrangements, so there is usually latitude for adjustments.

Facilities and equipment controlled by adult education agencies are selected and maintained for the specific purposes of the adult education program and are not subject to limitations that arise when another agency's space is used. For example, a public school adult education program that depends on classroom space in a neighborhood elementary school may have to contend with neighborhood adults' image of the facility as a place just for children, the small size of the furniture, availability of space only during the late afternoons and evenings, lack of storage space, and possible objections of teachers who use the classrooms during the daytime. In addition, agencies that control their own adult education program space have a planning advantage over agencies that must depend upon space provided by other agencies. For example, colleges and universities that serve adults in off-campus continuing education programs frequently depend upon classroom space provided by public secondary schools or community colleges. In some states (Indiana, Wisconsin), the establishment of regional campuses or geographically distributed continuing education facilities has resolved the off-campus classroom space problem.

In spite of the limitations, being able to arrange for short-term use of free or rented space from the parent organization, cosponsor, or public building can provide a high degree of flexibility and cost effectiveness. This flexibility is exemplified by some university continuing education conference centers that are only large enough to accommodate the core functions of registration, meeting, dining, and sleeping and must rely on university facilities and local hotels and restaurants for the overflow. If the agency were to restrict conferences to its own facilities, there would be a necessity for larger facilities and either higher costs due to unused facilities during slack periods or pressure to add activities of questionable educational value during slack periods.

For agencies like museums and libraries, space and program are highly interrelated. Museum space and related exhibits provide an unique setting for informal adult education programs. Many museums are now taking an active role in providing informal adult education opportunities in addition to their traditional roles as repositories of collections (Zetterberg, 1969). Increasing use of electronic aids—such as films, slides, viewer-activated taped lectures, and demonstration or "working" exhibits—have enhanced the educational orientation of the gallery experience for adults (Smith, 1976). Libraries have also expanded from self-service agencies to providers of planning and material services to other community organizations and providers of their own educational services to other community organizations' programs for adults (Lee, 1966).

Many adult education administrators have become accustomed to "making do" with unsatisfactory facilities and equipment, and it is important to consider the impact of this adaptation on the achievement of agency objectives. Inadequate facilities may discourage participants because of image, comfort, or convenience. Unsatisfactory facilities, equipment, and materials may also discourage resource people who feel hampered by these restrictions. Administrators must consider facilities and equipment within this broader context of agency effectiveness.

Influences on Resource Acquisition

All agencies sponsoring adult education programs must acquire the necessary resources to support their program efforts. Their success in this acquisition is dependent upon those factors—often interrelated—which influence the resource acquisition process.

Agency Type and Public Image

The two types of adult education agencies that account for the largest proportions of enrollments (religious institutions and colleges and universities) have very different public images, which greatly affect resource acquisition and utilization (Kleis and Butcher, 1969). Religious institutions, although not primarily educational, have extensive informal adult education programs, which have been traditionally funded by member donations, either directly or indirectly. Recently, many religious denominations have broadened their adult education programs to give more attention to critical social and community problems and to make increasing use of lay discussion leaders in programs. This gradual shift of focus may eventually change the perceived image of church-sponsored adult education programs, but it is likely that self-funding will persist until religious adult education can be seen as achieving a desired level of acceptance, professionalism, institutionalization, and integration with adult education programs sponsored by other agencies (Ryan, 1974; Stokes, 1970).

Educational institutions (public schools, community colleges, colleges, and universities) have general public acceptance for their adult education function. However, this function must compete internally with other educational functions, and despite optimistic predictions about increased tax and institutional support for adult education programs, most remain heavily dependent upon student fees for support (Sheats, 1960; Luke, 1969; Fischer, 1976). In addition, adult part-time students have been willing, although often reluctant, to pay higher tuition or fees than full-time resident students, thus hampering efforts to increase institutional support for adult programs (Dhanidina and Griffith, 1975; Zelan and Gardner,

1975; Wilms, 1974). Major increases in federal support for adult
education in recent years have had less than the desired impact
because of fragmentation and compartmentalization at the federal
level (Fischer, 1976; Knowles, 1969). Increased tax support and
agency subsidy for adult education programs in public educational
institutions seem to be more dependent upon an enhanced image
of the adult education function within the institution than the external image of the agency (Fischer, 1976; Knowles, 1969; Luke,
1969; Sheats, 1960). The recent success of Proposition 13 in California and other tax reduction initiatives planned in several states
could substantially change this situation. However, assuming that
there will continue to be some level of resources available, the
public image of the adult education agency will continue to be an
important factor in the competition for both external and internal
funds.

Although the public image of labor unions does not generally include recognition of a role as a bona fide sponsor of adult
education programs, some labor unions provide adult education as
a secondary activity, and labor union adult education programs
have broadened considerably during the past ten years to include
"education of the whole person" in addition to traditional union
organizational goals (Dwyer, 1977). Labor unions also have benefited from the commitment of many universities to labor education
(Rogin, 1970). Labor education programs in universities not only
have brought a recognized level of professionalism to labor education but also have provided access to foundation and federal
grants. Despite this unique dual programming approach, labor
union programs attract only a small fraction of their potential audience; a greater level of acceptance by union members of the concept of lifelong education and its value to the individual must be
achieved before significant growth in labor union adult education
will take place (Dwyer, 1977; Rogin, 1970; Mire, 1960).

Business and industry also sponsor adult education programs. Because major corporations are highly visible and work
at image building, industry-sponsored programs typically enjoy a
high level of acceptance. Agency subsidy is the main source
of financing; in many instances, training department costs are
charged to the operating departments in which trainees work.

Major corporations have been willing (and able) to invest in their educational objectives, as indicated by the programs sponsored by private corporations (Culbertson, 1974). The size and organizational thrust of large industries, coupled with management development programs provided by universities, contribute to the growth of industry-sponsored adult education programming (Culbertson, 1974; Risley, 1960; Nadler, 1970). The success of these adult education programs is closely related to the carefully developed public image that business and industry is not only a legitimate sponsor for such programs but also represents an "expert" source for management-related programs. These generalizations also apply to educational programs conducted by other types of employers, such as government agencies and the military.

Demand and Competition

The absence of accessible programs and long-range corporate demands have led to the establishment of several industry-sponsored programs, such as Xerox's large residential campus near Washington, D.C. (Culbertson, 1974). Demand and competition are often interrelated, because where demand for an adult education program is higher, several agencies typically respond. Proprietary schools with a profit motive and a job-market orientation are very responsive to private adult education demand. A recent study (Wilms, 1974) reported that proprietary schools, despite higher fees, compete favorably with tax-supported programs. This same study revealed that proprietary schools, with programs geared more specifically to job opportunities, may actually attract a higher percentage of lower-income students than similar public institution-sponsored programs in the same area.

Legislation

Legislation, particularly at the state and federal level, has a definite influence on resource availability and acquisition by adult education agencies. Theoretically, legislation is related to demonstrated demand; however, the time delay from the original recognition to the passage of legislation and the actual disbursement of funds makes it difficult to recognize this cause-effect relationship. Further, the overall effect of increased federal funds for adult education programming has been tempered by the greater fragmentation of these funds (Knowles, 1969; Fischer, 1976). An example of this fragmentation is Title IA of the Higher Education Act of 1965. After the appropriation, funds to administer this program in the Department of Health, Education, and Welfare are taken off the top; after distribution to each state, another 10 to 15 percent is usually allocated by the state to fund an office to oversee and allocate funded projects; thus, a significant portion of Title IA funds is preallocated before adult programming agencies submit requests for resources under this act.

Most legislation with a direct impact on adult education provides funds for specified program areas in selected types of agencies. Examples are Smith-Lever Act federal funds for the Cooperative Extension Service of the Land Grant universities, which are matched with state and local funds; Smith-Hughes Act (and more recently Vocational Education Act) funds for adult education programs conducted mainly by public schools; adult basic education federal funds for programs conducted by schools and community colleges; and federal support for continuing higher education related to community problem solving provided by Title IA of the Higher Education Act of 1965. Financial support for these aspects of adult education is typically administered and sometimes supplemented at the state level. Because of the pluralistic nature of adult education, each form of government support for adult education tends to be viewed as desirable by the agencies that receive it and as unfair by some of the other types of agencies. These contrasting views pose policy dilemmas for adult educators. For example, most legislation has assumed that there are categories of adults (unemployed, rural, undereducated) that are underserved, that there are competencies (occupational, citizenship, parenthood) that these adults require, and that it is desirable to provide tax funds to subsidize such programs. While many practitioners agree that subsidy is desirable for programs to reach underserved adults, there is less agreement on which agencies should receive subsidy and on what basis. This lack of agreement has made it difficult to obtain a broad base of support from the entire field on specific legislative proposals (Dorland, 1969).

Other Influences

The long-standing assumption that adults will place greater value on educational experiences for which they pay than on free programs has created some difficulty for agencies seeking program subsidy. Wilms's (1974) study tends to support this assumption, but another recent study (Londoner, 1974) that compared valuation of education goals by fee-paying and by subsidized students in the same program showed that paying one's own program expenses did not result in high valuation of education goals.

In practice, pricing decisions reflect many considerations, including past fees charged by the agency, financial policies of the parent organization, availability of subsidy funds, fees charged by other local agencies, willingness of potential participants to pay, and anticipated cost of satisfactory program. Traditionally, adult education administrators have tried to keep fees as low as possible in order not to exclude interested adults with a limited ability to pay. In recent decades, as financially hard-pressed educational institutions have urged their adult education agencies to increase cost recovery from fees, administrators have been forced to use differential pricing. The literature related to financing adult education can provide useful guidance for these increasingly complex financial arrangements (Bell, 1960; Bowen, 1973; Fischer, 1976; Johnston, 1969; Kidd, 1962).

A final influence on resource acquisition—and one more difficult to specify in practice—is the perception of whether an agency is the best available provider of a particular adult education program. Failure of well-established adult education agencies to receive the "best available source" designation has contributed to increased competition: A public school adult education program that offers a review course for certified public accountants in the same location as a university with a prestigious accounting department is not likely to be seen as the best source for such a program. In addition, this competition often involves new agencies, some with questionable qualifications (Fischer, 1976).

The public image of an adult education agency is consistently important in developing its resource base. However, the internal support for adult education programs within the parent agency may be the single most important influence on resource acquisition. Effective administrators acquire a realistic sense of the competitive pressures and demands for resources both within and among agencies. In the highly competitive funding area, agencies that strive to document their role as the most appropriate sponsor for a proposed program will increase their chances for success in resource acquisition.

Proposal Preparation

Another way adult education administrators obtain resources is through the preparation and submission of proposals to appropriate funding organizations. A proposal is a means of linking needs and resources. It is usually helpful to involve both people who will benefit from the proposed project (potential participants, leaders of related groups) and people who will provide leadership to the proposed project (instructors, administrators) in the proposal planning and preparation process. This collaborative development will strengthen the plan and commitment to the project if it is funded.

Although specific contents of proposals vary depending upon the nature of the project and the requirements of the potential funding source, three components are common to strategies for project planning and proposal preparation: purpose, procedures, and selection of funding source. The purposes entail what the planners of the project expect to accomplish if the proposal is funded. The procedures detail how the project planners will seek to accomplish the purposes and goals of the project if funded. The selection of the funding source entails an extensive review of the various listings of available funding sources. Examples of listings available to all adult education agencies are the *Federal Register,* a periodical that announces requests for proposals; *Commerce and Business Daily,* which lists all federal government procurement requests; and the *Foundation Directory,* which provides general purposes and funding priorities of private philanthropic foundations. Once a potential funding source has been selected, the person preparing the proposal should obtain as much information as possible about the priorities, procedures, and proposal guidelines of the potential grantor to ensure that the proposal prepared will be attractive and likely to be funded. "Attractiveness" is based not on cosmetic appearance (paper quality, type style, charts, neatness) so much as on responsiveness to the funding guidelines, priorities, and purposes of the potential grantor.

Knowledge of the influences on resource acquisition, their interrelationship, and how they operate in relation to one's own adult education agency can lead to realistic funding expectations and effective resource use. Once program funding is made available, attention must focus on effective utilization, including budgeting, accounting, and reporting of resources.

Budgeting, Accounting, and Reporting

Budget preparation and management is basic to the administration of adult education programs. The budget process is of special importance for tax-supported agencies because of requirements for accountability and post-program audit. Audit findings contribute to the validity of cost comparisons among various programs operated by an agency.

Budget Preparation

The preparation and administration of an agency budget is a vehicle for both planning and coordination. In a small agency, the budget may be one account of a parent organization—perhaps a revolving fund if there is no subsidy. In a large agency, each major section of the program may have a separate budget and account. The annual agency budget would then be the composite of all the section budgets. Because few adult education agencies have a capital budget for building and operating facilities or accounts for investment funds, agency budgets usually consist of operating budgets for income and expenditures.

Income budgets reflect amounts anticipated from all revenue sources, including tax funds (for public institutions), tuition and fees, charges for materials and services, and external grants and contracts. Expense budgets reflect estimated expenditures for each program, section, or for the total agency. Typical expense categories are wages and salaries for administrators, support staff, and instructional personnel; employee benefits; supplies and materials; travel expense; and purchased services (such as computer time and advertising).

The use of program budgeting in adult education is increasing. This technique, which identifies precise categories of income and expense for each separate program, provides the basis for financial evaluation of program results, cost comparison among similar programs, and cost-benefit analysis if program goals and objectives are stated and measurable (Johnston, 1969). Program budgeting is particularly valuable in programs that have several distinct income sources, because each program budget can reflect the related income sources and expense items. A detailed program budget can be an important and effective document to support requests for additional agency funds and to justify income needs to external funding sources.

"Management by objectives" (MBO) is a procedure whereby budgets and goals are established and periodically reviewed together. At the end of the specific program—or at a previously specified date—budgets and goals are appraised and accomplishments are rewarded (Fuller, 1973). MBO procedures are not common in most adult education agencies; in fact, some adult educators resist them as somewhat artificial and inadequate for proper evaluation. In spite of these objections, however, the process of establishing both program goals and operating procedures to attain them is often handled by people who have nothing to do with budget responsibilities. Since neither budget nor program can stand alone, but must be integrated for overall program success, MBO offers a means for combining budgeting and programming. MBO tends to be most effective when it represents an informal emphasis rather than a rigid system. A major reason for the failure of some formal MBO systems is that the public announcement of objectives tends to reduce flexibility and to increase resistance to the achievement of some organizational objectives. As a result many administrators tend to state modest, easily achieved objectives.

There is a need for more detailed studies of adult education program financing, particularly in terms of cost comparisons with preparatory education programs, by student and by program. For example, comparative cost data have been useful in the establishment of several external degree programs (Commission on Nontraditional Study, 1973). Surveys have shown that the cost per full-time equivalent adult education student in external degree programs is significantly less than the cost per full-time preparatory education student in traditional resident degree programs. Because the same resource categories are potentially available for both programs, these cost comparisons are valuable for adult education administrators who are competing for limited resources (Bowen, 1973).

Although there is a great need for detailed cost studies on all aspects of adult education programs, it will be difficult to conduct these studies until attention is given to detailed program budgeting and specification of indirect and other contributed costs associated with adult education programs. Budget planning, management, and control in adult education programs has typically lagged behind other programs of the parent organization, such as preparatory education programs. Adult educators' assumptions that their programs are cost effective must be supported by hard evidence from valid studies. In small agencies, the use of money, staff time, and facilities is readily apparent to all concerned. In large decentralized agencies, however, it is sometimes unclear whether programs are effective and whether resources are being well managed. Some management information is usually available in all agencies, such as enrollment and financial figures. Other crucial information regarding resources, processes, and outcomes that could readily be made part of a management information system is often lacking. Much of the needed information could be accommodated in the administrative data processing unit of the parent organization (as long as it is collected by the agency). Information that is useful but that cannot be justified for routine collection might be collected on a special study basis from a representative sample of activities.

Accounting Concepts and Procedures

Adult education administrators deal with various types of information and systems, some of the most important of which are fiscal systems. Although accounting operations vary with type and size of agency, six basic accounting concepts constitute the foundation on which fiscal systems in adult education agencies operate: enterprise, continuity, fiscal condition, results of operation, present fairly, and audit. These concepts comprise a framework for classifying and using fiscal information, and they enable an administrator to summarize and deal with information about complex, specialized, and changing program areas and functions so that resources will be well allocated and used. This process requires that fiscal information be used in conjunction with information about purposes, programs, and personnel.

For accounting purposes, the *enterprise* is the organizational unit that enters into transactions. It may be a legally constituted entity, such as the parent organization, or some distinct part of it, such as the adult education agency within the larger organization. Some large adult education agencies may designate subunits, such as university conference centers, as enterprises for accounting purposes. Financial records are organized around separate enterprises, and accounting procedures are concerned mainly with transactions relating to the specific enterprise rather than with other parts of the parent organization or other organizations in the community.

Continuity assumes that the agency or enterprise will continue to function with its present purpose and in its present form far enough into the future that its assets will be used for the purpose for which they were acquired and that the enterprise's obligations will be paid in due course.

Fiscal condition is the conclusion to be drawn from a balanced array of an enterprise's assets and the claims against those assets. An asset is anything of use and likely benefit to future operations of the enterprise. They may be monetary or nonmonetary, tangible or intangible, owned or not owned—as long as the enterprise can use them to contribute to future operations. *Current assets* consist of cash and other resources likely to be sold or consumed during the fiscal year (or other normal operating cycle). All other assets are termed *fixed assets*. This distinction is important because current assets are the primary means by which the enterprise meets its impending financial obligations, and its ability to do so is referred to as its *current position*. Liabilities are claims against the enterprise payable in cash, in other assets, or in services. The term *fund balance* refers to the balance of a specified group of accounts; in solvent enterprises, the balance is positive. Assets are equal to liabilities plus the fund balance.

For nonprofit adult education agencies, *results of operations* is a term indicating how well the enterprise fulfilled its purpose during a given time period—the patterns of benefits that result from the expenditures of revenues. *Revenues* are increases in assets or decreases in liabilities that augment the fund balance. *Expenses* are decreases in assets or increases in liabilities that reduce the fund balance or charges incurred to help achieve enterprise objectives during the current fiscal year.

Accounting reports are designed to provide an accurate and balanced summary of the financial operations of an enterprise using procedures that are consistent over time. The concept *present fairly* includes a cluster of generally accepted accounting principles, consistency, and full disclosure. Accepted principles cover agreed-upon accounting practices which, in combination, have been found over time to be an effective way to summarize the status and progress of an enterprise. Preparation of accounting reports consistently over time allows the use of a series of comparable reports to interpret trends. Full disclosure means that the financial statements taken as a whole present a satisfactory overall impression of the current fiscal position of the enterprise.

The annual *audit* is a major factor in establishing and maintaining confidence in the financial reporting of the enterprise. An independent auditor examines the financial information, based on preset standards, and renders an opinion on the degree to which the enterprise has complied with the accounting rules and regulations governing its financial operation.

The foregoing accounting concepts and procedures organize financial information for use in administrative decision making. An understanding of these general concepts can enable the adult education administrator to adapt and use accounting systems to suit the distinctive purposes of a specific adult education agency and to provide effective supervision of people with specific responsibility for fiscal operations in sponsored programs (Hentschke, 1975).

Reporting

A management information system for an adult education agency yields information for decision making within the agency and each of its separate enterprises. It also provides the basis for reporting to the parent organization and professional associations and for other external purposes. Effective reporting, however, requires more than simply having the information available. The main ingredient in effective reporting is an understanding of the types of information that people outside the agency can use constructively and then the ability to provide that information on a timely basis and in a clear and understandable form. Knowing what type of report is timely and understandable for each audience is difficult, but experienced administrators find that if they are careful in fashioning reports, assessing results, and making modifications as needed, reporting can become an effective way to promote cooperation and support. For example, detailed financial reports that indicate trends may be best for the business manager or controller of the parent organization; a narrative summary of working relationships and accomplishments may be best for directors of cosponsoring organizations; and a brief summary of program trends along with representative case examples of the benefits to adults who enroll may be best for state agencies or other supporting organizations. Effective reporting is important to the acquisition, use, and evaluation of resources because it provides feedback regarding accountability and achievement of results that can influence continued or increased allocation of resources. Adult education agency administrators need not be certified public accountants; however, a working knowledge of budget preparation procedures, basic accounting concepts, and reporting requirements can help the administrator provide effective leadership in resource utilization and more readily assess the potential impact on programs of several new financial policies, which are discussed in the following section.

Potential New Financial Policies

Many new plans for adult education financing are in the discussion stage at any time. However, three types of plans have received considerable attention in recent years and provide comprehensive approaches to the financing of adult education through direct support of the individual student (American Council on Education, 1974; Kurland, 1977; Kurland and Comly, 1975; University of Notre Dame, 1973).

Voucher plans would provide employed persons with dollar credits, which could be applied toward a wide variety of educational and training programs at any time during their working careers. People could draw on voucher credits early in their working careers or allow the credits to accumulate for mid-career educational activities. Tuition costs, some living expenses, and a portion of wages lost during education periods would be allowed. Voucher plans typically include special provision for voucher credits for women reentering education after childrearing. Financing of a national voucher plan would be similar to the Social Security system, with both employers and employees contributing a percentage of wages to the plan (American Council on Education, 1974; Bushnell, 1973).

Entitlement programs are variations of the basic voucher plan. Similar to veterans' education, entitlement programs would provide educational subsistence grants to individuals who complete a specified period of employment. At retirement age, unused entitlement dollars would apply to retirement income (American Council on Education, 1974).

There are three primary variations on entitlement programs. One would provide individuals with one half of the tuition costs of education for up to four years. After entering the work force, a 4 percent surcharge on income would be charged and credited to the individual's entitlement account. Every five years of work would entitle the individual to a one-month study leave at half salary. At age sixty, the unexpended balance in the account would go either to pension credit or terminal employment leave. The study-leave portion of this program would be self-supporting; tuition grants would be offset by reduction or elimination of other federal programs such as veterans' education, dependents' social security, manpower programs, and unemployment compensation (Cartter, 1973). Another entitlement variation is a voluntary plan with a fixed endowment ($10,000 has been suggested) that an individual could use for educational purposes. For those who participate, a fixed percentage surcharge on income would provide the financial base for the program. After age forty-eight, the unused balance in the individual's entitlement account, with accrued interest, would become an unrestricted asset of the individual (Dresch, 1974). A final entitlement variation, modeled on programs in western Europe, would guarantee every worker two full years of education and training on a full-time basis, with all education costs and basic living costs paid. This plan would require federalization of state unemployment insurance funds and a payroll tax of about 1.5 percent shared equally by employer and employee to make the program self-supporting (Striner, 1972).

A third proposal for financing adult education involves expansion of the federal loan program in the following ways:

1. Low-interest government-guaranteed loans could be provided for adult part-time students, patterned on the National Defense Student Loan program.
2. An education opportunity bank could be created for adults. Individuals could borrow for educational purposes and agree to pay back a specified percentage (uniform for all borrowers) of income for a set number of years. Under this plan, high-income individuals would indirectly subsidize portions of loans to low-income individuals.
3. A slight variation of the education opportunity bank involves an income-contingent program with variable-term repayments inversely related to the borrower's age to ensure that loans are paid up by age sixty-five. Under this plan, older borrowers would repay at a significantly higher annual rate.
4. Under another variation of the educational opportunity bank, loan repayments would be contingent upon the estimated savings level of each borrower. As the loan increased, the repayment period would lengthen and place a heavier burden on

young adults for obligations of older borrowers who reach retirement age before repayment is completed.

These four variations of federal loan programs are representative
of a large number of proposals that would make federal loan programs accessible to adults seeking support for educational activities
(American Council on Education, 1974; Biederman and Billings,
1973).

None of these proposed plans for financing adult education
involves direct support for agency-sponsored adult education programs; rather, all of them direct financial aid to the individual, who
then can select from available programs. The unstated assumption
of these proposals is that individual selection of programs by adult
learners will promote sound programs and eliminate weak ones.

A shortcoming of many voucher plans tied to employment
or employer contribution is that they tend to exclude adults who
are not employed for salary or wages. Thus, a woman who completed school, was married, and raised a family without ever working full time outside the home would be excluded by many voucher
plans if, at age forty, she decided to pursue further education.

The voucher, entitlement, and federal loan proposals are
new financial policies in the sense that they have not been formally
adopted and implemented. Whether or not any of them become
operational in the future depends upon a variety of political and
economic factors. However, with recent increases in the number of
adults participating in educational programs on a part-time basis,
the continuing decrease in the traditional college age group (18 to
22 years of age), and the general concern of both taxpayers and
governmental representatives with funding for education, it is
likely that one or more of these proposed policies will receive serious consideration in the next few years.

Examples of Current Practices

Adult education programs are sponsored by a variety of
noneducational organizations (business and industry, labor unions,
associations, and religious institutions) as well as by educational
institutions (public schools, community colleges, and universities).

Innovations in resource utilization by both types of adult education agencies can be found.

Decreasing preparatory education enrollments in New York state public schools allowed educational space no longer needed for preparatory programs to be used for community-operated adult education centers (New York State Education Department, 1975). Similar circumstances in Virginia led to the conversion of under-utilized portions of existing buildings for adult education programs (Green, 1975). These two examples illustrate how adult education agency administrators can acquire an important non-financial resource—physical facilities for adult programs—by keeping up with trends and demands not only within their own parent organizations but also in other educational organizations in the same geographic area.

In the business and industry sector, Leeds and Northrup Company identified a critical need for management training for company supervisors and established a development institute. Located in a large residence adjacent to corporate headquarters, the institute, fully funded by the corporation, has already provided residential short courses in management for over 700 people, using both internal staff and outside consultants in the instructional program (Eddy and Kellow, 1977). An even more ambitious education and training project has been undertaken by Xerox Corporation, which has invested an estimated $75 million in its Leesburg, Virginia, residential training center. Operating on a $25 million annual budget, it is anticipated that about 20,000 Xerox employees (over 25 percent of Xerox's total work force) will attend short courses annually in subjects such as sales, marketing, management, and technical areas (Strobach, 1976). The development of these programs and facilities is illustrative of an adult education agency (an industry's training department) acquiring resources for a major program from its parent organization. The key factors in the success of these programs were the ability to convince the parent organization that provision of resources would enhance the achievement of its overall purposes and the justification that the industry itself was the best available provider of programs needed by the target audience—employees of the industry.

A consortium of midwestern universities, funded by the National Institute of Education, is active in the development of independent study courses in several subject areas utilizing broadcast television as the delivery system. Courses and companion study guides are developed and produced by the University of Mid-America for distribution to member institutions and for sale to other educational institutions. This approach may expand availability to adult learning experiences to a much greater number of potential adult students, but the long-range cost effectiveness of this method remains questionable (University of Mid-America, 1977). This project shows how collaboration by several adult education agencies in various universities can increase the visibility of their common purpose and result in the acquisition of resources for a new program designed to serve the adult clientele of all the cooperating agencies. These agencies would not have been able to garner the support necessary to acquire these resources—or even a pro rata share—on their own.

Forsyth Technical Institute and the Forsyth County Library have collaborated on a program to expand learning opportunities for adults in Winston-Salem, North Carolina. A learning laboratory under the direction of Forsyth Technical Institute was developed (at no charge to the adults who participated) in conjunction with a building renovation project in the downtown library. Over 100 independent study courses using audio and video cassettes and self-pacing study guides are available. The learning laboratory has dovetailed with a federally funded project that provides information services and academic counseling to users of the learning laboratory. Courses are geared to community interests; a recent influx of Vietnam refugees to the Winston-Salem area led to the addition of an audiotape course in English as a Second Language. All costs are borne by Forsyth Technical Institute and the public library (Tompkins, 1976). In this example, two separate adult education agencies serving overlapping clientele have combined complementary resources, resulting in a comprehensive program approach—one agency providing the academic development of the independent study materials and the other providing physical facilities, equipment, and public access for potential adult clients. The result was additional services provided at minimal cost by combining some aspects of a new program with a closely related, separately funded program.

The foregoing examples of current practice in the field include both long-standing programs and recent variations in resource utilization for adult education programming. There are few limits to the potential innovations that adult education administrators can make in regard to resource acquisition, allocation, and evaluation, as long as they pay careful attention to community interests, possible collaboration with other sponsors, and the needs of adults.

Future Directions

There are several ways in which adult education agencies can improve their identification, acquisition, and management of resources. Although specific resource-related practices vary among adult education agencies, several basic needs deserve further attention by most agencies.

Adult education agencies can use program budgeting procedures to provide an accurate record of direct costs and income for each major program area. Program budgeting also facilitates the use of valid audits and provides an excellent base for evaluation of each program. The budget preparation and administration process should be fully integrated with development and modification of program goals and objectives. The individual program administrator has a major role in both program planning and budget preparation, because both activities are integral to a successful program. An important (and often overlooked) part of the program budgeting process is the determination of an estimated cost value to all nonfinancial items—space, materials, equipment, personnel time—provided without charge to programs. Inclusion of these estimates not only provides a complete profile of total costs for programs but also indicates, in combination with specific financial data, the total level of resource commitment by the agency to its adult education program.

Along with the lack of sufficient attention to program budgeting procedures, the lack of valid cost studies in adult education programs contributes to confusion about their cost effectiveness. Accurate cost studies of representative adult education programs can provide data for comparison with preparatory education programs. Well-organized and selective financial studies can also yield significant infoⁿmation about the cost effectiveness of the various programming formats used in adult education.

Collaboration and cooperation among agencies in jointly sponsored programs also deserves emphasis. The increase in collaborative approaches in recent years is significant and should be encouraged. Each agency brings unique resources to adult education programming. Interagency cooperation can expand the available financial base and provide additional flexibility in the use of financial and nonfinancial resources. Collaboration among agency sponsors such as colleges and universities, business and industry, professional associations, and state and federal government may be the most effective approach in developing the continuing professional education programs currently needed—and in the near future likely to be mandated. There are limits to the desirability of cosponsorship, however. When colleagueship, compatibility, and complementarity do not contribute to collaboration, the costs of cosponsorship may exceed its benefits. Even under the best of circumstances, it usually takes a substantial amount of administrative time and effort to establish and maintain interagency cooperation. Cosponsorship has typically been most effective between educational institutions and noneducational institutions. For example, a college has experts, classrooms, libraries, and laboratories but requires adult participants for a successful program; a professional association or a labor union has members who want to increase their competence but lacks educational personnel and materials. Each has personnel to help plan and conduct the program; more importantly, each requires what the other has to offer. The basic ingredients necessary for an effective partnership are present.

A final suggestion concerns the new proposals for funding adult education programs through direct assistance to potential adult students. Adult educators and program administrators can assume greater leadership in the investigation of and support for entitlement or federal loan systems for adult students. Adult education personnel should recognize the positive impact of the availability of direct financial aid not only to current adult students but also to potential adult students. Efforts toward increased direct financial support for adult students require a concomitant decreased emphasis on external support for programs. This shift, which is viewed negatively by many administrators who have struggled to maintain a minimal financial base for existing programs, may be a critical element in the extension of educational opportunity to those adults currently unable to participate for financial reasons. However, care needs to be taken to ensure that direct financial assistance is not restricted to only those adults who have been employed as wage earners for an extended period of time.

The acquisition and use of resources by adult education agencies is as varied as the range of agencies' purposes and programs. Increased collaboration among agencies, implementation of program budgeting procedures, and accurate cost studies of adult education will bring needed emphasis to good practices and improve visibility of educationally sound, cost-effective adult education programs. Further, a more aggressive investigation of possible direct financial aid systems for adult students might lead to the resolution of many of the resource problems encountered by minimally funded programs.

Chapter Seven

Staffing

James C. Hall

Effective staffing is essential to any productive organization but it is not often accomplished well without a plan. Staffing procedures are typically used to implement personnel policy. Recommendations for developing personnel policy and suggestions for sound staffing practices found in recent literature on personnel administration can be applied to adult education agencies as well as to other organizations.

This chapter provides practical information on how to define jobs, how to recruit people to fill these jobs, and how to develop and retain effective employees. Before describing typical staff procedures, a caution is noted. Although effective administration requires sound personnel procedures, sound procedures alone will not ensure success. Staffing, by definition, means making

181

judgments about people, and given the complexity of people, personnel decisions are at best uncertain. Sound decisions must sometimes be reversed if people become less effective over time; conversely, questionable decisions may eventually appear sound as individuals develop in desirable but unexpected ways. As a result, the only guarantee is that decisions based on sound procedures tend to produce better results than decisions made without sound procedures.

Adult education agencies must hire instructional personnel, administrators, and support personnel. In small agencies, employees typically perform more than one function. For example, the same person may identify an audience, design a program addressing needs of that audience, write promotional copy for the program, and provide some of the instruction. In contrast, staff members in large agencies with broad missions tend to be specialized: different individuals teach, do clerical or technical work, market, evaluate, administer a program, counsel participants, and maintain the physical plant. The focus of this chapter is on similarities among staffing procedures regardless of type of job or size of agency. The procedures described in personnel management literature apply to jobs ranging from highly specialized faculty members to front office receptionists.

Describing the Position

Most of the literature upon which this chapter is based is outside the field of adult education, because little has been written specifically on staffing adult education agencies (Deppe, 1969; Farmer, 1970). Most of what has been written (Beckerman, 1972; ERIC Clearinghouse on Adult Education, 1970; Williams and Gillham, 1970) is descriptive or hortatory. Adult education administrators have been encouraged to hire instructors who understand adults and who have empathy for the problems that adult students face. Adult education practitioners are told that a counselor trained to work with children or adolescents will not necessarily work well with adults (Farmer, 1971; Thoroman, 1968). But adult education administrators are not told how to find people who have the skills and hold the values associated with effective performance in adult education. This chapter provides some specific suggestions on how to find appropriate staff members.

Before any steps are taken to recruit and hire a staff member, the position to be filled should be defined so that those responsible for recruitment and hiring understand what the potential staff person will be expected to do. In this first step of the staffing process, the emphasis is on describing the job and specifying the competencies required to do the job. Job titles alone are not sufficient.

Beach (1975), Flippo (1976), and others agree that jobs should be defined in two ways: through job descriptions and through job specifications. Flippo (1976, p. 111) defines a job description as "an organized, factual statement of the duties and responsibilities of a specific job" and a job specification as "a statement of the minimum acceptable human qualities necessary to perform a job properly." The creation of job descriptions and job specifications, taken together, are commonly referred to as the two parts of job analysis.

Job descriptions and job specifications are useful not only for recruitment and selection but also as a basis for job classification—the categorization of jobs by kind of work and pay level. However, job classification will not be treated in this chapter for three reasons: (1) Many adult education agencies are small enough so that a formal system of job classification is not needed for employees to understand where they fit into the organization or for the director to set salaries and perquisites. (2) Adult education agencies that are large enough to require job classifications are usually part of a larger organization, such as a school system or a university, that already has a job classification scheme. (3) Adult education agencies large enough to need a job classification system but lacking one will need more specific direction than is provided in this chapter. Administrators in such agencies should refer to any of the general texts on personnel management referred to in this chapter.

For the purposes of this discussion, we will assume that positions and salaries offered are at least minimally attractive and competitive with similar positions in other organizations. If this is the case, the following staffing procedures should help attract and retain satisfactory personnel. If the positions and salaries are not attractive and competitive, the agency needs distinctive inducements to recruit staff or it is likely to experience difficulty with staffing regardless of the thoroughness of its staffing procedures.

Job Descriptions

Job descriptions have at least three purposes: (1) to announce job vacancies to people looking for work, (2) to provide agencies with basic information for periodic evaluation of employees, and (3) to add detail to the job titles included in the organization charts of agencies. Job descriptions should use the minimum level of complexity that meets the agency's needs and should be uniform in format across the agency for ease of comparison and use. Most job descriptions are written for full-time positions, but because part-time employees are important to many adult education agencies, part-time positions receive special attention in this section. The following format for job descriptions should be sufficiently detailed for most adult education agencies. It can be used both for full-time and part-time positions and is similar to the format suggested by Flippo (1976).

1. Job Title. For most agencies the job title describes the job: "Coordinator of Women's Programs," "Assistant Dean for Student Services," "Receptionist." But for some agencies with a job classification system mandated by a legislature, civil service commission, or union, job titles may not be descriptive of the job. For example, the title "Extension Worker Assistant" in the Montana University System conveys little about the content of a job to an outsider applying for work. In contrast, "Assistant to the Dean for Conferences and Institutes"—the unofficial title for the same job—communicates a clear general impression of the job to potential employees. The title displayed most prominently on the job description should help prospective employees understand what the job is. Official titles, when they are not descriptive, should be included in the job description but in parentheses.

2. Job Summary. A simple, clear paragraph or two should summarize the content of the job. The summary is meant to provide a sense of what the job is, not to define the job in detail.

3. Duties Performed. Flippo emphasizes the importance of this part of the job description: "The duties-performed section is the heart of a job description and is the most difficult to write properly. It is supposed to tell what is being done, how it is done . . . and the purpose behind each duty" (Flippo, 1976, p. 115). It is also advisable to include in this section the percentage of time spent on each duty. This will have to be estimated for a new job, but employees in existing jobs can provide accurate information on the time spent in each type of duty.

4. Supervision Given and Received. A brief statement of supervision given and received helps applicants—especially for support staff and administrative positions—understand where a job fits into an organization.

5. Equipment and Materials Used. Equipment and materials are often important for clerical and technical workers. Adult education instructors ordinarily choose the equipment and materials they use.

6. Working Conditions. A statement on working conditions may be important for some jobs in adult education. For example, if an employee must keep the office open alone in the evening, work irregular hours, or travel on short notice, these working conditions should be described.

7. Additional Comments. Given the day-to-day variation in activities of people employed in adult education, it is often advisable to describe the "flavor" of working in an adult education agency. This section of a job description is not essential for personnel selection, but it can help candidates better understand the job being described and better evaluate their qualifications for particular jobs.

8. Salary or Hourly Wage. To attract desirable candidates to an agency, salaries and wages should be competitive with those of similar agencies and consistent within similar categories of positions. Wages or salaries are usually stated in one of three ways: as a "competitive" salary, a range (low to high); or a set salary or wage. The term *competitive* is almost never used in reference to wages. A "competitive salary" announcement allows maximum freedom in setting a salary likely to be attractive to a desirable candidate, but it may also attract applicants who require salaries in excess of what the agency can offer. If the maximum salary that can be offered is, in fact, less than what is paid at other agencies or institutions, the job description should include a more specific salary than "competitive." To state that the salary for a job is competitive when it is not will lead to disappointment and delay in filling a job. If salaries and wages are stated as a range, potential applicants are informed of what they can expect as a minimum and maximum. A maximum will help limit the applicants to those who are willing to work within the range; if the maximum is less than the market wage, one can assume that some of the most desirable candidates will not apply. Yet some candidates tend to see the maximum stated in the range as the minimum acceptable wage for the position. A maximum limit should be firm, and the range should be tied to the experience and qualifications stated in the job specifications. Finally, specific salaries or wages that the agency can live with should be set and announced. Clerical jobs are offered at set salaries or wages; administrative and faculty jobs, except part-time jobs, are usually offered with a salary range.

The foregoing procedures apply to most full-time positions, such as secretaries and administrators, and to full-time teachers of adults in a few agencies as well. But for most adult education agencies, position descriptions have to be modified and selectively used for what are often the most crucial staffing decisions—the selection of experts to teach for the agency on a part-time basis. Although arrangements vary from one kind of agency to another and from instance to instance, part-time and short-term appointments share several features. One is that no commitment is typically made to a part-time instructor beyond a single assignment—such as teaching one evening course for an academic term or conducting a three-day workshop. Whether experts are asked to work with an agency more than once depends on the perceived quality of their performance. Further, administrators and planning committees have specific expectations for experts who serve as teachers in adult education programs; in contrast, they have more general expectations for most full-time employees, who have a variety of assignments that may change over time. Finally, part-time instructors can be selected from within or outside the parent organization. The education and training department of a business may select a manager or a specialist from within the company to conduct a session in management development or may select an outside expert from a university, professional association, or government agency. A community college continuing education division may select a full-time faculty member to teach a noncredit course for adults or may select an accountant, attorney, insurance agent, or realtor to teach the course.

In the case of part-time and short-term instructional appointments, it is unlikely that an administrator would prepare and announce a complete position description. However, the essential ingredients of the position description are still desirable, even though the procedures used may be less formal than they would be for a full-time faculty member. For example, the planning committee for a weekend marriage enrichment retreat sponsored by a religious organization may spend many hours deciding on the qualifications, expectations, and remuneration for a consultant to conduct the program. The statement the committee devises may be sent to several potential consultants prior to any actual interviews, and even if only one person is seriously considered, the main points of the statement may be reflected in a detailed letter of confirmation.

Some adult and continuing education divisions at universities encourage hiring of full-time faculty members from the parent organization to teach evening or off-campus credit courses on an overload basis for extra compensation. A job description related to the teaching of adults may help to convey the adult education agency's expectations regarding matters such as instructional style, travel, materials, advising, and grading. An appointment letter may confirm additional expectations and a specific stipend. When someone other than a full-time faculty member teaches a continuing education credit course on an adjunct appointment, the academic department involved often has some statement of qualifications and expectations, which can be included in a letter of appointment and can also function as a kind of job description.

The quality and responsiveness of much adult education teaching can be attributed to the practice of reappointing only those who perform well; and adult education administrators traditionally have had wide latitude in making part-time and short-term instructional appointments. However, in recent years some teachers' organizations have imposed restrictions on hiring of outsiders to teach courses to adults, in part by giving full-time faculty members "first refusal." Some states have established teaching credentials for instructors of adults, motivated at least partially by a desire to limit the hiring of "outsiders." If these restrictions become widespread and result in a decline in the quality of teaching for adults, new ways to maintain high quality and responsiveness will have to be developed. Job descriptions for part-time teaching appointments and a review of the performance expectations they reflect may help accomplish the goal of high-quality instruction for adult students.

Job Specifications

A job description reflects what a job is. A job specification, in contrast, reflects the knowledge, skills, and experience needed to do a job. Job specifications are not used as often as job descriptions for staffing decisions, perhaps because describing tasks is often easier than describing the human characteristics needed to accomplish those tasks. For example, specifying that a clerk-typist must be able to type sixty words per minute with fewer than three errors is a simple matter and easily measurable. However, specifying that an administrative assistant for program development must have the ability to work effectively under pressure with adult students, instructors, and administrators is very important for the success of the employee and the agency but is not as easily measured as typing speed.

Many jobs in adult education agencies require cognitive and affective proficiency more than psychomotor skills. Many people who work in adult education must not only know a subject matter well but must also be able to work well with a wide range of people. Thus, the job specifications needed to staff adult education agencies, though difficult to write, should nevertheless be written to provide a basis for selecting people for jobs and evaluating people once they are on the job. The particular format chosen to state job specifications is not important, but it should be used consistently within the agency and should include at least the minimal knowledge, skills, and experience that are necessary to do the job.

The adjectives *specific* and *necessary* must be stressed. The knowledge, skills, and experience required of job applicants should be as *specific* as possible, both to help potential applicants decide whether to apply for a job and to help those involved in the hiring process identify which applications warrant further scrutiny. The knowledge, skills, and experience required of applicants for a job should also be *necessary* for that job. It is unfair, imprudent, and illegal, for example, to require a masters degree for a routine typing job even though, given the current crowded job market, one could almost certainly hire someone with a M.A. tor just such a job. Job specifications should reflect *minimal* job requirements, although job specifications may allow for reasonable variation above the minimum. The components of each of the three general categories of job specifications follow.

1. Knowledge. This category ordinarily refers to the highest level of formal education required of applicants. Traditionally, clerical staff members have been expected to have a high school diploma or a general educational development equivalency certificate (GED); administrative assistants are expected to have some college or a baccalaureate degree; directors or deans a master's or doctorate; and instructors a level of knowledge commensurate with the subject matter being taught. However, given the wide range of topics taught in adult education agencies, knowledge might well include not only information gained in the classroom but also knowledge gained outside the formal educational system and unrelated to degrees earned. A guru trained in India, it might be argued, might be at least as well equipped to teach meditative techniques as a person with a Ph.D. in clinical psychology who has studied meditation as a therapeutic technique. Similarly, a sheep rancher might be able to teach a practical course in shearing techniques as well as or better than a professor of animal husbandry from a land grant university.

2. Skills. The skills included in job specifications are usually technical skills related to the use of machinery; secretarial skills in transcription and typing are familiar examples. However, skills are also part of the proficiency required of administrators and instructors. In the selection of part-time teachers in adult education agencies, skills are typically subsumed in global judgments about past teaching performance. Some search committees may ask candidates to demonstrate their teaching ability in a brief presentation before the screening committee or a group of subject matter experts in order to measure applicants' teaching ability in a simulated instructional situation. Letters of reference from (or, better yet, conversations with) people who supervised or observed a candidate teaching adults may yield similar global information about teaching proficiency. Interpersonal skills often are not included in job specifications except in general expectations that applicants should "like people" or "enjoy working with a diverse student body" to be considered for the job. Some day it may be possible to screen applicants effectively for interpersonal skills; staffing decisions would become more certain if such screening were possible.

3. *Experience.* Experience, like knowledge, provides an estimate of likely employee performance. Evidence of successful management of an office in the past indicates to search committees and administrators that an applicant should be able to manage a similar office in the future. Evidence of successful instruction of accounting courses for small businesses or courses in watercolor painting indicates that an applicant should be able to teach successfully in similar areas in the future. But predicting performance in a new situation from past experience is uncertain in at least two ways. First, because no two situations are exactly alike, it is difficult to know if past experience can be meaningfully related to present and future needs. (The relevance of formal schooling is equally difficult to judge for this same reason.) Second, gathering reliable information on the success of an applicant's past experience is very difficult, although following up on references and interviewing candidates can provide some useful information on past performance. (Both references and interviewing are discussed in a later section.)

The ability of adult education administrators or search committees to select staff members effectively depends in part on their conception of the proficiencies that are important for a position. For example, some secretaries of adult education agency directors devote a major portion of their time to informal conversations with current and potential participants, with other staff members, and with the general public. A director who appreciates the importance of this informal contact for solving problems, recognizing opportunities, and enhancing the image of the agency will give special attention to proficiency in interpersonal relations and communication in addition to clerical skills. Experienced adult education administrators also understand that helping adults to learn requires both subject matter expertise and process proficiency in instructional methods and interpersonal relations. Most adult education participants prefer resource people who have something of value to offer and who relate to them as adults and not as large children. Selection criteria for instructors and other experts tend to emphasize only subject matter expertise, but administrators who recognize the importance of process proficiency for teachers of adults can obtain information on this proficiency during recruitment and selection.

Several proficiencies are crucial in the selection of adult education program administrators. As with most administrators, an orientation toward action and results, effective interpersonal relations, and integrity are important personal qualities. Another important proficiency for adult education administrators in particular is an understanding of issues and trends in the broad field of adult and continuing education to serve as a foundation for goal setting and relations with other agencies. An understanding of adult development and learning can be applied by administrators in their work with resource people and clients. Proficiency in program development is most fundamental for program administrators, entailing attention to both planning and conducting educational programs, including tasks related to educational context, needs, objectives, learning activities, and evaluation. In addition to developing programs, effective adult education administrators engage in tasks related to goals and policy, staffing, finance, facilities, organizational relations, and coordination of all these components. If people who select adult education program administrators recognize that these proficiencies are crucial, they will write position descriptions and selection criteria to reflect the proficiencies and will limit consideration to candidates who have these skills or are likely to acquire them in the near future.

Job Design

Setting forth tasks and proficiencies are not the only concerns administrators have with job design. For humane and managerial reasons it is often important for jobs to be as interesting and
rewarding to the person doing them as possible because, as Beach
puts it (1975, p. 195), "the design of jobs—their content and structure—affects both productivity and employee motivation and
morale."

Some employees do not care whether their jobs are interesting or challenging; but too many jobs are designed more narrowly
than is necessary, and productivity, morale, and motivation can
suffer accordingly. Examples include clerical employees who do
nothing but post grades on transcripts in an extension division;
secretaries grouped in "word processing units" with the sole task of
transcribing dictated tapes; administrators of continuing education
programs in business management, who are discouraged from involving disciplines outside the business school; and faculty members assigned to teach the same introductory course over and over
in an evening program.

Jobs should be designed to challenge the people doing them
and broaden their skills while addressing productivity needs. As
much autonomy, responsibility, and judgment as possible should
be delegated to staff members to provide challenge and to create
interest. If at all possible, employees should be encouraged to exer-
cise responsibility and judgment beyond their own jobs in some of
the agency-wide decisions that affect them, such as the scheduling
of working hours and vacations, working on a full-time or part-
time basis, and determining fringe benefits. The more employees
are involved in their total working environments, the more likely
they are to be satisfied and productive workers (Werther, 1975, pp.
438–439). Further, by providing jobs that help staff members grow
through learning new skills, adult education agencies can create a
learning environment for their staff members that mirrors the environment the agencies attempt to create for their clients.

Recruitment

The goals of recruitment are to develop a pool of qualified
applicants for a specific job, to screen applicants, and to select the

best applicant from the pool. When job description and job specification have been formulated, recruitment is likely to be effective because the expectations of the agency are clear, and potential applicants can decide whether they are interested and qualified.

The way in which a pool of applicants is developed will vary from agency to agency and from job to job within an agency. In agencies that are part of large parent organizations (such as a large business, major university, or large school system), administrators may have access to a central personnel office with procedures for developing applicant pools and for initial screening of applicants for clerical and entry-level administrative jobs. (Most central personnel offices to which adult education agencies have access do not recruit faculty members or high-level administrators.) Even if an adult education agency has access to a central personnel office, however, the agency is usually still responsible for writing the job descriptions and specifications for most, if not all, jobs within the agency. Administrators in small adult education agencies—such as those associated with a community agency, a labor union, or a voluntary association—may not have access to any central personnel office and, consequently, must do all of their own personnel work. Thus, whether or not a central personnel office is available, each adult education agency must have a plan for searching for and selecting among applicants for jobs.

Recruitment can be divided into at least three distinct phases: (1) the search phase, during which the job is advertised and a pool of applicants is developed; (2) the screening phase, during which the number of applicants in the pool is successively reduced; and (3) the selection phase, in which an applicant is offered and accepts the job.

Searching

During all phases of recruitment, most adult education agencies have a legal responsibility—and all have a moral responsibility—to offer employment equally to all qualified people regardless of their race, color, religion, sex, national origin, or age. The basic laws on which equal employment opportunity is based are the Civil Rights Act of 1964, the Equal Employment Act of 1972 (which amended the 1974 act), and the Age Discrimination in

Employment Act of 1967. While the point of these three laws is simple to state—employers are required to recruit broadly and to select employees solely on the basis of reasonable qualifications for the job—the interpretation of the laws is complex and their interpretation changes subtly over time. For technical advice on compliance with the provisions of equal opportunity legislation and administrative orders, adult education administrators can consult legal counsel, refer to personnel journals such as the *Labor Law Journal,* and rely on their institution's Equal Employment Opportunity Officer or personnel officer (if such positions exist in their organizations). More important than understanding the latest interpretations of the law, however, is the implementation of its intent: to provide an equal chance for employment to all qualified applicants.

In attempting to meet the intent of the law, two principles for searching for, screening, and selecting job applicants should be followed: (1) all job openings should be advertised widely in media that will reach a diverse but appropriate audience, and (2) all applicants should be equally judged against the expectations stated in the advertised job specifications. If these two principles are followed—and if the agency does not have a preexisting imbalance in the composition of its work force—there is little danger that an unsuccessful job applicant would either claim discrimination or be able to support that claim. If an imbalance in the composition of an agency's work force has been demonstrated, however, the burden of proof against a charge of discrimination becomes the agency's and may be difficult and costly to refute (Holley and Field, 1976; Portwood and Schmidt, 1977).

Not all jobs need to be advertised equally; rather, the scope of a job advertisement should be related to the level of the job, and in this case the level of the job can be readily judged by the level of salary offered. Local advertising is usually adequate for relatively low-salary jobs. Regional and national advertising is wise for middle- and high-salary jobs, respectively. The advertising media chosen—newspapers, employment agencies, newsletters, journals, letters to colleagues, job markets at professional meetings, and the like—should be selected to assure the hiring agency of reaching a wide range of qualified people. Ordinarily, a good-faith effort to advertise widely and to select according to stated criteria will lead to a heterogeneous and well-balanced staff and will limit the probability of discrimination claims.

Major administrative positions in the field can be publicized in several ways to enrich the pool of candidates who apply. The parent organization usually has standard procedures for informing people within the organization about openings. If a college education is an important qualification, announcements might be sent to placement offices and schools of education, especially those associated with the approximately eighty graduate programs in North America offering a major in adult and continuing education. Most professional associations in the field (for example, the Adult Education Association of the U.S.A., the American Society for Training and Development, the Association for Continuing Higher Education, the National Association for Public Continuing and Adult Education, the National University Extension Association, and the Canadian Association for Adult Education) have publications, listings at a national office, and arrangements at annual meetings to help employers and potential staff members find each other. Information about periodicals, associations, and graduate programs related to the field is contained in the *Directory of Resources in Adult Education,* published every year or two (Niemi and Jessen, 1976). Especially for continuing higher education positions, the *Chronicle of Higher Education* is frequently used.

For the most demanding positions in the field, it may be that many of the people best qualified are already successful and satisfied in similar positions elsewhere. Under these circumstances, those who apply spontaneously for the position are less likely to be the best qualified, and a personalized effort may be necessary to identify prime prospects and encourage them to apply.

In many adult education agencies, search committees help attract applicants for full-time administrative or instructional positions and screen the pool to eliminate less qualified applicants. Some administrators also ask search committees to select a few finalists—ordinarily three to five—from which the administrator chooses. The use of search committees in adult education recruitment is a sound administrative practice for several reasons. First, using a search committee to describe a job, set the specifications for it, and evaluate its total design reduces the likelihood that an administrator's personal biases will affect job description or lead to unreasonable job specifications. Second, a search committee, especially if its membership is varied, can often more effectively publicize a job to a diverse audience than can an administrator working alone. Third, a search committee can relieve an administrator of the routine screening of applications, although the administrator should take care that the criteria for screening are based on the advertised job specifications and that the criteria are applied equally to each applicant. Fourth, service on a search committee often helps staff members understand at least the personnel aspect of administration and may prepare them for new responsibilities in the future. Finally, being involved in hiring decisions often evokes a sense of responsibility from search committee members for new staff members and for the welfare of the total agency.

The size, composition, and responsibilities of search committees should be reasonably related to the importance of the search to the agency. A search for an entry-level clerk should be a relatively simple procedure involving probably no more than the person who will supervise the new employee and perhaps one or two others. A search for a new dean, director, or full-time faculty member, in contrast, should probably involve a search committee representing the agency's staff as well as the parent organization (if there is one), the agency's clientele, and perhaps the community at large.

Whatever specific role they play, search committees have the potential for helping administrators make sound personnel choices through a collegial deliberative process that precedes the selection of staff members. The use of search committees, of course, can and often does slow down the selection process, but the opportunity for increasing the quality of personnel decisions seems worth the extra time.

The information provided by a person applying for a job is often the only information an administrator or search committee has on which to decide, at least initially, whether an applicant should remain in the pool or should be eliminated from consideration. Applications for clerical and entry-level administrative positions are usually taken on a form provided by the employing agency. Because the categories of information requested are the same for each applicant completing the form, comparisons among applicants can be readily made when forms are used. These application forms should request information relevant to the particular job but should not request information that might discriminate among applicants on grounds that are ordinarily not relevant to the job—such as race, color, religion, or national origin. Age and sex may be requested on application forms, but the Age Discrimination in Employment Act of 1967 forbids discrimination on the basis of age for persons forty to sixty-five years of age, and many states have even broader laws against age discrimination. Discrimination on the basis of sex is generally illegal. Application forms should include requests for the applicant's name, address, social security number, telephone numbers both at home and at work, age, sex, education, training, and work experience (including employer's name, address, telephone number, dates employed, full time or part time, job title, and supervisor's name for each job). While information about marital status, number of dependents, hobbies and recreational interests, and other personal matters has often been requested in the past, this information is seldom relevant to the qualifications necessary to do a particular job and is seldom needed to make a selection decision.

Application forms are not used for most administrative, teaching, or other professional jobs; rather, applicants are asked to provide a résumé or curriculum vitae containing information relevant to the description and specification of the job for which they are applying. Information similar to that requested on an application form should be culled from the information provided by applicants for professional jobs and may reasonably be augmented by information on professional activities not related directly to a prior job, by titles of publications and other professional products, and by honors and awards related to the applicant's professional performance. In the case of applicants for professional jobs, references are ordinarily requested and provided. In general, irrelevant information should be disregarded, and deviations from the job specifications should be avoided in the screening and selection process.

Some kinds of information tend to be especially valuable for the selection of teachers, counselors, and administrators and should be requested as a part of application procedures. Information about college degrees, work experience, and publications provides an indication of subject matter expertise for teachers or process proficiency for counselors and administrators. Letters of recommendation tend also to focus on expertise. A less easy to obtain but equally important aspect of successful performance by adult education administrators, counselors, and teachers is the ability to work effectively with adults. The best evidence is based on actual adult education experience, and in the selection of part-time instructional staff for adult education workshops and courses, experienced administrators tend to rely heavily on conversations with people who have observed a potential instructor in action. If candidates for administrative, counseling, or teaching positions lack experience in adult education, useful predictions of how they are likely to perform can often be derived from their experience in other kinds of interactions with adults, such as participation in professional associations and community groups.

Screening

When the application deadline has passed, the administrator or screening committee sorts the applications by the apparent qualifications of the applicants, based on the job specifications. Usually many applicants can be eliminated on an initial screening because they do not meet the stated educational or experience requirements. Applications that are eliminated should be kept so that all applicants can be notified of the results of the search when it is completed and so that all applications will be available for scrutiny should a charge of discrimination be filed in connection with the search and selection process.

The screening process should continue until five to ten well-qualified applicants remain. Additional information should be obtained about the finalists from former supervisors, people listed as references, and perhaps mutual acquaintances. If a finalist is currently employed, it is courteous to request permission of the applicant before contacting his current supervisor in order to avoid punitive action by a supervisor who does not know that an employee has applied for another job.

Background checks are essential to sound staff selection. No applicant should ever be offered a job without a background check, made either in person or by telephone—inquiries by letter, evaluative checklists, or general letters of reference are often not reliable (Flippo, 1976). Because the information sought in a background check should be related to the job for which the applicant is being considered, a brief description of the job can help a current or former supervisor respond specifically to the inquiry. General questions about an applicant's performance on a past or present job—such as attention to detail, leadership ability, creativity, or absenteeism—are appropriate in a background check. Special attention should be given to past performance in tasks that are crucial to success in the position to be filled. Examples of tasks that indicate successful teaching performance are presenting clear and interesting course or program descriptions, developing useful instructional materials, encouraging self-directed learning by adult participants, and providing program evaluation findings that help learners and teachers to improve learning activities. Examples indicating successful administrative performance are delegation of responsibility and authority, sufficient attention to basic organizational functioning so that time and resources are available for improvement of the agency, helping those associated with the agency to agree on the priority of objectives, and advocacy for agency mission and requirements.

Information from a background check should be evaluated in relation to a finalist's general pattern of performance. If one source presents unfavorable information that is not corroborated by at least one other source, a finalist should not be eliminated but instead should be questioned about the unfavorable information in an interview. However, if substantial unfavorable information about a finalist is corroborated in a background check by at least two independent sources, the finalist should probably be eliminated from the pool.

Background checks should follow an established format to ensure that similar information is collected about all finalists. If one person can check the backgrounds of all finalists using such a format, the reliability and comparability of the information gathered should be greater than if two people collect information on different candidates in nonstandardized ways.

In the staffing procedures described so far, an administrator or search committee has gathered (1) information provided by the applicants in their applications and (2) information about finalists provided by people who are familiar with the quality of their performance. Testing and interviewing provide two additional sources of information.

Many tests are available to assess intelligence, personality, aptitudes for various kinds of work, and other psychological variables. But because valid psychological testing sometimes requires proficiency in test administration and interpretation, testing is often delegated to specialists. In addition to considering the use of standardized psychological tests, employers can also create their own performance tests to simulate crucial tasks of the job to be filled. For example, it is relatively simple to test typists by asking them to type a brief report; each applicant should, of course, be given the same assignment and be tested under similar conditions. A potential instructor can be asked to conduct a brief seminar session in his field for instructors and students from the same field, who can evaluate the applicant's performance. Applicants for counseling and administrative jobs can also be placed in a simulated situation relevant to their potential responsibilities and be observed as they perform. A program development case study can be used as a work sample for applicants for a program administration position. The applicant can be asked to prepare a written response to the case study, which can then be discussed with the search committee.

If applicants are to take either psychological or simulated performance tests, they should be notified beforehand so that they can come prepared. Testing, especially performance testing conducted at little cost to the agency, should be seriously considered as part of the selection process, because it can provide a readily observable sample of a finalist's proficiency. However, care should be given to preparation of a valid simulation or work sample.

Although the validity of information related to job performance that is gathered through selection interviews has been seriously questioned (Mayfield, 1964, and earlier studies cited therein), administrators and search committees almost universally use personal interviews as part of the selection process. One reason interview data may not be as valid in predicting subsequent performance as data gathered from written applications or preemployment testing is that many interviews are poorly conducted, poorly evaluated, and poorly reported.

The style of interviewing used to screen finalists for a job can range from highly structured to totally unstructured. In a series of studies performed for the Life Insurance Agency Management Association (Carlson and others, 1971), structured interviews involving simultaneous note-taking seemed superior to semi-structured and unstructured interviews regardless of the experience of the interviewer. Flippo (1976) also strongly advises the use of a structure in which the interviewers generate a set of questions to be used in each interview before it begins, reviewing each finalist's materials thoroughly before meeting with the finalists, and recording an evaluation of the interview based on answers to the predetermined questions immediately after each interview is concluded. Using such a structured approach tends to generate information that is comparable from interview to interview, saves time by focusing the interviews, and reduces to a minimum the skill necessary to interview successfully.

Goodale (1976) agrees that a structured approach is best and provides a six-part framework for a selection interview. First, the interviewer establishes a personal rapport with the applicant with a bit of "small talk." Second, the interviewer explains the purpose of the interview and sets the agenda for the rest of the interview. The purpose of the interview in Goodale's opinion is to gather specific information about the applicant and the applicant's background that may be predictive of future performance on the job. In step three, the interviewer asks the predetermined questions to gather information which, it is hoped, will be predictive of future performance. Fourth, the interviewer describes the job thoroughly and places the job in the hierarchy of the organization. Fifth, the interviewer offers to answer any questions the applicant wishes to ask and allows the applicant to add any information he feels is pertinent. Sixth, the interviewer terminates the interview and indicates to the applicant an approximate time by which the applicant will know whether he has been selected.

When all interviews are complete, the interviewers should discuss the results of the interviews with each other and make recommendations, usually in priority order, to the search committee, the administrator, or both. Before making recommendations, any unfavorable information uncovered during the interviews should be investigated by telephone or a personal visit in a manner similar to that used in the background check. It is possible at this stage that no acceptable candidate emerges; in that case, the search process is extended and a renewed effort is made to enrich the pool of applicants. In the case of some major positions, it may be necessary to identify and contact persons who are well qualified and satisfied in their present position who would not apply spontaneously.

After the interviewers have made their recommendation, they may wish to meet to discuss discrepancies in the information they gathered. Such a "debriefing" may help the interviewers improve their own interviewing skills and may lead to increased reliability of information gathered by them in future interviews.

Selecting

The top applicant should be made a specific offer including a statement of salary, benefits, vacations and holidays, starting date, and all other relevant conditions of work (even if prior discussions have included all of these facts). Often the initial offer is made by telephone and, if accepted, followed by a confirming letter with each of the pertinent aspects of the offer repeated in writing. When an offer is formally accepted, the search is finished and all other applicants should be notified in writing that the position has been filled. Notifications to unsuccessful candidates should be unequivocal and as brief as possible. If the top applicant declines the offer, it is usual to proceed down the priority list of desirable applicants until one accepts or no acceptable applicants remain and the search process is extended.

Orientation, Staff Development, and Organization Development

Orientation and staff development focus on individual staff members and their ability to do a particular job. Orientation occurs in the first few days on the job. Staff development begins as orientation is completed and continues throughout a staff member's association with an agency. Staff development is especially important when new duties are added to an individual's job or when a staff member's performance falls below an acceptable level. Organization development has as its focus the improvement of the entire staff of an agency, with emphasis on the human aspects of the organization and its ability to adapt to change. Organization development in an agency involves either the entire staff of an agency or, if the staff is large, major subsets of that staff, and it should be continuous.

Much has been written about staff and organization development. The programs described in the literature range from relatively simple, short-term approaches, such as on-the-job training, to complex, long-term approaches. Special emphasis is given here to simple, inexpensive approaches to orientation and development. It is assumed that many readers are adult educators in relatively small agencies and that adult educators from large, complex agencies will go substantially beyond the overview in this chapter to design detailed staff and organization development programs for their agencies. The references cited in this chapter contain detailed information on the design of development processes for large, complex organizations.

Orientation

Orientation has three goals: to help new staff members feel comfortable during their first few days on the job, to teach them the essential routines of the job, and to introduce them to the style of the organization. Orientation as described here is a simple but important process, which seldom needs to last more than a few days. Much of a helpful orientation process seems to be common sense—and it is—but too many agencies fail to get new staff members off to a good start, resulting in unneeded stress at best and early resignations at worst.

A new clerical or administrative staff member should be met on the first day of work by a staff member assigned to the task of orientation. Introductions to other staff members who work in the same general area should be made as soon as possible. Too many introductions at once, however, can be baffling to a new staff member. Judgment needs to be exercised in helping new people get acquainted. Identifying the roles of staff members to whom a new person is introduced often helps the newcomer identify them later, when names alone may have been forgotten or confused.

New instructors, especially when they are part-time staff members, are often overlooked in the orientation and staff development processes. Overlooking the orientation of new faculty members can make them feel unconnected with the total agency, with possible unfortunate consequences. In some large agencies, part-time instructors have taught courses several terms without having met the administrator or having received any explanation of basic procedures. Instructors should be welcomed into the agency and helped to understand the agency's mission and their responsibilities as staff members in accomplishing that mission. The orientation of a new instructor, especially a part-time instructor, need not take more than a few hours, but it should not be overlooked.

A new clerical employee or entry-level administrative staff member should be shown his office or work space, provided with materials and equipment customary for the job, and allowed some time alone to become comfortable with the new physical environment. When the new staff member is settled in, an assignment should be given, followed by a thorough explanation of how to complete the assignment. Questions should be encouraged before, during, and after the assignment. The assignment should be evaluated as soon as it is completed; whatever honest praise is deserved should be given, along with advice on how to improve performance in the future. With the completion of each task another assignment should be given; honest compliments and helpful criticism should be provided so that within a few days the new staff member begins to function satisfactorily. The new staff member should be consciously integrated into the rest of the staff in social activities such as group luncheons and after-work entertainment. It is also often helpful to provide the new staff member with a brief tour of the building in which the agency is housed and of the surrounding neighborhood. This attention helps the new staff member feel at home and overcome the anxiety that often accompanies a new job.

The style of orientation will, of course, depend upon the role and place of the new staff member in the hierarchy of the agency. New clerks are typically oriented in more structured, supervised fashion than new agency directors, for example. But the goals of the orientation are similar at all levels of an organization. New staff members want to feel part of the group and want to know what is expected of them. The process of integrating a new member into the staff certainly cannot be accomplished in a few days of orientation, but the first few days on the job can be critical to the new person's view of the job and the agency. After the effort and expense of a careful recruitment process, an agency administrator will want to make the first few days on the job as pleasant and productive for a new staff member as possible.

Staff Development

Kozoll (1974) makes three assumptions about staff development that help put the process into perspective. Although Kozoll's assumptions are not based on empirical evidence, they are plausible and, unlike most systems of staff development, emphasize simple, inexpensive approaches to improving a staff member's performance. (1) Staff development should be continuous because it gains greatly in effectiveness from continuity and, conversely, suffers greatly from discontinuity and sporadic scheduling. (2) Staff development need not entail highly-structured, formal events but can be accomplished well through frequent, relatively informal sessions. The goals of the process and the purpose of the sessions, however, must be clearly defined. (3) Staff development need not rely on outside experts. Productive, well prepared staff members can provide the foundation for a staff development program, augmented from time to time with specially skilled outsiders. Given these assumptions, virtually all agencies have the potential and resources for adequate staff development regardless of the size of their staff or budget.

Staff development may be viewed as an extension of the orientation process in which new staff members are taught their jobs and other staff members are retrained. If a number of staff members are beginning in similar jobs at the same time or if some duties of a number of jobs are similar, staff development may be accomplished in groups. In small agencies with relatively few staff members and low-turnover, staff development is typically provided on an individual basis. The job description, which sets forth the job duties to be mastered, serves as the basis for staff development; the job specification, which sets minimum levels of performance, provides a framework for evaluation. Additional written and oral explanations of duties—and in some cases demonstrations of performance—are also usually needed. These explanations and demonstrations should build on the description created at the beginning of the staffing process.

In the process of staff development, clerical staff members may learn how to maintain the appointment calendar and filing system of an adult basic education program. A new instructor may learn how to evaluate students in a competency-based baccalaureate degree program for adults. An administrative assistant for information services may learn the routines connected with placing an ad in a local paper. Initial staff development for each new staff member ends when the basics of the new job have been mastered. Similar staff development episodes may take place whenever new skills or procedures are needed or whenever performance falls below acceptable levels. Subsequent staff development is designed to enhance the individual's career and to prepare him for future responsibilities.

During the past decade, increasing attention has been paid to faculty development in adult education as well as at all levels of formal education. As a result, much has been written on how teachers of adults can become more effective (Havelock and Havelock, 1972; Hoyt and Howard, 1978; Knox, 1971; Kozoll, 1972; Spear, 1976). Several generalizations on faculty development are broadly applicable. For example, staff development programs intended to increase the proficiency of teachers of adults in program planning and implementation ought themselves to be excellently planned and implemented programs. Their objectives should be specific and clearly stated, and faculty participants in the programs should be involved in the planning process. Appropriate and varied instructional methods should be used in faculty development programs, and the programs should be models of evaluation in terms of both outcome and process.

Many approaches and resources are suitable for staff development, and not all need to be implemented by an agency to meet its own staff development needs. The use of professional libraries and materials resource centers; observation of outstanding teachers, counselors and administrators, or clerical workers; attendance at the meetings of appropriate professional associations; involvement in staff meetings devoted to new concepts and practices; association with visiting scholars and practitioners; and involvement in coaching relationships are a few of the ways in which staff members can help and be helped to improve their performance on the job.

Organization Development

In contrast to staff development—which is based on the assumption that the better technical skills staff members have, the better they will perform on the job—organization development is based on the assumption that to be successful in a changing and competitive environment, technically skilled individuals are not enough. Individuals must be helped to improve not only their technical skills but also their ability to work productively with each other for the good of the organization. In the words of Argyris (1971, p. ix), "At the heart of organizational development is the concern for vitalizing, energizing, actualizing, activating, and renewing of organizations through technical and human resources. Technical development is achieved through areas of marketing, finance, engineering, and manufacturing. Human-resource development concerns people, interpersonal relationships, small groups, intergroups, and organizational norms and values." While Argyris describes organization development in industrial terms, "program planning" and "program implementation" can readily be substituted for "engineering" and "manufacturing" in applying the description to adult education agencies.

With so many technical and human variables included in organization development, it is clear that organization development is a complex process aimed at planned change within organizations. Bennis (1969), who tends (in his earlier writing on organization development) to emphasize the human aspects of the process more than the technical aspect, provides seven characteristics of the organization development process. These characteristics are presented in the following paragraphs, supplemented by applications to adult education.

Bennis suggests first that organization development "is an *educational strategy* adopted to bring about a *planned organizational change*" (1969, p. 10). A variety of educational strategies can be used in organization development. For example, information about communication problems among staff members in a geographically decentralized community education program could be gathered by questionnaire and later discussed in a series of meetings. Staff members from the various program sites and the central program coordinator could receive the results of the questionnaire in these meetings, define problems, and begin to develop new modes of communication. In a more complicated situation, training sessions for the senior staff of a statewide cooperative extension service program might be led by a specialist enlisted from outside the organization to help increase the quality of communication among staff members and to help the organization adapt to increasing urbanization in its state. In the first example, an outside change agent is probably not needed; in the second example, a trained outsider can help minimize the risk of psychological injury to staff members during training sessions that deal with interpersonal processes. Both examples, and organization development in general, focus on the "human side" of the organization. Organization development assumes that organizations change for the better or the worse as the human climate within them changes.

Bennis's second characteristic of organization development is that "the changes sought for are coupled directly with the *exigency* or demand the organization is trying to cope with" (1969, p. 11–12). Bennis lists three categories of "exigencies," each of which is a familiar source of organizational problems for experienced staff members in adult education agencies. The first category includes "problems of destiny—growth, identity, and revitalization." (In today's environment, one might add "decline" as a problem of destiny as well.) An example is the redirection of a university division of continuing education which, because of a change in state funding policy, must shift from its traditional focus on degree-oriented credit extension courses to more professionally oriented conferences and institutes in order to maintain its staff and survive as an organization. The second category of organizational exigencies includes "problems of human satisfaction and development," which are exemplified by a high turnover rate of key staff members in a successful professional organization that provides postlicensure training for real estate brokers. If exit interviews reveal that departing staff members are bored with their jobs or feel they have learned as much as they could, a program of organization development might be able to identify ways to increase job satisfaction or provide opportunities for continued development, leading in turn to increased stability within the staff and perhaps to increased vitality for the agency as well. Bennis's third category of exigencies is "problems of organizational effectiveness." Declining enrollments in almost any adult education program would be an example of this kind of exigency. Unless declining enrollments are part of an agency's plan vis-à-vis a particular program or are accounted for by a well-documented change in the environment, they almost always suggest a need to improve organizational effectiveness. More subtle measures of organizational effectiveness may also signal a need for change: declining posttest scores in an adult basic education program may suggest a renewal process for the program's faculty or for the whole organization staff. Declining funding from a parent organization or legislative body may also indicate a need for change. In assessing an organization's effectiveness and need for improvement, more than one measure of effectiveness is almost always appropriate. Further, the alternative strategies of organizational improvement are directly related in number and in quality to the sensitivity of the measures used for assessing the organization's effectiveness.

Bennis's third characteristic of organization development is that it "relies on an educational strategy which emphasizes *experienced behavior*" (p. 12). Unlike staff development, which emphasizes technical skills and knowledge from outside sources, organization development initially focuses on the experience of the staff members in the organization. Problems that arise—such as the breakdown of clerical support services in an educational brokering agency or the lack of supervision of new instructors in a community college literacy program—are described by those staff members who experience the problems, and their descriptions become the starting points for discussion and change.

A fourth characteristic of organizational development, Bennis claims, is that most agents whose task it is to lead an organization toward change are outsiders and not part of the organization undergoing development, because "the external consultant can manage to affect . . . the power structure in a way that most internal change agents cannot. This again may be related to the aura created by an external (often highly paid) consultant, but is equally related to the ability of the external change agent to 'see' with more innocence and clarity the problems which the insiders may have long learned to avoid or overlook and most certainly regard with anxiety" (pp. 12–13). Fortunately for those adult education agencies that cannot afford to pay consultants, Bennis admits that the advantage of an outsider over an insider in the role of change agent disappears once the organization development process is accepted and initiated by the members of the organization. Administrators of adult education agencies that cannot afford outside change agents but who see the need for organization development may either act as change agents themselves—particularly early in their tenure at the agency, when they still have some of the aura of an outsider—or they may assign as change agent a talented newcomer to their agency or some other staff member who is both sensitive and productive. In short, arguments in favor of outside change agents should not preclude organization development in an agency where an outsider is financially impossible.

"Fifth, organization development implies a *collaborative relationship* between change agent and constituents of the client system" (Bennis, 1969, p. 13). Collaboration, in this sense, "involves mutual trust, joint determination of goals and means, and high mutual influence" (p. 13). If, for example, the staff members of an extension program and the staff members of a conference and institute program who in the same university office of continuing education have no contact during a typical working day, a change agent (insider or outsider) will have to develop a collaborative relationship with the staff members of each program and engineer the development of trust between the two groups before organization development will have a chance of succeeding. Reasonably honest communication among at least most parties involved in an organization development process is essential to its success.

Bennis's sixth characteristic is that change agents exhibit "a set of values about the world in general and human organizations in particular which shape their strategies, determine their interventions, and largely govern their responses to client systems" (pp. 13–14). The values to which Bennis and others refer (see Argyris, 1971, for example) are humanistic and democratic in their orientation, in contrast to the impersonal, rational, and task-oriented values that have been the basis for early industrial and bureaucratic organizations. As we saw in Argyris's definition, organization development is concerned with the human dimensions of organization as well as the technical dimensions. Change agents, the chief actors of organization development, must hold similar concerns.

"The seventh characteristic is that change agents share a set of *normative goals* based on their philosophy" (p. 15). The goals that Bennis lists (p. 15) are:

- Improvement in interpersonal competence
- A shift in values so that human factors and feelings come to be considered legitimate within the organization
- Development of increased understanding between and within working groups in order to reduce tensions
- Development of "team management"—the capacity for functional groups to work with increased competence
- Development of better methods of "conflict resolution"— rational, open methods of conflict resolution rather than usual bureaucratic methods that rely on suppression, compromise, and unprincipled power
- Development of organic systems—in which staff members share in decisions on work and organizational goals—rather than mechanical systems—in which managers control methods of work and set goals as if the organization were a machine rather than a human group

Having set forth some of the characteristics of organization development and the assumptions on which it is based, the issue of implementing organization development remains. It is essential that at least some staff members feel that their organization is not reaching its full potential; further, the implementation of organization development depends most critically on the approval, support, and appropriate involvement of those at the top of an organization. "Change must begin where the power lies. Those that presently hold responsible positions and control organizations are also responsible for beginning the change" (Argyris, 1973, p. 27). Without approval from the top, the organization development process should not be started, because it has little chance of success. To succeed, however, those at the top must not only approve but also support the process through an allocation of resources sufficient to carry out the complex process to completion. The dollar value of this support depends upon the size of the organization and the complexity of problems being addressed; but whether the cost is high or low, those at the top must be willing to pay the price of organization development if it is to succeed.

Finally, in addition to approval and support, those at the top of the organization must become involved in the organization development process in a manner consistent with their own roles. For example, if the staff of a university extension division is contemplating an organization development process, the dean of the extension division would have to approve of the process, be ready to provide the resources to carry it out, and be willing to take an active part in the process. The academic vice president, to whom the dean reports, would need to approve of the process and agree to the use of supporting university funds, but the academic vice president probably would not have to be involved regularly as a participant in the process. The university's president might be informed of the process and give his tacit approval but would probably not be involved in the process at all unless the whole institution is engaged in an organization development process.

Conclusions

Most administrators of adult education programs assent to the usefulness of the staffing and development processes described in this chapter. Many of the same administrators, however, do not have current job descriptions in their agencies, do not have current specifications, and do not review descriptions and specifications carefully—both on a periodic basis and when positions become vacant—to decide whether the jobs are accurately defined. Many adult education administrators do not have routine procedures for search, screening, and selection of applicants for positions within their agencies. Few adult education administrators adequately orient new staff members (particularly new part-time instructors), and few have established plans for either staff or organization development.

Why is there such disparity between recommendations in the literature and general practice? No single explanation is adequate. Most adult education administrators are kept busy with the day-to-day operation of their agency. Problems of staffing are often not visible until a vacancy occurs or a new staff member is needed. Staffing problems often must compete for the administrator's attention with program development problems, financial problems, or student problems, to name a few. When a new staff member is needed, it often seems more important to fill one vacancy than to take the time to develop sound staffing procedures, which could be used to select all new staff members. When the immediate problem has been solved by hiring a new person, staffing once again recedes as an active concern.

Administrators of adult education agencies often have so many opportunities for success in this burgeoning field that they can achieve some degree of success even though their organizations are not producing at full potential. A haphazard approach to staffing and a lack of regular orientation, staff development, and organization development programs do not automatically lead to failure. On the contrary, in the present environment of growth within adult education, staffing deficiencies may be compounded by other problems without spelling doom for a particular agency.

The ad hoc nature of many adult education agencies contributes to deficient staffing practices. Many adult education agencies are truly created to meet a temporary need or are organized around short-term funding; others carry with them an ethos of being ad hoc compared with other parts of their parent organizations. A literacy program for Southeast Asian immigrants in an Iowa farming community is an example of the former; continuing education offices in research-oriented universities are examples of the latter. Given this sense of being temporary or of not fitting into the primary mission of the parent organization, some adult education administrators feel justified in operating their agencies without establishing staffing policies and procedures, even though such policies would facilitate the success of staffing decisions by increasing the consistency and rationality of those decisions.

Some adult education administrators fail to follow sound staffing procedures because they are not certain which procedures to establish in their agencies and because they cannot find models to follow in their colleagues' agencies. Many adult educators still enter the field "through the back door," without benefit of administrative training and without having learned how their most successful colleagues administer their agencies. Perhaps preservice and in-service preparation in administration of adult education—which is becoming more readily available than it has been in the past—will help focus attention on effective policies and procedures for staffing adult education agencies. Also, books such as this one may facilitate self-directed learning, which may provide the basis for improved staffing practice.

Developing sound staffing practices where they do not presently exist can improve productivity of the agency and its administrator in at least four important ways. First, stated staffing procedures that are consistently followed make the chances of finding the best person for each job more likely than do haphazard procedures. Second, accurate job descriptions and specifications are by-products of sound staffing procedures that lead in turn to sound procedures for evaluating performance on the job. Evaluations of performance based on accurate job descriptions and specifications not only help the agency maintain or improve its productivity but also help staff members understand what is expected of them on the job. Third, initial orientation and subsequent staff development help maintain and increase an agency's productivity by (1) helping staff members develop their technical skills and (2) providing a relatively nonthreatening opportunity for supervisors to assess the performance of their subordinates and to intervene with appropriate assistance when necessary. Fourth, when organization development is approved of, supported by, and participated in by those at the top of the organization, organization development can help an agency define, understand, and move toward a resolution of its problems in a relatively open manner. Organization development may also help staff members, including administrators, deal successfully with the human aspects of their organizations and consequently may help their organizations become or remain productive in a constantly changing environment.

Each of these four benefits of sound staffing procedures can save time and irritation in the long run for administrators and other staff members in adult education agencies, may contribute to a sense of equanimity within an agency, and may allow adult education administrators and staff members to direct their energy toward creating new programs and services and improving existing programs and services instead of wasting their energy on staffing procedures that have gone awry.

◆◆◆◆◆◆◆◆◆◆◆◆◆◆◆◆◆◆◆◆◆◆◆
◆◆◆◆◆◆◆◆◆◆◆◆◆◆◆◆◆◆◆◆◆◆

Chapter Eight

Leadership

◆◆◆◆◆◆◆◆◆◆◆◆◆◆◆◆◆◆◆◆◆◆◆
◆◆◆◆◆◆◆◆◆◆◆◆◆◆◆◆◆◆◆◆◆◆

Thurman J. White
Joy Reed Belt

Administrative leadership is critical to the future of adult education. Richman and Farmer (1974, p. 14), in applying their expertise in business administration to the management of institutions of higher education, explain that administration "involves strategy, innovation, initiating and bringing about change, creative problem solving and decision making, actively seeking out alternatives and opportunities, reforming goals and priorities, redeploying resources, negotiating, resolving conflicts, dynamic or active leadership, diplomacy, statesmanship, and a high degree of risk taking and entrepreneurship." Robbins (1976, p. 7) notes that "those who have the responsibility for deciding the direction an organization will take, and who hold the authority to move it toward its goals, are the single most important ingredient in determining the organization's success or failure." This chapter is concerned with some of the major concepts of administration as they apply to leadership in adult education agencies.

The adult or continuing education agency is typically a dependent unit of a parent organization with major purposes other than educating adults on a part-time or short-term basis. The adult education agency may be part of an educational institution, as is the case of the adult education division of a school or community college, or it may be part of an organization whose major purpose is noneducational, such as the education and training department of a business or the education committee of a labor union. The agency may be large and stable, like the cooperative extension services of the land grant universities, or it may be small and variable, as often occurs in libraries, YMCA-YWCAs, and religious institutions. Not only are the adult participants part time but the teachers and planners of adult education activities also usually work on a part-time basis.

If the adult education agency is associated with an educational institution, many of the part-time adult education teachers also teach in the parent organization. Therefore, administrators of adult education divisions must understand fully how their parent organization functions if they are to relate to it effectively. In large organizations, a number of professionals in addition to the director—for example, conference coordinators in university conference centers and program coordinators in large public school agencies—work with participants and teachers in planning and conducting various educational activities. Within business and industry, adult education professionals work in specialized activities such as sales and marketing training, safety training, supervisory training, and management and organization training. Because most adult education programs, regardless of size, lack expressed policy, permanent facilities, and adequate or stable funding, adult education administrators become the "human cement" that binds the agency together. The overview of administration presented in this chapter can be applied to positions of leadership in adult education agencies of all kinds.

Background

There have always been administrators—military leaders, statesmen, merchants, and people associated with religious organizations all functioned as administrators. However, it was not until the twentieth century that administrative theory developed into a written body of knowledge and inquiry. Several schools of administrative thought have developed that are worthy of note. Taylor's *Principles of Scientific Management* (1919) established him as the father of scientific management. Fayol (1949), a contemporary of Taylor, was one of the first administrative theorists. Both postulated that people are expected to perform effectively when work functions are highly specialized and standardized. Proponents of scientific management believe that people will work effectively if they are sufficiently well paid. Contributors to this school throughout the years include Max Weber, Oliver Sheldon, James D. Mooney, Lyndall Urwick, Chester Barnard, and Herbert Simon.

Most writers of administrative theory credit Mary Parker Follett with being the first great exponent of the human relations point of view in administration. Systematic empirical data in support of the importance of human relations in administration was provided by Mayo (1949) and by Roethlisberger and Dickson (1939). From 1923 to 1932, they performed the now-famous series of experiments at the Hawthorne plant of the Western Electric Company concerning group attitudes, feelings, group behavior, and social grouping. As a result, management was alerted to the need to develop social skills in the handling of working groups.

Some theorists argue that administrative leadership is primarily concerned with decision making, and decision-making processes have become central in the study of administrative theory. Herbert Simon, James G. March, Russell Ackoff, Jay Forrester, Martin Starr, and Kenneth Boulding have made major contributions to the understanding of administrative decision making.

As mentioned earlier, most adult education agencies are dependent units of parent organizations with a major purpose other than the education of adults. The relationships and functioning of both the parent organizations and the dependent agencies can be better understood by use of general systems theory as developed by Von Bertalanffy (1951). A system is typically thought of as "a set of components surrounded by a boundary which accepts input from other systems and discharges output into another system" (Berrien, 1968, p. 111). When we talk about organizations as systems, we are attending to the combination of parts and elements that form a unique whole. The focus is not on a part as it stands by itself but rather on how the part interacts with and is related to other parts. Systems concepts provide a basis for studying administrative relationships and facilitate an understanding of the function of leadership in adult education administration (Katz and Kahn, 1978).

The most recent direction taken by administrative theory is the increased emphasis on a situational or contingency approach. This emphasis stems from theorists' search for some common characteristics that might exist in a number of situations and that could make it possible to adjust the theory to the specifics of the situation. Situationalists believe that there is no one best way to manage. They define the supervision problem as twofold: (1) knowing the concepts, principles, and techniques that are available to the manager and (2) being able to analyze the particular situation as a basis for deciding which of the available concepts, principles, and techniques will be the most effective in that situation" (Carlisle, 1973, p. 6).

Adult education administrators seek to accomplish objectives with and through other people, as do other professionals in leadership positions. This accomplishment depends heavily on effective communication and coordination if one is to achieve consensus on major shared objectives and successfully encourage contributions needed to achieve the objectives. Stated objectives, staffing practices, resource allocation, and informal working relationships all contribute to team building and to achievement of results. Teamwork requires particular attention to the individual satisfaction of those associated with the educational program as well as organizational productivity. The managerial grid concept, which was developed by two professors at the University of Texas (Blake and Mouton, 1964), provides a way to analyze attention to individual satisfaction and organization productivity and helps identify needed adjustments of emphasis for one or the other.

Most administrators of adult education agencies enter organizations with established standard operating procedures and political pressures that reflect various factions and viewpoints. These influences on the decision-making process are realities that an effective administrator must come to understand and manage. Formal models or rationales for policy making and decision making are useful not so much as an alternative to the bureaucratic and political realities but as a way of diagnosing inadequacies in the agency's functioning. They also facilitate more public and shared objectives that are of high priority and assist in initiating concerted efforts to achieve these objectives (Allison, 1971).

People with substantial experience in the administration of adult education have developed methodologies that provide a valuable supplement to the general literature on administration in other settings. Smith, Aker, and Kidd (1970) provide a useful overview of providing agencies, program areas, legislation, finance, program development, and agency relationships. Similar overviews emphasize programs sponsored by schools and community colleges (Shaw, 1969) and programs conducted by business, industry, hospitals, government, and the military (Craig, 1976).

Robbins (1976, p. 15) defines administration as a "process of functions: It is planning, organizing, leading and evaluating of others so as to achieve specific ends." To give order to our discussion of leadership, we shall use Robbins's four categories: planning, organizing, leading, and evaluating. *Administration* as it is used in this chapter will refer to "leadership in an organizational context."

Planning

Planning is determining in advance the objectives to be accomplished and the means by which these objectives are to be attained. Cohen and March (1974, p. 12) stress that "planning is the primary responsibility of executive leadership and is so certified by traditional administrative theory and by innumerable modern treatments." There are two basic types of planning: (1) strategic or long-range and (2) operational or short-range, both of which begin with the establishment of objectives. Many authors agree that the principal defect in leadership is the failure to set goals. Without goals, the reason for the organization's existence is not clear: "Achievement is never possible except against specific, limited, clearly defined targets, in business as well as in a service institution. . . . Only if targets are defined can resources be allocated to their attainment, priorities and deadlines set, and somebody be held accountable for results" (Drucker, 1973, pp. 139, 140).

Why There Is So Little Long-Range Planning

The lack of long-range planning in most adult education agencies is a reflection of various factors. Most agencies have no separate policy board to establish long-range purposes, plans, and policies. An exception is the Cooperative Extension Service with an annual state plan and local or county councils to set priorities. For agencies that are part of noneducation organizations—such as business, military, labor unions, religious institutions, and professional associations—it is often assumed that adult education activities for the members simply serve the purposes of the parent organization. For agencies that are part of educational institutions, it is assumed at the operational level that there are important distinctions between continuing education of adults and preparatory education of children and youth, but boards of trustees and school boards seldom give much attention to these distinctions. An additional factor accounting for the lack of long-range planning is the typical approach to program development that emphasizes individual courses and workshops for separate clienteles rather than total curriculum development for the student body. In fact, many practitioners believe that being responsive to market demand and learner needs is the main purpose of their agency and that the profile of aggregate agency offerings is of little consequence. In most adult education agencies, the level of financial support fluctuates with enrollments, especially in agencies that derive full cost recovery from fees paid by participants but also in agencies that receive full or partial reimbursement based on enrollments.

The lack of full-time staff and facilities also inhibits long-range planning. With the exception of daytime adult basic education programs for full-time participants and education and training programs in work settings, most adult education agencies have little meeting space of their own but instead must arrange for part-time use of facilities that belong to the parent organization or to outside organizations. Most of the people who serve as adult education teachers and resource people do so on a part-time, short-term basis. Thus, the number and characteristics of instructional staff can easily fluctuate with the specific programs that are conducted.

Consequences of Lack of Long-Range Goals

Cohen and March (1974, p. 2) have classified institutions that lack clearly defined goals as "prototypic organized anarchy"; most universities do not know what they are doing and exhibit the general properties of "problematic goals, unclear technology, and fluid participation" (Cohen and March, 1974, pp. 2, 3). Robert Hutchins, president of the University of Chicago from 1929 to 1945, commented that without a comprehensive long-range plan, "quite often a university becomes a loose collection of competing departments, schools, institutes, committees, centers, programs, largely noncommunicating because of the multiplicity of specialist jargons and interests and held together chiefly by a central heating system" (Lassey, 1971, p. 154). And Clark Kerr, chairman of the Carnegie Commission, amended that statement by saying that "universities are held together by what to do about the parking problem."

Most agencies have placed a premium on being responsive and timely, and many adult education administrators have sought to modify parent organization purposes, plans, and policies that seem inappropriate for the adult education function. Although planning problems and procedures vary among various types of agencies, there are some basic planning concepts that can be useful to most agencies.

Nature of Long-Range Planning

A comprehensive long-range plan should involve academic, fiscal, physical, personnel, research organizational, and evaluation concerns. Administrators of adult education agencies that are situated in universities should understand the extent and type of long-range planning that occurs within the parent organization so that they can contribute to the process, benefit from the results, and anticipate likely impact.

In the past, most adult education agencies engaged in little long-range planning; their lack of full-time facilities and faculty, fluctuations in program offerings, and rapid growth trends make coping with current adjustments more urgent than planning for the future. However, planning has been done by adult education agencies, especially with regard to program development and to staffing, and the information derived from this planning can help the agency director make decisions about marketing and resource allocation and also make staffing decisions regarding numbers and qualifications of full-time program administrators and part-time instructors to fit program requirements. For example, the director of a training program in a manufacturing plant might work closely with supervisors and with the personnel department to anticipate shifts in personnel and procedures that have implications for education and training; the director of a community college continuing education division might periodically review needs assessment information and enrollment trends in an effort to anticipate likely trends in various components of the program during the next few years.

Uses of Long-Range Planning

The increase in the number of active providers of adult education programs, the interest of legislatures and state coordinating boards, and the interest of accrediting associations in the relationships among providers of adult education have all contributed to an increase in planning and collaboration, as reflected in the efforts by adult education associations and councils at regional, state, and local levels to work together on tasks related to needs assessment, marketing, financing, policy making, and coordination. Part of this cooperation has occurred because agency administrators prefer voluntary collaboration to externally imposed regulation (Knox, 1975a).

In university settings there is an observable tendency for long-range planning to be used for purposes other than long-range planning. Cohen and March (1974, pp. 114–116) have identified four ways in which plans are sometimes used:

1. Plans become symbols: An organization that is failing can announce a plan to succeed.
2. Plans become advertisements: What is frequently called a plan by a university is really an investment brochure—an attempt to persuade private and public donors of the attractiveness of an institution.
3. Plans become games: plans become an administrative test of will.
4. Plans become excuses for interaction: the results of the planning *process* become more important than the plan.

Leadership and Goals

Attention to future directions for an adult education agency is the responsibility of administrative leadership. Several approaches can be used to chart future directions for these agencies. One is to arrange for applied social research on policy issues, as is thoroughly discussed by Cohen and Garet (1975). Another is to consider alternative futures so that current efforts will increase the likelihood that desirable futures occur (Ziegler, 1970). Neither of these approaches is frequently employed in the field of adult education. Perhaps the most widely used and successful mechanism for future planning of adult education agencies is to identify specific trends and issues in the field. Current trends and issues are usually identified in professional publications and in meetings, and many of these issues recur over the years. A particularly useful statement on trends and issues is provided by Blakely and Lappin (1969). With awareness of these trends and issues, adult education administrators can recognize emerging trends early enough to capitalize on the desirable effects and can try to avoid the undesirable ones.

Leadership entails reaching consensus on desirable goals among those who contribute to their achievement. This consensus can be facilitated by an understanding of trends and issues and by interpreting current circumstances in order to propose future directions. This sense of purpose and direction enables an administrator to persist in the face of inertia and resistance; without such a sense of direction, administrators tend only to react to external pressures.

The Process of Planning

Dedication to Purpose and Mission. Drucker (1973) illustrates the importance of organizational and individual goals in his discussion of the history of the modern American university from 1860 to World War I. The American university during that period was primarily the work of a small number of men (Andrew W. White, Charles W. Eliot, and Daniel Coit Gilman, to name a few), all of whom had in common "one basic insight: the traditional college—essentially an eighteenth-century seminary to train preachers—had become totally obsolete, sterile, and unproductive. The men who built the new universities shared a common objective: to create a new institution, a true university. Beyond these shared beliefs, they differed sharply on what a university should be and what its purpose and mission were" (Drucker, 1973, p. 150). Each gave priority to his definition of the university's purpose and mission.

The Danish Folk High School is an example of an adult education agency that has enjoyed unusual achievement for over 150 years because of its dedication to purpose and mission. The first of these schools was founded in 1844 and was the first attempt by a national government to establish an organized adult education program. The schools are community based and are simply begun when a group of people decides that something needs to be taught. The schools are controlled by the local community and are directly responsive to the needs of the community. The community focus and control has kept the Danish Folk High School viable since its beginning.

Relationship of Boards to the Planning Process. An effective administrator develops plans for decision making, objective setting, forecasting, and implementation processes. (The final category—implementation processes—includes policies, procedures, methods, standards, and rules.) Together, these four types of supporting plans free the administrator from making repetitive decisions. Governing boards develop these supporting plans that help to guide administrative decisions. Houle (1960, p. 95) states that "the board should establish such broad policies governing the program as may be necessary to cover continuing or recurrent situations in which uniformity of action is desirable.

. . . It is the duty of the executive to administer the program in terms of policies, to understand the degree of latitude which is allowed to him in making exceptions in some cases, to know when a policy applies and when it does not, and to deal with situations not covered by policy."

Adult education administrators should understand how the policy board of their parent organization functions and how it affects the adult education agency. Many adult education organizations relate to councils for university or community college continuing education divisions; citizen's advisory committees for public school adult education programs or libraries; and local extension councils for cooperative extension service. Effective adult education administrators can work with various advisory and policy groups to set priorities, identify promising directions, assess client needs, locate resource people, facilitate cosponsorship, acquire resources, and increase understanding and support for the adult education agency. (Typologies and an excellent discussion of boards can be found in Houle, 1960.)

Revision of Policies. Missions, goals, policies, and procedures must be constantly revised. Drucker (1973, p. 159) finds that "in service institutions particularly, yesterday's success becomes . . . holy writ unless the institution imposes on itself the discipline of thinking through its mission, its objectives, and its priorities, and of building feedback control from results and performance on policies, priorities, and action."

Many institutions by their very design obstruct change rather than facilitate it. One of the great strengths of adult education agencies, however, has been their responsiveness to their clientele and their willingness to innovate. Adult education agencies associated with larger education institutions have pioneered many delivery systems, such as correspondence study, closed-circuit telephone networks, conference centers, television courses, and lay-led discussion groups. These delivery systems were operative long before most resident instruction programs discovered the concept of nontraditional study. In addition, the adult education agencies of some firms and museums have developed attractive audiovisual presentations. Some subject matter areas, including social work, labor relations, and criminal justice, were first introduced in the adult education component of the larger institutions because of the agency's flexibility and willingness to innovate. Effective administrators of adult education appreciate their agencies' potential for innovation and organizational renewal.

Management by Objectives. Management by objectives (MBO) can be particularly effective in the administration of adult education, because it devises controls that stress procedures and methods. One of the reasons that MBO is such a widely used approach to goal setting and control in contemporary management is that it tends to orient administrators to results. Once the reason for the organization's existence is made clear through the statement of major objectives, administrators can establish subobjectives and can forecast—that is, formulate assumptions about the future. We often talk about objectives "as if everyone in the organization participated and fully accepted the goals of the organization" (Robbins, 1976, p. 133). This is rarely the case, however. Organizational objectives are not the same as individual objectives, and successful administrative decision making must take both into account.

Detailed Program Planning. The success or failure of an adult education agency typically depends on the success of various programs. Thus, in addition to the types of planning already discussed, effective administrators of adult education agencies must insist on detailed program planning. Many programming models are available to the adult educator, including Houle (1972), Knowles (1970), and, for nontraditional study, Cross, Valley, and Associates (1974).

Organizing

The second function of the administrative process is that of organizing. Robbins (1976, p. 17) defines organizing as the "establishment of relationships between the activities to be performed, the personnel to perform them, and the physical factors needed." In adult education, often the organizing function becomes a coordinating function, because the participants and the resource people are part time and the facilities are not exclusively those of the adult education agency.

Most adult education agencies have small staffs, and as a

result the administrators and supporting clerical staff tend to perform a variety of tasks, with considerable flexibility among administrative, clerical, and instructional tasks. Even larger adult education agencies tend to be less "institutionalized" than their parent organizations. Some agencies are large enough to be organized into sections—such as a university continuing education division with sections for correspondence study, off-campus or evening courses, conferences, and community development. When each section has its own staff and procedures, effective interchange among sections depends on informal interaction, administrative coordination, and overlapping functions such as marketing, counseling, client services, and program development. An administrator who is familiar with the various administrative practices will have available alternative ways to organize agency functions and make useful adjustments in agency organization.

The core of organizational theory is division of labor. Simon (1947, p. 12) notes that "the administrative organization is characterized by specialization—particular tasks are delegated to particular parts of the organization. . . . A pyramid or hierarchy of authority may be established, with greater or less formality, and decision-making functions may be specialized among the members of this hierarchy." Several contemporary writers of administrative thought have made contributions to organizational theory that are significant for adult education agencies. Hefferlin (1969, pp. 10–16), in particular, provides us with a classic list of organizational characteristics of educational institutions:

1. Organizations are inherently passive.
2. Voluntary organizations attract members who agree with their activities.
3. Organizations tend toward institutionalization and ritualism.
4. Organizations that are livelihoods for people tend to come to exist only as livelihoods for those people.
5. The maintenance of institutional effectiveness or achievement (such as students' learning) is only one problem that organizations must face in order to survive. Other problems may take precedence over it.
6. Their purposes and support are basically conservative.

7. The educational system is vertically fragmented.
8. Within higher education, institutional reputation is not based on innovation.
9. The ideology of the academic profession treats professors as independent professionals.
10. Academics are skeptical about the idea of efficiency in academic life.
11. Academic institutions are deliberately structured to resist precipitant change.

An administrator of an adult education agency usually deals with the structure of two organizations, his own agency and the parent organization. Within this relationship, the purpose of the adult education agency can vary from being marginal to the purpose of the parent organization to being auxiliary, where the unit of adult education is designed to facilitate the parent organization's purpose. In many cases, the successful administrator deals with the organizational attitude of "we versus them" and endeavors not only to coordinate activities within the agency but also to coordinate the agency's activities with the parent organization.

A generation ago, Clark (1956) documented the marginality of the adult education agency in contrast to the core concerns of the school system and noted some trends in relations between agency and parent institution. A few years later Carey (1963) reported a tendency for adult education agencies to become differentiated from the preparatory education resident instruction program and then for the function to become reintegrated with the academic units. These general issues regarding relationships between the adult education agency and the parent organization continue to be central in the administration of adult education in educational institutions, although the specifics have changed in recent years.

Leading

The third function of the administrative process is leading, the various aspects of which have been explored by numerous authors. Robbins (1976, p. 18) states that in the "leading function, we guide and supervise subordinates. This function carries out the objectives established in planning. . . . Basically, leading consists of supervision, motivation, and communication." Bass (in Lassey, 1971) sees leadership as the effort of one member of a group to change other members' behavior by altering their motivation or their habits. McGregor (1960, p. 33) says that "leadership is basically a relationship between the person assigned to leadership responsibility or who emerges as a leader and those with whom he must collaborate in achieving prescribed and collaboratively selected goals." Richman and Farmer (1974, p. 15) assert that "effective leadership is often based more on influence than on formal authority or power, especially in academic institutions." The essential task of leadership is "to arrange organizational conditions and methods of operation so that people can achieve their own goals best by directing their own efforts toward organizational objectives" (Lassey, 1971, p. 43).

Leadership Patterns

Most adult education administrators have relatively little formal power compared with administrators elsewhere in the parent organization. Thus, persuasion and influence tend to constitute more critical ingredients in effective leadership of adult education agencies than is typically the case for many other types of administrative positions. The administrator who is best able to influence, guide, and direct—in short, to communicate with the individual participants in an organization—is the one who has developed a sensitivity to the participants' needs and goals. The professional performance of adult education administrators is also influenced by expectations—their own and those of others. A study of role theory can contribute to an understanding of relationships between expectations and performance (Biddle and Thomas, 1966). Each administrator has a pattern of strengths and weaknesses. Administrative effectiveness depends upon fitting this pattern to agency objectives and to complementary contributions by others in the organization.

Organizations do not exist in a vacuum. Tannenbaum and

Schmidt (1973) list four social developments that have an impact on effective leadership styles:

1. the youth revolution, which expresses distrust and even contempt for organizations identified with the establishment
2. the civil rights movement, which demands that all minority groups be given a greater opportunity for participation and influence in the organizational processes
3. the ecology and consumer movements, which challenge the rights of managers to make decisions without considering the interest of people outside the organization
4. the increasing national concern with the quality of working life and its relationship to worker productivity, participation, and satisfaction.

These societal changes "make effective leadership in this decade a more challenging task, requiring even greater sensitivity and flexibility than was needed in the 1950s" (Tannenbaum and Schmidt, 1973, p. 17).

Figure 1 presents the "continuum of leadership behavior" which Tannenbaum and Schmidt published in an earlier article (1959). In this model, the administrator initiates and determines group functions, assumes responsibility, and exercises control. Later, the authors present a new behavior continuum for leadership, which illustrates a more participative style of leadership behavior. The terms *boss-centered leadership* and *subordinate-centered leadership* are changed to *manager* and *nonmanager power and influence* (Tannenbaum and Schmidt, 1973, p. 17). Because leadership in adult education is leadership of equals, the new range of leadership behavior is certainly more appropriate for administrators of adult education tnan that presented in Figure 1.

One approach adult education administrators might consider is organizing their agencies around "problems to be solved," using groups of relative strangers with diverse professional skills. In this kind of organization structure "the groups will be arranged on organic rather than mechanical models; they will evolve in response to problems rather than programmed expectations. People will be evaluated not in a rigid vertical hierarchy, according to rank

Figure 1. Continuum of Leadership Behavior

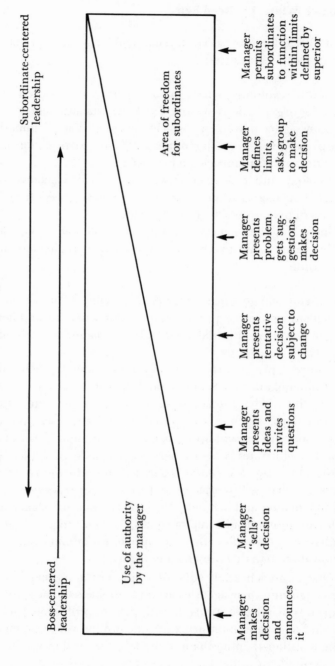

Source: Tannenbaum and Schmidt, 1958, p. 164.

and status, but flexibly, according to proficiency. Organizational charts will consist of project groups rather than stratified functional groups as is now the case. Adaptive, problem-solving, temporary systems of diverse specialists, linked together by coordinating executives in an organizational flux . . ." (Bennis, 1971, p. 146).

Flexible arrangements like this are fairly common in adult education. For example, in university continuing education, conference coordinators organize ad hoc planning committees that function for only one conference or workshop. Education and training departments of companies organize task forces as part of organizational development; these groups also disband when project objectives have been met.

Administrative Influence

Administrative influence is highly related to personal time allocation. That is, if an administrator devotes time to the decision-making activities of the organization, he will have considerable influence on the system (1) by providing decision-making energy and (2) by becoming the major source of information about particular decisions (Cohen and March, 1974). Some leaders try to anticipate when and where a particular issue will be discussed, but these times are difficult to predict because much critical discussion is unscheduled. An administrator who devotes time to the system will not only have access to important discussions but can also be around to give encouragement when it is most needed, further contributing to administrative influence.

An effective administrator must use time wisely. Many adult education administrators, especially those in small and rapidly expanding agencies, feel overwhelmed by the torrent of competing tasks. The management of time is problematic for most administrators, and numerous studies have been made of both the basic concepts of administrative time and specific time-management techniques (Drucker, 1966; Mintzberg, 1973).

Innovation and Change

Adult education agencies historically have been in a state of continuous adaptability, and one of the important functions of leadership is to direct innovation and change. As Hefferlin (1969, p. 20) says, "We hope for continual academic change beyond sporadic and occasional reform, beyond reacting to crisis or near bankruptcy or an exodus of staff or an explosive split among key personnel, beyond the fits and starts and spurts of housecleaning followed by years of inertia." Cohen and March (1974) have identi- fied two ways an administrator can foster innovation within an organization: (1) by putting the creative person in touch with the right resources within the organization and (2) by "supplementing the technology of reason with the technology of foolishness" (p. 208). *Foolishness* is defined as "temporary relaxation of rules in order to explore the possibility of alternative rules" (p. 209).

Creative program development is especially important for adult education agencies whose survival depends upon initiating new educational activities in response to timely issues. Adult educa- tion administrators can encourage creative program development by giving encouragement, release time, and venture capital. Ven- ture capital is difficult to secure, but it is especially important in agencies where full cost recovery of programs is required.

Several excellent books have been written to guide admin- istrators who are locked in the struggle of reforming educational institutions: Argyris (1965), Baldridge and Deal (1975), Hefferlin (1969), Lahti (1973), and Havelock (1973). Bennis and others (1976) is required reading for the change agent; and Richman and Farmer (1974) present a strategy for locating and analyzing power in an educational institution.

Motivation

The provision of incentives and rewards, especially for teachers and other resource people, is an important aspect of ad- ministration. An excellent discussion of rewards and punishments as incentives can be found in McGregor (1967), which stresses two distinct motivational relationships: (1) Extrinsic relationships are characteristics of the environment. Money is the most obvious, but fringe benefits, promotion, praise, recognition, criticism, and social acceptance and rejection are other examples. (2) Intrinsic relation- ships are inherent in the activity itself. The reward is the achievement of the goal. Intrinsic rewards cannot be directly controlled externally, although characteristics of the environment can enhance or limit one's opportunities to obtain them. Attainment of knowledge or skill, autonomy, self-respect, and solutions to problems are examples. Management has exploited the influence of extrinsic rewards but has paid less attention to intrinsic rewards because it is more difficult to establish links between rewards and performance. Bennis (1971, p. 23) reminds us that "professionalization and higher educational levels have produced a new kind of employee who is motivated less by extrinsic rewards, such as money, and more by challenge, independence, further learning, and a professional career; the new employee is more committed to his profession than to any particular organization." Drucker goes even further, warning against the use of extrinsic rewards: "The closer a need comes to being satisfied, the larger an increment of additional gratification will be required to produce the same satisfaction." He believes that in successful contemporary management, psychological manipulation replaces incentive of financial rewards; and empathy (that is, the exploitation of individual fears, anxieties, and personality needs) replaces the old fear of being punished or of losing one's job" (1973, p. 239).

Modern administrative theorists generally conclude that people do what they want to do because they find it rewarding. If organizational goals are to be obtained, individual performance must be measurable; performance must in some way respond to effort; and management must support such a system. "The task is to provide an appropriate environment—one that will permit and encourage employees to seek intrinsic rewards at work" (McGregor, 1967, p. 24). For adult education agencies, especially university continuing education divisions, the provision of both monetary and nonmonetary incentives is an important way in which administrators can improve program functioning.

Equitable pay for resource people is, of course, always desirable (although sometimes difficult to achieve). As an example of nonmonetary incentives, university faculty members who devote a substantial portion of their time teaching in the adult and continuing education program, can receive consideration for this effort in promotion and tenure decisions. These nonmonetary incentives

can be facilitated by specific standards of excellence and by evaluation evidence indicating whether performance meets the standards. Performance standards and evaluation procedures can be
applied to teachers of adults whether or not teaching of adults is
their only contact with the parent organization.

Some of the most effective teachers of adults do so for
reasons other than remuneration and promotion. Some receive a
sense of satisfaction from seeing increased competence of adult
learners; others wish to maintain contact with concerns and procedures in their field; and teaching in some continuing professional
education programs provides visibility in the field that leads to
referrals or consultations. Effective adult education administrators
use multiple incentives and rewards to attract and retain effective
teachers and other resource people (Votruba, 1978).

Evaluating

The fourth function of the administrative process is evaluating. Robbins (1976, p. 413) reminds us that "evaluation is the final
link in the functional chain of administration—checking up on
activities to ensure that they are going as planned and, in those
instances where there are significant deviations, taking the necessary action to correct the deviations." The evaluation process consists of three activities: (1) measuring actual performance, (2) comparing performance with a standard to determine whether there is
any difference, and (3) correcting any significant deviations
through remedial action.

An adult education agency administrator typically applies
these evaluation activities to faculty and staff, programs, and the
entire organization or agency. Program evaluation is discussed in
detail in Chapter Four of this book. Consequently, this section of
the chapter on leadership will focus only on methods that can help
the administrator conduct organizational evaluation.

The four most common methods that administrators use to
measure actual performance are personal evaluation, statistical reports, oral reports, and written reports. Service institutions have
long been under attack for not being managed more like business—that is, for being concerned only with control of cost while

neglecting control of performance and results. Drucker (1973, p. 138) adds that service institutions need "to use these measurements for *feedback* on their efforts, that is, to build *self-control* from *results*."

Carlisle (1973, pp. 167–168) lists some planning and scheduling methods and some budget and accounting methods which can assist the administrator in the evaluation process:

Planning and Scheduling Methods

The *Gantt chart* is a scheduling technique developed by H. L. Gantt in about 1910. It is a flexible, schematic method based on horizontal and vertical axes representing two related sets of information. Normally, time is expressed in a linear fashion horizontally, and the work to be done or activities to be performed are listed vertically in the order of their performance. Gantt charts can be used to portray schematically time-oriented planning information of all types. They are fairly simple and widely used; many more recent scheduling techniques are adaptations of them.

Milestone charts are adaptations of the Gantt chart and are somewhat more sophisticated. The operations are not simply shown as bars on the time lines; they are subdivided into "milestones" within the programs or major activity phases. A milestone is a discrete event that signals the accomplishment of a significant portion of a program; it marks completion of a goal or task that represents an important point in overall progress. A milestone chart records the sequencing and timing of events from both a planning and control standpoint.

Network analyses are planning techniques in which the schedule for a project is shown in network form (that is, it is designed to show *all* dependent relationships rather than simple linear relationships between each pair of events). Network analysis has been widely used since the initiation of PERT (see next item) in 1958. The techniques represent an advance over milestone scheduling because they permit the identification of dependent relationships among events. Time is not shown linearly as on Gantt and milestone charts but is instead indicated in numerical figures on the lines that represent dependent relationships.

PERT (Program Evaluation and Review Techniques) is a particular form of network analysis that consists of activities, events, and time estimates. An event, which is represented by a circle in the network, is much the same as a milestone; it marks the completion of a significant phase of the total project. Activity is represented by a line between dependent events; it is the work that must be done to complete an event. The time estimate—the time units necessary to complete an activity—is shown above the activity line.

Flow control is a scheduling technique utilized when resource inputs, manpower inputs, and time increments are known, so that only the flow of the different types of components or parts must be continuously scheduled to regulate day-to-day operations. An example is an automotive assembly line: flow control scheduling coordinates colors and accessories on each automobile.

Budget and Accounting Methods

Fixed budgets do not adjust to changes from the planned level of activity; they are fixed in relation to the original plan and established periods of time. They are sometimes called "appropriation budgets" because of their use in government. They are common in such areas as research and development, where activity is difficult to measure.

Variable or flexible budgets adjust to levels of activity or production; they are normally associated with units of production, not time. Standard costs make variable budgets feasible. If a certain number of units are produced during a given time period, a specific budget is "earned." The basis of earning is the standard cost of the units produced. Variable budgets are also developed by estimating different projected volume levels. The actual budget is then calculated from the estimate that corresponds with the actual volume achieved. This would occur, for example, in a public educational institution in which tax funds support an evening course program depending on the number of reimbursable courses offered.

Standard cost systems use predetermined costs of production as the basis for recording costs. A standard represents what the cost of one unit of a product should be under normal operating conditions. Standardized costs are associated with continuous production operations for which there is considerable cost experience. They are extremely useful as a basis for evaluating operations.

The final step in the evaluation process is taking the necessary action to correct the deviations from the plan. Even if there were no changes in the organization's goals, the procedures which had been devised to accomplish them would gradually become inadequate because of the changes that occur in the environment. So even if an organization seeks to serve the same set of goals over a period of years, it cannot do so in a changing environment unless it is willing to alter its methods to accommodate to those changes. The leadership role in a dynamic society demands a willingness to help others to see the need for changes and then a capacity to direct the process of innovation. Outstanding leadership is characterized as employing evaluation not only to correct deviations from a planned course of action but also as developing new standards of performance and engineering their acceptance among the members of an organization.

Suggestions for Implementation

Adult education administrators have access in the literature to broad administrative concepts such as planning, organizing, and evaluating. However, to benefit agency leadership, these concepts must be applied. Generalizations about organizational behavior can help practitioners adapt concepts from one segment of the field to another (for example, from adult religious education or labor education to continuing higher education or adult basic education). Generalizations about contingency management can help practitioners find concepts in the literature and apply them to specific circumstances. In the following pages, applications of concepts presented earlier in the chapter to professional practice in various segments of the field will be discussed.

Planning

An administrator with a sense of direction is committed to establishing goals for the agency and for adult education in general, understands trends in the larger society, field, and parent organization, and is able to distinguish important issues from trivial ones and progress from change. A sense of direction can suggest to an administrator content and methods of agency planning involving various categories of people.

There are several ways in which an administrator can establish a sense of direction for an agency. One is to involve members of the organization in identifying improvements in the agency that entail increased commitment to setting goals and priorities. For example, the executive director of a professional association might work with the education committee to conduct a study of standards of professional practice. The study results could provide the basis for a self-assessment inventory and guidelines for peer review in order to evaluate members whose performance is substandard. Another example is an industrial training director who works with first- and second-line managers on problems of production and quality control for which education and development are most needed. In both instances, the administrator involves other people whose ideas could enrich planning and whose commitment could improve implementation. Additional activities that increase a sense of direction are staff retreats on goals and clients, informal work with policy makers to increase their role in priority setting for the adult education function, and circulating among the staff excerpts from the professional literature that suggest desirable future directions.

Coordinating various program areas is a major planning task in large agencies. For example, the director of a large and diverse community college continuing education division might coordinate evening and off-campus credit courses for part-time students, noncredit courses, and community service projects. Staff members who work with each of these program areas might be encouraged to concentrate on operational planning: for example, the staff members who plan credit courses might try to schedule courses so that the adult student can complete a certificate program or an associate degree on a part-time basis. The staff member who works with community service projects might try to identify spin-off activities from successful projects. An administrator who understands the concept of coordination can work with the program administrators in the division to help them recognize how planning and coordination can contribute to agency vitality (through marketing and counseling efforts that span program areas) and can reduce problems (by avoiding overuse of a few visible resource people). Effective administrators use their broad perspective on the total agency to achieve this coordination.

Another planning concern is accountability, which includes both agency planning and commitment to objectives. The predominance of voluntary participation by adults in most agencies often results in accountability at the level of the individual course or workshop. Management by objectives and program budgeting easily fit the process of planning and conducting individual conferences and institutes. Even at the agency level, where the expectations of the parent organization and community focus mainly on enrollments, the director can establish planning targets in terms of numbers of participants or dollars. Prior to the 1960s, administrators were free to plan programs with the idea that all they would be required to report would be income and enrollment data, and such an approach to client responsiveness and organizational accountability was fairly satisfactory. However, as the adult education function has become more visible and interrelated with the parent organization, more detailed forms of agency accountability are being imposed. An emerging issue is how greater accountability can be achieved without too great a loss of flexibility. Manifestations of demands for accountability exacted by state education departments and teachers' unions include imposition of management by objectives and imposition of first refusal rights to teach adult education courses by full-time faculty members who do so several times. Such constraints can impose strict limits on the freedom of the planner and in so doing may unintentionally reduce the institution's responsiveness to emerging opportunities.

Adult education directors can use staff and organization development procedures usually aimed at external clients to increase the proficiency of their own agency staff (Beder, 1978). Such procedures and the concepts from which they flow can alert practitioners to distinctive issues regarding planned change within their agency. In attempting to induce planned change administrators should consider both individual preferences and organizational purposes (Schein, 1978). Even in a small agency, a director can discuss expectations and performance periodically with each staff member in a way that helps to establish growth goals to which both are committed. Staff meetings, temporary committees, reassignments, special projects, collaborative efforts, and periodic reorganization can contribute to agency renewal and increase agency effectiveness. Slow growth, limited staff turnover, compulsory adult education, and lack of challenge can all make agencies stagnate. Administrative planning for agency development is likely to be a crucial antidote to rigidity as the adult education function becomes increasingly institutionalized.

Collaboration is another important concept related to planning procedures. When an individual or agency independently engages in an activity, less planning is required than in a collaborative activity. The trend in many agencies is toward greater collaboration in relation to both the parent organization and external groups such as cosponsors. Effective administrative planning entails consideration of the purposes and resources of potential collaborative groups and assessment of their likely impact on agency goals and procedures. For example, a community college adult education director might recognize that cosponsorship of a workshop with a professional association might help recruit participants but might be concerned about influences on program planning, finances, and institutional image if the association had been domineering and insensitive to the felt needs of the target audience. A minister considering cosponsorshop of an adult basic education program in church facilities might recognize the benefits to undereducated members of the congregation but be concerned about possible restrictions on the presentation of ideas because of cosponsorship with the local school system. Cooperating agencies often complement each other because one has members and the other has teachers. This complementarity is less evident in the case of a consortium of higher education institutions to provide continuing education courses for adults. A director of continuing higher education who is considering joining the consortium should weigh the advantages (possible improvement in community awareness of extent of higher adult education programming; improved service to community by offering courses jointly that could not be supported by a single institution alone) and disadvantages (possible loss of a share of a limited market; possible loss of distinctive identity) of doing so from a long-range planning perspective.

Organizing

The three major organizing tasks of the administrator are provision for specialization, alternative organizational structure arrangements, and extent of centralization.

An administrator of adult education activities for a small agency tends to be a generalist, and there tends to be a good deal of overlap among tasks such as assessing needs, teaching, evaluating, marketing, counseling, staffing, and allocating resources. This overlap occurs, for example, in a one-person training department in a small business, in which the trainer handles most of the orientation, supervision, sales, and safety education. It also occurs for the coordinator of adult services in a library or community agency, who arranges for discussion groups, materials, and other educational activities. In larger adult education agencies, with multiple program administrators and multiple target markets, each staff member tends to perform specialized standardized tasks. The director of a large agency should understand this specialization in order to provide assistance and coordination. Systems concepts are of help in the analysis of specialized functions and how they fit together in an organization. An analysis of who makes decisions about what also helps specify organizational structure. The literature on adult education program development and administration can help a director recognize the extent and type of specialization that exists in the agency and identify specialized tasks that are not adequately performed. For example, creative program development to generate new activities tends to be supplanted by time-consuming routine tasks such as budgeting and scheduling. If inadequate attention is being given to new program development, staff time can be set aside for the purpose and someone can be designated to provide leadership for initiation of new programs; in a large agency, a separate program development staff might be created. As adult education agencies become larger, personnel more proficient, and agencies more competitive, it seems likely that attention to staff specialization will increase.

The second organizing task of the administrator has to do with various ways in which subunits are organized within a large agency. The nature of the parent organization and changes in the interests of clients and funding agencies influence organizational patterns. There are three main bases for differentiating subunits within a large agency—structure of the parent organization, delivery systems within the agency, and clientele groups. A director who parallels the structure of the parent organization in creating sections within the adult education agency strengthens connections with the resource system. For example, the training and development department of a large manufacturing company might be decentralized, with training staff located in each of the operating divisions, as well as in marketing, personnel, and finance. A university continuing education division might have sections associated with each of the major professional schools and the college of arts and sciences. Staff members associated with each section of the agency would interact extensively with people in the corresponding division of the parent organization to ensure close and responsive working relationships.

A director who creates sections corresponding to the delivery systems of the agency emphasizes the distinctive contribution of program staff members along with supporting facilities and services and assumes that relationships can be maintained with both resource systems and client systems. The most widespread use of agency delivery systems as the basis for organization occurs in the university continuing education division, in which there are sections for evening credit courses, off-campus courses, and conferences. These sections become permanent parts of organization structure with the help of specialized facilities or services, such as conference centers, television stations, or offices to handle duplicating, mailing, and scoring of correspondence study lessons.

A director who organizes sections in relation to categories of clients emphasizes the main client systems. An example is the Cooperative Extension Service with divisions for people engaged in farming and agribusiness, for homemakers, and for leaders of youth groups. Another example is a training department with sections for first-line supervisors, middle management, sales personnel, secretarial staff, and technicians.

In practice, each administrator must attend to all three relationships. Whether or not formal procedures are used (such as matrix management), program administrators should give adequate attention to resources, delivery, and clients. This perspective is even more valuable when cosponsorship with other agencies is entailed.

An emerging organizational issue, especially for agencies associated with educational institutions, is extent of centralization. As the adult education function has become more visible and has moved from the margin toward the core of the parent organization, and as support for preparatory education of young people has declined, the issue of centralization of adult education programs, budgets, and decision making within the parent organization has arisen as one of the most contentious issues confronting practitioners. It is likely that there will be increasing centralization within separate adult education divisions and decentralization of both personnel and program responsibilities from the extension unit to academic departments and colleges. For example, in many community colleges the adult education function does not rest with a director of adult education, instead division directors and the academic dean have responsibility for the continuing education and community service function as well as resident instruction for full-time students.

Leading

In contrast to planning and organizing, leading emphasizes implementation. Three major concepts related to leading are influence, style, and innovation.

Administrators function primarily with and through other people—by achieving consensus on desirable goals and by encouraging contributions to goal achievement. Often the administrator must influence other people in order to overcome inertia. For example, an adult religious education administrator working with a local congregation might meet resistance from members when attempting to explore moral issues through direct contact with community problems. Likewise, a director of adult basic education who seeks to consolidate separately funded programs in order to increase service to harder to reach adults might meet considerable staff resistance to the change. Administrators with a commitment to progress and an understanding of the need for administrative influence are willing and able to use staffing, resource allocation, and channeling of external influences in dynamic ways to produce results. They realize, however, that lasting change can best be produced through persuasion—by convincing those who are affected that the change will advance their own goals.

Leadership style depends on characteristics of both the administrator and the situation and is the foundation of the contingency management approach. Each situation requires some attention to stability and to change, to productivity and to satisfaction by people associated with the agency. Each administrator is able to perform some tasks with greater effectiveness and enthusiasm than others, and search committees recruiting administrators must consider the fit between organizational and personal characteristics. In the past, there have been studies of important areas of proficiency for effective adult education administrators (Knox, 1979a); in the future, more attention should be given to achieving a good match between personal and situation characteristics.

Fortunately there is an extensive, growing body of professional literature on innovation and organizational change. However, many adult education practitioners deal with these concepts for client groups but not for their own agency. Attention to innovation within the adult education agency is becoming more important as the adult education function is becoming more institutionalized. Innovation encompasses an agency's traditional outlook regarding innovation, the available incentives and rewards for innovation by staff members, and the extent to which role models and encouragement are available in the agency to stimulate new program directions. For instance, a labor education coordinator of a union who wants to broaden the scope of its education program might organize a task force composed of members of the union's education committee and several adult education staff members from the community college. This committee could explore new program directions on social and economic issues, which would supplement the traditional emphasis on apprenticeships, collective bargaining, and orientation for business managers and stewards. A continuing higher education administrator might provide better incentives and rewards to faculty members as a way of encouraging more innovative attention to continuing education.

Evaluating

Most adult education agencies have available a considerable amount of information that can be used for agency evaluation, including brochures, course evaluations, position descriptions, staff performance reviews, listing of scheduled activities, enrollment reports, budgets, and accounting reports. Some large agencies have complex management information systems that contain data about plans, resources, activities, and results. These data can be easily summarized to prepare reports, discern trends, and make decisions. In most instances, however, available data for agency evaluation are fragmentary and underutilized. In many agencies, more could be done to use existing information selectively for purposes of agency evaluation and to supplement it with information collected specifically for the purpose of evaluation. For example, the director of a large public school adult education program might assemble statements about agency goals, conclusions from a clientele analysis based on enrollment records, and minutes from a staff meeting on reaching underserved adults and decide to conduct a follow-up study of a small but representative sample of former participants.

Many people can contribute to the collection and analysis of agency evaluation data. Usually the director, who depends on the conclusions for decision making, is in a central role; an advisory committee can help with the process, as can an institutional research office in the parent organization. The director's clerical and part-time or short-term staff can assemble and summarize much of the information once an evaluation plan is prepared. Agency staff members can yield much of the information as a by-product of their own evaluation, recordkeeping, and reporting activities. Cooperation depends on a clear and attractive evaluation plan and selective data collection.

The role of the director is even more crucial in the process of reporting evaluation conclusions and encouraging use of findings to make needed adjustments in agency functioning. Perhaps the most important concept in this regard is involving in the evaluation process the people whose cooperation is necessary if the findings are to be utilized. The growing visibility of the adult education function and increasing concern for accountability are placing a premium on agency evaluation. Research and demonstration projects are needed that yield overviews of agency evaluation rationales and procedures, along with instruments and normative information to collect and interpret data.

The effective administrator, concerned with the satisfaction of his staff as well as the productivity of his institution, has a wealth of literature to draw upon as he strives to improve his own performance in carrying out his leadership, planning, and policy functions. By drawing upon the concepts and procedures developed by others he can increase his capacity to achieve planned institutional change and that is the challenge to those who aspire to set the pace in adult education in the 1980s.

Chapter Nine

Future Directions

Alan B. Knox

The policy issues for the future presented in this chapter are largely extrapolated from the preceding chapters. More attention to identification of emerging issues and a more proactive approach by practitioners is clearly warranted, although there have been a few efforts to do so (such as USOE, 1972; Broschart, 1977). The utility of this book—especially this concluding chapter—lies in the stimulation it provides the practitioner to reflect on current practice, to consider concepts and practices that have been helpful to others in the field, and to use the resulting perspective and proficiency to provide more dedicated and effective leadership for the agency, field, and society.

Origins

One of the most urgent concerns of adult education practitioners is the identification of promising new program ideas,
which are the prerequisites of effective objective setting, marketing, and resource acquisition. What is needed is a general
strategy for generation of new program ideas and establishment of
priorities.

The most comprehensive approach to program origination
consists of matching societal needs with agency purposes. This entails scanning for promising new program ideas in the parent organization and in the service area and learning from the program
development experience of other practitioners. Included in this
approach are adult education needs assessment activities related to
the client system and resource inventory activities related to the
agency, parent organization, and cosponsors.

Mandatory continuing professional education is an issue
that appears to evoke a programming response but that has more
disadvantages than advantages. Some practitioners favor regulations requiring a certain number of hours each year as a condition
of relicensure or recertification. However, requiring all members
of a field to participate in education activities does not in fact pro-
tect the public against substandard performance by a few members
of a profession and leads to some undesirable by-products, such as
more rigid and unresponsive programs, less public esteem for
adult education, and avoidance by professional associations in dealing directly with substandard performance (Knox, 1975b).

As a field that has depended on voluntary participation,
adult education has long given attention to the needs and interests
of potential participants, and there has been a moderate accumula-
tion of research on adult education needs assessment. The purposes
and resources of the sponsoring agency and the sponsor's relationship with community groups in its service area have a major influence on needs assessments. Unfortunately there is very little research on how the characteristics of sponsoring agencies and
cosponsoring groups influence program priorities and objectives.
Usually program administrators lead from their own strengths
when they develop new programs that relate to agency purposes

and resources. The use of information from potential participants and from experts in the field provides cross-validation that the new programs are responsive to the educational needs of adults and are based on the necessary resources and congruence with agency purposes. The possession of authoritative information about client needs and preferences can also provide adult education practitioners with valuable leverage in some instances (Knox, 1979b); data-based generalizations about needs can enable the administrator to have more influence on decisions about objectives and marketing than would be the case with unsupported opinion.

An exceedingly cost-beneficial way to facilitate the development of adult education programs is to share needs assessment and resource inventory information. This could be readily accomplished if professional associations and journals would seek out successful practitioners and arrange for them to prepare brief descriptions of purposes, materials, rationale, and evidence of results. A collection of case descriptions can stimulate practitioners to adapt some practices to their own purposes and situation and can serve as a spawning ground for research and evaluation projects.

Objectives and Activities

The most familiar aspect of adult education program development is the implementation of objectives and learning activities. The process of objective setting is especially important because of the different expectations of participants and resource people, the utility of consensus for cooperative efforts, and the relevance to participants of their increased proficiency beyond the educational activity. Attention should be given to the information and people to include in the objective-setting process. For example, the expectations, needs, and motives of potential participants are important but often ignored aspects of objective setting that can be collected by needs assessment studies and by inclusion of representative potential participants on planning committees. Professional values regarding lifelong learning and self-directed study should emphasize an active learner role in program development generally.

One of the major problems likely to confront agency administrators in coming years is how to set program priorities at the agency level. In the past, priorities were set almost exclusively for separate activities, and the profile of aggregate program offerings was of little consequence. When adult education was marginal to the parent organization and so small in scale that few people worried about duplication, practitioners could concentrate on responsiveness to client demand and give little attention to priority setting. However, increasing concern with resource allocation and decentralization in the parent organization and with duplication and accountability in the community service area are raising the issue of priority setting for adult education agencies. The setting of priorities at the agency level while retaining responsiveness at the activity level constitutes a challenging task for administrators. Some research questions related to setting high-priority objectives follow:

1. Within broad program areas, what do policy makers, practitioners, and potential participants perceive as high-priority objectives for adult education programs?
2. What is the relative effectiveness of various procedures for exploring potential adult education objectives and for gaining consensus on high-priority objectives?
3. What patterns of representation and tasks by representatives of learners, teachers, and administrators tend to be especially effective in the program planning process?
4. For various types of adult education programs, how do the preferences of participants, resources people, administrators, and policy makers influence objective priorities?

    Practitioners would benefit from greater understanding of how to incorporate research findings into strategies for selecting and organizing learning activities. It would be helpful to identify the design criteria that have been used by effective practitioners, such as provision of adequate opportunity for the learner to practice the desired behavior, reinforcement of desired performance, continuity, and sequencing. Research findings on relationships between types of objectives and types of learning activities can be disseminated within the field and serve as guides for optimal effectiveness. A reassessment, on involvement of learners in program development and especially objective setting, on self-directed learning, and on increased proficiency and improved performance is called for if the programs are to be focused on the needs and interests of the learners. Voluntary participation in adult education, which enables dissatisfied learners to withdraw from programs that do not meet their felt needs, has helped maintain this emphasis on learner-centered education. In the past, teacher-centered and agency-centered trends have resulted in overemphasis on content expertise, standards, organizational goals, and enrollments. Trends toward institutionalization of agencies and compulsory adult education could erode the learner-centered orientation unless adult education administrators preserve it through staffing, policies, and procedures.

Overviews of organization development and community development contain many generalizations about these processes that could be tested by research, but few of them have been tested (Beckhard, 1969; Bennis, 1969; Bennis, Benne, and Chin, 1969; Biddle and Biddle, 1965). Some suggested research questions related to the teaching-learning transaction, self-directed learning, and innovative methods and materials follow.

1. What are the relationships among teaching style, adult learning style, and learner achievement?
2. What is the relative effectiveness (as reflected in achievement and satisfaction) of various instructional methods and materials in relation to adult education objectives and adult learner characteristics (such as educational level, personality rigidity, or age)?
3. What is the relative extent of use and effectiveness of procedures for self-directed study by adults?
4. What is the cost effectiveness of adult education courses that entail major investments in instructional materials?
5. What procedures (review, simulation, praise, external recognition) provide the most effective reinforcement for adult learners with various characteristics?

The rationales for organization development and for community development have tended to emphasize the resolution of societal problems and to view learning activities as ways for participants to understand problems, solutions, and the problem-solving process. The rationale for self-directed learning, in contrast, has emphasized personal growth. This distinction is analogous to the emphases of productivity and satisfaction in administrative style. In settings such as personnel development, program development procedures should give attention to both individual and organization/community goals (Schein, 1978).

Evaluation

Program evaluation tends to intimidate practitioners, with the paradoxical result that they often feel guilty about not engaging in more sophisticated evaluation while ignoring opportunities to use simple and practical evaluation activities. One of the most intimidating points about program evaluation is that often it appears that conducting a thorough evaluation of an adult education program entails more time and expense than conducting the program itself. Except in some pilot projects, such an expenditure is not justified. The practitioner, therefore, needs to decide on a focus and scale for an evaluation activity so that the benefits are likely to exceed the costs.

Practitioners must also coordinate evaluation activities with the remainder of the program, and their own leadership role regarding evaluation—in contrast with that of the evaluation specialist—is important in this regard. Evaluation activities can cause organizational conflict as well as help to reduce it. How can program administrators benefit from program evaluation without allowing it to disrupt agency functioning? One way is to include in evaluation plans and implementation those people who are associated with the program, those who will be affected by its activity, and those who must use the findings to reduce it.

A related issue is the evaluation of the evaluator. In most cases people associated with an agency or program lack sound bases for evaluating the validity of the evidence, the soundness of the conclusions, and the implications for action. A major need pertaining to evaluation concerns sharing of experience with program evaluation. The evaluation of effective evaluation strategies and instruments is so costly and rare that it seems desirable for there to be greater sharing of the results, including summary findings that might be helpful to those attempting to interpret findings in similar settings.

The greatest need for research on evaluation procedures is for validation studies that develop feasible outcome measures for adult education programs. Some research questions related to evaluation procedures—with an emphasis on outcome measures—follow:

1. What efficient and valid evaluation instruments can be developed and used to assess the outcomes of major types of systematic adult learning activities including social, occupational, academic, and personal?
2. How valid are adult education participant satisfaction forms for various categories of learners?
3. What cognitive and noncognitive measures are useful to predict adult participant persistence and achievement in systematic learning activities?
4. How can adult education program evaluation reporting effectively serve multiple audiences?

Adult education program evaluation has emphasized program improvement. In the future, more attention should be given to accountability and evaluation of impact. As adult education becomes more visible, central, and anticipated, people ask whether it has an impact. Does an unemployed thirty-year-old who finally completes a high school equivalency diploma benefit in terms of subsequent employment? Does a forty-year-old physician who completes a continuing medical education workshop actually modify performance as a result? Convincing answers to these questions require a well-designed evaluation study as well as a well-designed educational program.

Participation

One administrative function of adult education is the provision of information and counseling services to attract and retain adult participants. Public information specialists help program administrators with marketing activities that attract participants and support. An overview of marketing concepts and procedures for nonprofit organizations (Kotler, 1974) points out general marketing trends and suggests tests of their application to adult education. Some research questions related to adult participation in education follow:

1. What have been the trends in recent decades regarding the extent and type of participation by adults in part-time or short-term systematic learning activities?
2. What are the major personal and situational correlates of adults' decisions to participate in systematic learning activities? Particular attention should be given to the influence of "important others" to the potential participant, to incentives for participation, and to ways of restructuring the potential participant's environment to make it supportive of participation.
3. What are the main reasons for nonparticipation in lifelong learning during the adult years for various categories of learners, and what can be done to reduce barriers to participation?
4. What is the impact of mandatory adult education requirements on extent of participation, types of participants, program topics, and level of performance?
5. What are the relative advantages and disadvantages of community-based educational counseling for adults (educational brokering) in contrast to agency-based counseling for adult learners?
6. What characteristics of sponsoring agencies are especially effective in reaching specialized and underserved target markets (less educated, older, minorities, remote)?
7. How can practitioners identify elements of successful marketing and counseling services for adult learners, and then share their conclusions with others?

Practitioners can consider many questions as they analyze current efforts and explore future directions. Are more or different counseling services needed? How can the underserved be more effectively reached and served? How can marketing, counseling, and program development activities be more effectively inter-related? What marketing and counseling services can best be provided by other organizations, such as advertising agencies and community-based educational information centers?

Another policy issue is how much field-wide marketing of adult education should occur. Each agency tends to engage in marketing activities to establish and maintain a favorable image in its service area and to recruit participants to individual programs. Over the past four decades, some metropolitan adult education councils have conducted marketing projects on behalf of many local agencies. During the past decade, there have been several instances in which agencies within a given category (such as public school adult education divisions) have joined forces in a statewide marketing effort. Perhaps the time has come for various segments of the field to make a concerted field-wide marketing effort to increase public understanding of the scope and diversity of the entire field of adult education (Blakely and Lappin, 1969).

Resources

Adult education administrators deal with physical and financial resources, including money, facilities, equipment, and materials. Each agency director must obtain a distinctive mix of resources in order for the agency to function. Various influences on resource acquisition have been identified, including agency type and public image, demand, competition, pertinent legislation, and expertise in proposal preparation. Practitioners would benefit from greater understanding of the relative importance of each of these types of influence on resource acquisition.

Agency administrators use various practices to control and evaluate resource acquisition, allocation, and utilization, many of which are from the general accounting field. It would be helpful to know whether these practices are generic or are unique to the administration of adult education.

Some research questions related to acquisition, allocation, and accountability of financial and physical resources in adult education follow:

1. What is the monetary and nonmonetary return on the investment in continuing education for the individual, organization, and society?
2. What combinations of financial and other resources are especially effective for continuing education programs?
3. What policies and practices of financial assistance to adult learners are associated with effectiveness in reaching the target markets?
4. How satisfactory is the current mix of sources of financial assistance to adult education participants in terms of minimizing barriers for high-priority members of the target market?

Many practitioners enter the field of adult education because of a missionary commitment to social equity but because of low participation rates by adults with little formal education and high participation rates by adults with much formal education, there is a widening of the gap between the educational "haves" and "have nots." This makes resource allocation to subsidize adult education for less advantaged adults especially important.

Staffing

Agency effectiveness is closely associated with the caliber of staff that is attracted and retained. The staffing process includes preparation of job descriptions and specifications, job design, personnel recruitment and selection, supervision, and staff and organization development. In addition, there are several policy and research issues related to staffing.

Effective staffing takes into account both individual and organizational considerations. In adult education, however, uncertain enrollment and funding patterns interfere with the regular application of staffing procedures. In addition, procedures that are standard for full-time staff are not always applicable without adaptation to part-time and short-term staff commitments. The issue of what to emphasize in adult education staffing warrants further research.

Although adult education staff selection and development is a crucial administrative function, there has been relatively little research on it. Of course, all of the generalizations about adult education in organizational settings can be applied to staff development activities for adult education staff. Some research questions related to adult education staff selection and development follow:

1. What are effective procedures for the identification of talent pools of potential resource people and other staff to plan and conduct adult education programs and to prepare educational materials?
2. What are effective procedures for the selection of people from those pools to help plan and conduct adult education activities with an emphasis on work samples?
3. What incentives and rewards attract and retain effective teachers and resource people in adult education programs?

Leadership

Leadership involves attention to goals, planning, results, and coordination of various agency functions to produce results. Efforts by adult education practitioners to reflect goals and priorities in plans and decisions have been little studied and deserve much more attention. A sense of professionalism and direction on the part of the agency director has appreciable influence on agency success, especially if an understanding of relevant social and philosophical issues can be related to some planning mechanism within the agency. Multiple agency goals and programs make both long-term planning and precise evaluation difficult. The creation of procedures for agency priority setting is one of the major challenges to practitioners in the field.

Another important leadership concern is the provision of incentives and rewards for agency personnel, especially resource people. In many parent organizations, improvement of faculty rewards for teaching adults is likely to entail policy changes and much informal effort. Particular attention should be given to the quality of performance in conducting adult education activities as a basic criterion for promotion, tenure, and increases in base salary.

Some research questions regarding administrative leadership within the agency, parent organization, community, and nation follow:

1. What is the typical work distribution—in terms of content and time—of continuing education administrators?
2. What are the main sources of role conflict for continuing education program administrators?
3. What are the main functional and dysfunctional relationships between the organizational agencies that provide continuing education for adults and the remainder of the parent organization of which they are a part?
4. What are the typical cooperative, complementary, and competitive functions of various types of continuing education sponsoring agencies?
5. What are the main costs and benefits of agency cosponsorship arrangements?

Adult education administration is leadership in an organizational setting and includes attention to organizational functioning. Effective practitioners find it necessary to analyze system functioning, partly because they often operate from a power-poor position and therefore require a detailed and accurate understanding of relations with the parent organization. They must also develop effective interpersonal relationships if they are to negotiate flexible and responsive organizational relationships for the agency. Sometimes this negotiation is directed toward policy changes within the parent organization. In this context, policy makers must be helped to understand the adult education function and become committed to purposes, procedures, and support that will strengthen it. Some research questions related to general organizational functioning of the adult education agency follow:

1. How institutionalized—in terms of policy base, automatic provision of resources, responsiveness to clientele, and administrative flexibility—are the organizational units that sponsor adult education programs compared with the remainder of the organization?
2. What characteristics of sponsoring agencies are generic to all sponsors, are distinctive to the type of parent institution (school, employer, association, university), and are idiocyncratic?
3. To what extent is achievement of adult education agency goals

associated with participant satisfaction, achievement of participant objectives, satisfaction of resource people, program growth, program responsiveness and change, and program visibility?
4. What factors influence government and foundation funding of local adult education programs?
5. What are the major sources of knowledge adult education administrators utilize and to what extent and in what ways do they share their knowledge with other adult educators?
6. In what ways can adult education agencies support and complement each other's work?

Summary

The adult education function seems finally to be coming into its own. However, it is likely that some of its forms will change. During generations of marginality, practitioners innovated methods and gained satisfaction from service to adult learners. As the adult education function shifts from the margin toward the center of parent organizations and society in general, the field is becoming more competitive. Practitioners in related fields who a few years ago could not be bothered with adult education now claim it as their own. Supremacy will go to those who are able and well prepared.

Adult education is the goal and the means. Effective agencies and programs for adult learners depend on practitioner proficiency. Lifelong learning is crucial for practitioners as well as participants. The professional literature now contains a pool of concepts and procedures from which practitioners can draw. Associations in the field facilitate sharing. Expertise on clientele, goals, program development, interpersonal relations, and administration provides practitioners with the strategic advantage. The essential ingredient is the practitioners' commitment to personal and professional development.

One benefit of professional proficiency is that it enables practitioners to take the initiative in response to policy issues and program priorities. For example, practitioners who go beyond a generalized responsiveness to adult learners and acquire a detailed understanding of adult development and learning are likely to be effective in reaching and serving harder-to-reach adults. Professional proficiency can also provide leverage for program administrators: they can attract talented resource people to work on a part-time or short-term basis and they can be more effective in helping adults learn. An understanding of marketing can help attract participants and resource people as well as can enhance the public image of adult education generally. An understanding of the interweaving of stability and change in agency functioning can enable practitioners to innovate through exposure to promising practices, staff development for agency personnel, focused evaluation and research activities, and an unrelenting concern for impact. An understanding of relationships among an agency, the parent organization, and the community can facilitate work with policy makers and colleagues in other agencies.

Adult education is an action-oriented field. Increased understanding from the professional literature is most useful when it is related to the actual problems and opportunities that practitioners confront. Applying theory to practice entails consideration of effective interpersonal relations and ongoing strategies for interrelating knowledge and action. Adult education participants tend to benefit most when there is a creative tension between knowledge and action; the same is true for adult education administrators.

References

ADAMS, J. L. *Conceptual Blockbusting.* Stanford, Calif.: Stanford Alumni Association, 1974.

ALFORD, H. *Continuing Education in Action.* New York: Wiley, 1968.

ALKIN, M. C. *Toward an Evaluation Model: A Systems Approach.* Working Paper No. 4. Los Angeles: Center for the Study of Evaluation, University of California, December 1967.

ALLISON, G. T. *Essence of Decision.* Boston: Little, Brown, 1971.

American Council on Education. *Financing Part-Time Students: The New Majority in Postsecondary Education.* Washington, D.C.: American Council on Education, 1974.

ANASTASI, A. *Psychological Testing.* (4th ed.) New York: Macmillan, 1976.

ANDERSON, D., and NIEMI, J. A. *Adult Education and the Disadvantaged Adult.* Syracuse, N.Y.: ERIC Clearinghouse on Adult Education, 1969.

APPS, J. W. *Toward a Working Philosophy of Education.* Syracuse University Publications in Continuing Education, Occasional Paper No. 36. Syracuse, N.Y.: Syracuse University Press, 1973.

ARGYRIS, C. *Integrating the Individual and the Organization.* New York: Wiley, 1964.

ARGYRIS, C. *Organization and Innovation.* Homewood, Ill.: Irwin, 1965.

ARGYRIS, C. *Management and Organizational Development.* New York: McGraw-Hill, 1971.

ARGYRIS, C. *On Organizations of the Future.* Beverly Hills, Calif.: Sage, 1973.

ARGYRIS, C., and SCHÖN, D. A. *Theory in Practice: Increasing Professional Effectiveness.* San Francisco: Jossey-Bass, 1976.

ATKIN, J. M. "Some Evaluation Problems in a Course-Content Improvement Project." *Journal of Research in Science Teaching,* 1963, *1,* 129–132.

ATWOOD, H. M. "Diagnostic Procedure in Adult Education." *Viewpoints* (Bulletin of the School of Education, Indiana University), 1973, *49* (5), 3–6.

ATWOOD, H. M., and ELLIS, J. "Concept of Need: An Analysis for Adult Education." *Viewpoints* (Bulletin of the School of Education, Indiana University), 1973, *49* (5), 7–16.

AXFORD, R. W. "Curriculum and Content." In R. M. Smith, G. F. Aker, and J. R. Kidd (Eds.), *Handbook of Adult Education.* New York: Macmillan, 1970.

BALDRIDGE, J. V., and DEAL, T. E. *Managing Change in Education Organizations.* Berkley, Calif.: McCutchan, 1975.

BAREITHER, H. D., and SCHILLINGER, J. L. *University Space Planning.* Urbana: University of Illinois Press, 1968.

BEACH, D. S. *Personnel: The Management of People at Work.* (3rd ed.) New York: Macmillan, 1975.

BECKER, H. S., and GEER, B. "Participant Observation: The Analysis of Qualitative Field Data." In R. N. Adams and J. J. Preiss (Eds.), *Human Organization Research.* Homewood, Ill.: Dorsey Press, 1960.

BECKER, J. W. "Architecture for Adult Education." In M. S. Knowles

(Ed.), *Handbook of Adult Education in the United States.* Washington, D.C.: Adult Education Association of the U.S.A., 1960.

BECKERMAN, M. M. "Educational Change Agent: A New University Extension Professional Role." *Adult Leadership,* 1972, *21* (2), 39–40.

BECKHARD, R. *Organization Development: Strategies and Models.* Reading, Mass.: Addison-Wesley, 1969.

BEDER, H. "An Environmental Interaction Model for Agency Development in Adult Education." *Adult Education,* 1978, *28* (3), 176–190.

BEDER, H., and SMITH, F. *Developing an Adult Education Program Through Community Linkages.* Washington, D.C.: Adult Education Association of the U.S.A., 1977.

BELASCO, J. A., and TRICE, H. M. *The Assessment of Change in Training and Therapy.* New York: McGraw-Hill, 1969.

BELL, C. R. "Career Planning and Development: A Resource System." *Training and Development Journal,* 1975, *29* (8), 32–35.

BELL, W. V. "Finance, Legislation, and Public Policy for Adult Education." In M. S. Knowles (Ed.), *Handbook of Adult Education in the United States.* Washington, D.C.: Adult Education Association of the U.S.A., 1960.

BENNIS, W. G. *Organization Development: Its Nature, Origins, and Prospects.* Reading, Mass.: Addison-Wesley, 1969.

BENNIS, W. G. "Post-Bureaucratic Leadership." In W. R. Lassey (Ed.), *Leadership and Social Change.* Iowa City, Iowa: University Associates, 1971.

BENNIS, W. G., BENNE, K., and CHIN, R. (Eds.). *The Planning of Change.* New York: Holt, Rinehart and Winston, 1969.

BENNIS, W. G., and SCHEIN, E. H. (Eds.). *Leadership and Motivation.* Cambridge, Mass.: M.I.T. Press, 1966.

BENNIS, W. G., and others (Eds.). *The Planning of Change.* New York: Holt, Rinehart and Winston, 1976.

BERDIE, D. R., and ANDERSON, J. F. *Questionnaires: Design and Use.* Metuchen, N.J.: Scarecrow Press, 1974.

BERGEVIN, P., MORRIS, D., and SMITH, R. *Adult Education Procedures.* New York: Seabury Press, 1963.

BERRIEN, F. K. "A General Systems Approach to Social Taxonomy." In B. P. Indik and F. K. Berrien (Eds.), *People, Groups, and Organizations.* New York: Teachers College Press, 1968.

BIDDLE, W., and BIDDLE, L. *The Community Development Process.* New York: Holt, Rinehart and Winston, 1965.

BIDDLE, B. J., and THOMAS, E. J. (Eds.). *Role Theory: Concepts and Research.* New York: Wiley, 1966.

BIEDERMAN, K. R., and BILLINGS, B. B. "Loan Programs for Recurring Education." Paper presented at Recurring Education Conference, Washington, D.C., 1973.

BLAKE, R. R., and MOUTON, J. S. *The Managerial Grid.* Houston: Gulf Publishing, 1964.

BLAKELY, R. J., and LAPPIN, I. M. *Knowledge Is Power to Control Power.* Syracuse University Publications in Continuing Education, Notes and Essays on Education for Adults, No. 63. Syracuse, N.Y.: Syracuse University Press, 1969.

BLANEY, J. P., and MC KIE, D. "Knowledge of Conference Objectives and Effect Upon Learning." *Adult Education,* 1969, *19* (2), 98–105.

BOAZ, R. L. *Participation in Adult Education.* National Center for Education Statistics, Final Report 1975. Washington, D.C.: U.S. Government Printing Office, 1978.

BOCK, L. K. *Teaching Adults in Continuing Education.* Readings in Program Development, No. 1. Urbana: Office of Continuing Education and Public Service, University of Illinois, 1979.

BOOTH, A. *Diffusion and Adoption of Educational Programs.* Final Report, National Science Foundation Study GS-698. Lincoln: Bureau of Sociological Research, University of Nebraska, 1967.

BOOTH, A., and KNOX, A. "Participation in Adult Education Agencies and Personal Influence." *Sociology of Education,* 1967, *40* (3), 275–277.

BOSHIER, R. "Educational Participation and Dropout: A Theoretical Model." *Adult Education,* 1973, *23* (4), 255–282.

BOSHIER, R. "Motivational Orientations Revisited: Life-Space Motives and the Education Participation Scale." *Adult Education,* 1977, *27* (2), 89–115.

BOWEN, H. R. "Financing the External Degree." In Commission on Non-Traditional Study, *Diversity by Design.* San Francisco: Jossey-Bass, 1973.

BOYLE, P. G., and JAHNS, I. R. "Program Development and Evaluation." In R. M. Smith, G. F. Aker, and J. R. Kidd (Eds.), *Handbook of Adult Education.* New York: Macmillan, 1970.

BRADFORD, L. P. "Report of the Division of Adult Education Services of the National Education Services of the National Education Association." *Adult Education Bulletin*, 1947, *11*, 167–170.

BRADFORD, L. P., GIBB, J. R., and BENNE, K. D. (Eds.). *T-Group Theory and Laboratory Method*. New York: Wiley, 1964.

BRADSHAW, J. "The Concept of Social Need." *Ekistics*, 1974, *220*, 184–187.

BROPHY, K., GROTELUESCHEN, A., and GOOLER, D. D. "A Blueprint for Program Evaluation." In A. Grotelueschen, D. D. Gooler, and A. B. Knox, *Evaluation in Adult Basic Education: How and Why*. Danville, Ill.: Interstate, 1976.

BROSCHART, J. R. *Lifelong Learning in the Nation's Third Century*. U.S. Office of Education, publication no. OE 76-09102. Washington, D.C.: U.S. Government Printing Office, 1977.

BRUNNER, E. DE S., and Associates. *An Overview of Adult Education Research*. Chicago: Adult Education Association of the U.S.A., 1959.

BUCHANAN, W. W., and BARKSDALE, H. C. "Marketing's Broadening Concept Is Real in University Extension." *Adult Education*, 1974, *25* (1), 34–46.

BURGESS, P. "Reasons for Adult Participation in Group Educational Activities." *Adult Education*, 1971, *22* (1), 3–29.

BURTON, W. H. "Basic Principles in a Good Teaching-Learning Situation." *Phi Delta Kappan*, 1958, *39* (6), 242–248.

BUSHNELL, D. S. "Needed: A Voucher Plan for Adults." *Education*, 1973, *94*, 3–11.

BYRN, D. (Ed.). *Evaluation in Extension*. Topeka, Kans.: Ives, 1959.

CAPLOW, T. *How to Run Any Organization*. Hinsdale, Ill.: Dryden Press, 1967.

CAREY, J. T. *Forms and Forces in University Adult Education*. Chicago: Center for the Study of Liberal Education for Adults, 1963.

CARLISLE, H. M. *Situational Management*. New York: AMACOM, 1973.

CARLSON, R. E., and others. "Improvements in the Selection Interview." *Personal Journal*, 1971, *50*, 268–275.

Carnegie Commission on Higher Education. *Less Time, More Options*. New York: McGraw-Hill, 1971.

CARP, A., PETERSON, R. E., and ROELFS, P. J. "Adult Learning Interests and Experiences." In K. P. Cross, J. R. Valley, and Associates (Eds.), *Planning Non-Traditional Programs: An Analysis of the Issues for Postsecondary Education.* San Francisco: Jossey-Bass, 1974.

CARTTER, A. M. *The Future Financing of Postsecondary Education.* Washington, D.C.: American Council on Education, 1973.

CASTALDI, B. *Creative Planning of Educational Facilities.* Chicago: Rand McNally, 1969.

CAULLEY, D. N., and GROTELUESCHEN, A. D. "The Illusions of Learner Accomplishment." *Educational Leadership,* 1978, *35,* 280–283.

CHIN, R. "The Utility of System Models and Developmental Models for Practitioners." In W. G. Bennis, K. D. Benne, and R. Chin (Eds.), *The Planning of Change.* (2nd ed.) New York: Holt, Rinehart and Winston, 1969.

CLARK, B. R. *Adult Education in Transition.* Berkeley: University of California Press, 1956.

COHEN, D. K., and GARET, M. S. "Reforming Educational Policy with Applied Social Research." *Harvard Educational Review,* 1975, *45* (1), 17–43.

COHEN, M. D., and MARCH, J. G. *Leadership and Ambiguity.* New York: McGraw-Hill, 1974.

COMMISSION ON NONTRADITIONAL STUDY. *Diversity by Design.* San Francisco: Jossey-Bass, 1973.

COOK, T. D., and GRUDER, C. L. "Meta-Evaluation Research." *Evaluation Quarterly,* 1978, *2,* 5–51.

CORSON, J. J. *The Governance of Colleges and Universities.* (Rev. ed.) New York: McGraw-Hill, 1975.

Counseling Psychologist, 1976, *6* (1), entire issue. Special issue on counseling adults.

CRAIG, R. L. (Ed.). *Training and Development Handbook.* (2nd ed.) New York: McGraw-Hill, 1976.

CRONBACH, L. J. "Course Improvement Through Evaluation." *Teachers College Record,* 1963, *64,* 672–683.

CRONBACH, L. J. *Designing Educational Evaluations.* Unpublished manuscript. Palo Alto, Calif: Stanford University, 1978.

CRONBACH, L. J., and SUPPES, P. (Eds.). *Research for Tomorrow's Schools: Disciplined Inquiry for Education.* Toronto: Macmillan, 1969.

CROSS, K. P., VALLEY, J. R., and Associates. *Planning Non-Traditional Programs: An Analysis of the Issues for Postsecondary Education.* San Francisco: Jossey-Bass, 1974.

CULBERTSON, D. J. "Corporate Role in Lifelong Learning." In D. W. Vermilye (Ed.), *Lifelong Learners—A New Clientele for Higher Education: Current Issues in Higher Education 1974.* San Francisco: Jossey-Bass, 1974.

DAIGNEAULT, G. H. *Decision Making in the University Evening College.* Chicago: Center for the Study of Liberal Education of Adults, 1963.

DARKENWALD, G. G. "Innovation in Adult Education: An Organizational Analysis." *Adult Education,* 1977, *27* (3), 156–172.

DAVIS, L. N., and MC CALLON, E. *Planning, Conducting, and Evaluating Workshops.* Austin, Tex.: Learning Concepts, 1974.

DEPPE, D. A. "The Adult Educator: Marginal Man and Boundary Definer." *Adult Leadership,* 1969, *18* (4), 119–120, 192, 130.

DHANIDINA, L., and GRIFFITH, W. S. "Costs and Benefits of Delayed High School Completion." *Adult Education,* 1975, *25* (4), 217–230.

DICKINSON, G. *Teaching Adults: A Handbook for Instructors.* Toronto: New Press, 1973.

DICKINSON, G., and CLARK, K. M. "Learning Orientations and Participation in Self Education and Continuing Education." *Adult Education,* 1975, *16* (1), 3–15.

DORLAND, J. R. "The Impact of Legislation on Adult Education." In N. C. Shaw (Ed.), *Administration of Continuing Education.* Washington, D.C.: National Association for Public School Adult Education, 1969.

DRESCH, S. P. "U.S. Public Policy and the Evolutionary Adaptability of Postsecondary Education." In S. J. Mushkin (Ed.), *Recurrent Education.* Washington, D.C.: U.S. Government Printing Office, 1974.

DRUCKER, P. F. *The Effective Executive.* New York: Harper & Row, 1966.

DRUCKER, P. F. *Management: Tasks, Responsibilities, Practices.* New York: Harper & Row, 1973.

DWYER, R. "Workers Education, Labor Education, Labor Studies: An Historical Delineation." *Review of Educational Research,* 1977, *47* (1), 179–207.

EDDY, B., and KELLOW, J. "Training Facilities." *Training and Development Journal*, 1977, *31* (5), 32–36.

EISNER, E. W. "Educational Objectives: Help or Hindrance?" *School Review*, 1967, *75*, 250–260.

EISNER, E. W. "Educational Connoisseurship and Criticism: Their Form and Functions in Educational Evaluation." *Journal of Aesthetic Education*, 1976, *10* (3 and 4), 135–150.

ERDOS, R. F. *Teaching by Correspondence*. New York: Longmans, Green (for UNESCO), 1967.

ERIC Clearinghouse on Adult Education. *Personnel Development in Adult Education*. Current Information Sources, No. 31. Syracuse, N.Y.: ERIC Clearinghouse on Adult Education, 1970.

FARMER, J. A., JR. "Professionalization in Higher Adult Education Administration." *Adult Education*, 1970, *21* (1), 29–34.

FARMER, J. A., JR., and KNOX, A. B. *Alternative Patterns for Strengthening Community Service Programs in Institutions of Higher Education*. Urbana: Office for the Study of Continuing Professional Education, University of Illinois, 1977.

FARMER, M. L. *Counseling Services for Adults in Higher Education*. Metuchen, N.J.: Scarecrow Press, 1971.

FAYOL, H. *General and Industrial Management*. (Trans. by C. Stours). London: Pitman, 1949.

FISCHER, F. B. "Financing Continuing Higher Education: One Perspective of the Present and Future." *Continuum*, 1976, *41* (2), 9–11.

FLIPPO, E. B. *Principles of Personnel Management*. (4th ed.) New York: McGraw-Hill, 1976.

FORDYCE, J. K., and WEIL, R. *A Manager's Handbook of Organization Development Methods*. Reading, Mass.: Addison-Wesley, 1971.

FREEMAN, H. E. "The Present Status of Evaluation Research." In M. Guttentag (Ed.), *Evaluation Studies Review Annual*. Vol. 2. Beverly Hills, Calif.: Sage, 1977.

FREIRE, P. "The Adult Literacy Process and Cultural Action for Freedom." *Harvard Educational Review*, 1970, *40* (2), 205–225.

FRENCH, W. L., and BELL, C. H., JR. *Organization Development: Behavioral Science Interventions for Organization Improvement*. Englewood Cliffs, N.J.: Prentice-Hall, 1973.

FULLER, J. W. "MBO Revisited." *Adult Leadership*, 1973, *22*, 112–114.

GAGE, N. L. *Handbook of Research on Teaching.* Chicago: Rand McNally, 1963.

GARDNER, J. W. *Self-Renewal: The Individual and the Innovative Society.* New York: Harper & Row, 1964.

GETZELS, J. W., LIPHAM, J. M., and CAMPBELL, R. F. *Educational Administration as a Social Process.* New York: Harper & Row, 1968.

GLASS, G. V., and WORTHEN, B. R. "Educational Evaluation and Research: Similarities and Differences." In J. Weiss (Ed.), *Curriculum Theory Network.* Monograph Supplement on Curriculum Evaluation: Potentiality and Reality. Toronto: Ontario Institute for Studies in Education, 1972.

GOLDSTEIN, A. P., and SORCHER, M. *Changing Supervisor Behavior.* Elmsford, N.Y.: Pergamon Press, 1973.

GOOD, C. V. (Ed.). *Dictionary of Education.* (3rd ed.) New York: McGraw-Hill, 1973.

GOODALE, J. G. "Tailoring the Selection Interview to the Job." *Personnel Journal,* 1976, *55,* 62–65.

GOOLER, D. D., and GROTELUESCHEN, A. D. "Curriculum Development Accountability." *Educational Leadership,* 1971, *29* (2), 165–169.

GORDON, R. L. *Interviewing: Strategy, Techniques, and Tactics.* (Rev. ed.) Homewood, Ill.: Dorsey Press, 1975.

GRABOWSKI, S. M. "Educational Counseling of Adults." *Adult Leadership,* 1976, *24* (7), 225–227, 249.

GRATTAN, H. *In Quest of Knowledge.* New York: Association Press, 1955.

GRAY, W., JR. *Manual for Discussion Moderators.* Oklahoma City: American Institute of Discussion, 1964.

GREEN, P. "Community Programs Occupy Empty School Spaces in Virginia." *Schoolhouse,* 1975, *21,* 1–8.

GRIFFITHS, D. E. *Administrative Theory.* New York: Appleton-Century-Crofts, 1959.

GROSS, R. *The Lifelong Learner.* New York: Simon & Schuster, 1977.

GROTELUESCHEN, A. D., and GOOLER, D. D. "Evaluation in Curriculum Development." In J. Weiss (Ed.), *Curriculum Theory Network.* Monograph Supplement on Curriculum Evaluation: Potentiality and Reality. Toronto: Ontario Institute for Studies in Education, 1972.

GROTELUESCHEN, A. D., GOOLER, D. D., and KNOX, A. B. *Evaluation in Adult Basic Education: How and Why.* Danville, Ill.: Interstate, 1976.

GROTELUESCHEN, A. D., and KNOX, A. B. "Analysis of the Quick Word Test as an Estimate of Adult Mental Ability." *Journal of Educational Measurement,* 1967, *4,* 169–177.

GROTELUESCHEN, A. D., and others. *An Evaluation Planner.* Urbana: Office for the Study of Continuing Professional Education, University of Illinois, 1974.

GUBA, E. G. "Significant Differences." *Educational Research Newsletter,* 1969, *20* (3), 4–5.

GUBA, E. G. *Toward a Theory of Naturalistic Inquiry in Educational Evaluation.* Center for the Study of Evaluation Monograph No. 8. Los Angeles: University of California Press, 1978.

HAMPTON, D. R., SUMMER, C. E., and WEBBER, R. A. *Organizational Behavior and the Practice of Management.* Glenview, Ill.: Scott, Foresman, 1973.

HARRIS, B. M., and BESSENT, W. *In-Service Education.* Englewood Cliffs, N.J.: Prentice-Hall, 1969.

HAVELOCK, R. G. *Planning for Innovation.* Ann Arbor: Center for Research on Utilization of Scientific Knowledge, Institute for Social Research, University of Michigan Press, 1969.

HAVELOCK, R. G. *The Change Agent's Guide to Innovation in Education.* Englewood Cliffs, N.J.: Educational Technology, 1973.

HAVELOCK, R. G., and HAVELOCK, M. *Training for Change Agents.* Ann Arbor: Center for Research on Utilization of Scientific Knowledge, University of Michigan Press, 1972.

HAVIGHURST, R. J., and ORR, B. *Adult Education and Adult Needs.* Chicago: Center for the Study of Liberal Education for Adults, 1956.

HEFFERLIN, JB L. *Dynamics of Academic Reform.* San Francisco: Jossey-Bass, 1969.

HEFFERNAN, J. M., MACY, F. V., and VICKERS, D. F. *Educational Brokering: A New Service for Adult Learners.* Syracuse, N.Y.: National Center for Educational Brokering, 1976.

HEMPHILL, J. K. "The Relationships Between Research and Evaluation Studies." In R. W. Tyler (Ed.), *Educational Evaluation: New Roles, New Means.* 68th Yearbook of the National Society for the

Study of Education, Part II. Chicago: University of Chicago Press, 1969.

HENTSCHKE, G. C. *Management Operations in Education.* Berkeley, Calif.: McCutchan, 1975.

HERTLING, J., and GREENBURG, R. "Determining Continuing Education Needs and Interests." *National University Extension Association Spectator,* 1974, *38* (15), 7–14.

HESBURGH, T. M., MILLER, P. A., and WHARTON, C. R., JR. *Patterns for Lifelong Learning.* San Francisco: Jossey-Bass, 1973.

HIEMSTRA, R. *The Older Adult and Learning.* Lincoln: Department of Adult and Continuing Education, University of Nebraska, 1975.

HILL, R. J. *A Comparative Study of Lecture and Discussion Methods.* New York: Fund for Adult Education, 1960.

HOHMAN, L. "Education Directors in Professional Associations: Their Preparation, Role, and Function." In cooperation with the American Society of Association Executives. Washington, D.C., 1977 (mimeo).

HOLLEY, W. H., and FIELD, H. S. "Equal Employment Opportunity and its Implications for Personnel Practices." *Labor Law Journal,* 1976, *27,* 278–286.

HOPKINS, K. D., and GLASS, G. V. *Basic Statistics for the Behavioral Sciences.* Englewood Cliffs, N.J.: Prentice-Hall, 1978.

HOPPE, W. W. (Ed.). *Policies and Practices in Evening Colleges.* Metuchen, N.J.: Scarecrow Press, 1969.

HOULE, C. O. *The Effective Board.* New York: Association Press, 1960.

HOULE, C. O. *The Inquiring Mind.* Madison: University of Wisconsin Press, 1961.

HOULE, C. O. "Who Stays and Why?" *Adult Education,* 1964, *14* (4), 225–233.

HOULE, C. O. *The Design of Education.* San Francisco: Jossey-Bass, 1972.

HOULE, C. O. *The External Degree.* San Francisco: Jossey-Bass, 1973.

HOUSE, E. R. "Justice in Evaluation." In G. V. Glass (Ed.), *Evaluation Studies Review Annual.* Vol. 1. Beverly Hills, Calif.: Sage, 1976.

HOUSE, E. R. "Assumptions Underlying Evaluation Models." *Educational Researcher,* 1978, *7,* 4–12.

HOUSE, E. R. "The Objectivity, Fairness, and Justice of Federal Evaluation Policy as Reflected in the Follow-Through Evaluation." *Educational Evaluation and Policy Analysis,* 1979, *1,* 28–42.

HOYT, D. P., and HOWARD, G. S. "The Evaluation of Faculty Development Programs." *Research in Higher Education,* 1978, *8,* 25–28.

HUNSAKER, H., and PIERCE, R. (Eds.). *Creating a Climate for Adult Learning.* Report of a National Conference on Architecture for Adult Education. West Lafayette, Ind.: Purdue University, 1959.

HYMAN, H. H., LEVINE, G. N., and WRIGHT, C. R. *Methods to Induce Change at the Local Level: A Survey of Expert Opinion.* Report No. 2, first report and annex. Geneva, Switzerland: Research Institute for Social Development, United Nations, 1965.

HYMAN, H. H., WRIGHT, C. R., and SHELTON, J. *The Enduring Effects of Education.* Chicago: University of Chicago Press, 1975.

INSKO, C. A. *Theories of Attitude Change.* New York: Appleton-Century-Crofts, 1967.

IRONSIDE, D., and JACOBS, D. *Trends in Counseling and Information Services for the Adult Learner.* Toronto: Ontario Institute for Studies in Education, 1977.

JACOBS, H. L., MASON, W. D., and KAUFFMAN, E. *Education for Aging: A Review of Recent Literature.* Syracuse, N.Y.: ERIC Clearinghouse on Adult Education, 1970.

JACOBS, T. O. *Developing Questionnaire Items: How to Do It Well.* Alexandria, Va.: Human Resources Research Organization, 1974.

JENSEN, G., LIVERIGHT, A. A., and HALLENBECK, W. (Eds.). *Adult Education: Outlines of an Emerging Field of University Study.* Washington, D.C.: Adult Education Association of the U.S.A., 1964.

JOHNSON, E. I. *Metroplex Assembly: An Experiment on Community Education.* Report No. 213. Boston: Center for the Study of Liberal Education for Adults, 1965.

JOHNSON, E. I. "Technology in Adult Education." In R. M. Smith, G. F. Aker, and J. R. Kidd (Eds.), *Handbook of Adult Education.* New York: Macmillan, 1970.

JOHNSTON, W. J. "Finance and Budget Development." In N. C. Shaw (Ed.), *Administration of Continuing Education.* Washington, D.C.: National Association for Public School Adult Education, 1969.

JOHNSTONE, J. W. C., and RIVERA, R. *Volunteers for Learning.* Chicago: Aldine, 1965.

Joint Committee on Standards for Educational Evaluation. *Standards for Evaluations of Educational Programs, Projects, and Materi-*

als. Unpublished manuscript. Kalamazoo: Western Michigan University Evaluation Center, 1978.

KALLEN, H. M. *Philosophical Issues in Adult Education.* Springfield, Ill.: Thomas, 1962.

KATZ, D., and KAHN, R. L. *The Social Psychology of Organizations.* (Rev. ed.) New York: Wiley, 1978.

KATZ, E., and LAZARSFELD, P. F. *Personal Influence.* New York: Free Press, 1955.

KELLEY, E. C. *The Workshop Way of Learning.* New York: Harper & Row, 1951.

KERLINGER, F. N. *Foundations of Behavioral Research.* (2nd ed.) New York: Holt, Rinehart and Winston, 1973.

KIDD, J. R. *Financing Continuing Education.* New York: Scarecrow Press, 1962.

KIDD, J. R. *How Adults Learn.* (Rev. ed.) New York: Association Press, 1973.

KLEIS, R., and BUTCHER, D. "Roles and Interrelationships of Continuing Education Institutions." In N. C. Shaw (Ed.), *Administration of Continuing Education.* Washington, D.C.: National Association for Public School Adult Education, 1969.

KLEVINS, C. (Ed.). *Materials and Methods in Adult Education.* New York: Klevens, 1972.

KNOWLES, M. S. "Historical Development of the Adult Education Movement in the United States." In M. S. Knowles (Ed.), *Handbook of Adult Education in the United States.* Washington, D.C.: Adult Education Association of the U.S.A., 1960.

KNOWLES, M. S. *Higher Adult Education in the United States.* Washington, D.C.: American Council on Education, 1969.

KNOWLES, M. S. *The Modern Practice of Adult Education.* New York: Association Press, 1970.

KNOWLES, M. S. *Self-Directed Learning.* New York: Association Press, 1975.

KNOWLES, M. S. *A History of the Adult Education Movement in the United States.* (Rev. ed.) Huntington, N.Y.: Krieger, 1977.

KNOX, A. B. "Adult Education Agency Clientele Analysis." *Review of Educational Research,* 1965a, *35,* 231–239.

KNOX, A. B. "Current Needs in Adult Education Research." *Journal of Education* (Boston University), 1965b, *147* (3), 21–31.

KNOX, A. B. "Critical Appraisal of the Needs of Adults for Educational Experiences as a Basis for Program Development." New York: Teachers College, Columbia University, 1968a (mimeo).

KNOX, A. B. "Interests and Adult Education." *Journal of Learning Disabilities*, 1968b, *1* (2), 6–15.

KNOX, A. B. "Continuous Program Evaluation." In N. Shaw (Ed.), *Administration of Continuing Education*. Washington, D.C.: National Association for Public School Adult Education, 1969.

KNOX, A. B. *Factors Related to Educative Activity by Non-College-Bound Young Adults*. Final Report, U.S. Office of Education Project 6–1826. New York: Center for Adult Education, Teachers College, Columbia University, 1970.

KNOX, A. B. *In-Service Education in Adult Basic Education*. Tallahassee: Florida State University, 1971.

KNOX, A. B. *Development of Adult Education Graduate Programs*. Washington, D.C.: Commission of the Professors of Adult Education, Adult Education Association of the U.S.A., 1973.

KNOX, A. B. "Life-Long Self-Directed Education." In R. J. Blakely (Ed.), *Fostering the Growing Need to Learn*. Rockville, Md.: Division of Regional Medical Programs, Bureau of Health Resources Development, 1974.

KNOX, A. B. "New Realities in the Administration of Continuing Higher Education." *National University Extension Association Spectator*, 1975a, *39* (22), 6–9.

KNOX, A. B. "Professional Competence Means and Ends." *Professional Engineer*, 1975b, *45* (11), 49–52.

KNOX, A. B. *Helping Adults to Learn*. Concept Paper #4. Washington, D.C.: Continuing Library Education Network and Exchange, 1976.

KNOX, A. B. *Adult Development and Learning: A Handbook on Individual Growth and Competence in the Adult Years for Education and the Helping Professions*. San Francisco: Jossey-Bass, 1977a.

KNOX, A. B. *Current Research Needs Related to Systematic Learning by Adults*. Occasional Paper No. 4. Urbana: Office for the Study of Continuing Professional Education, University of Illinois, 1977b.

KNOX, A. B. (Ed.). *New Directions for Continuing Education: Enhancing Proficiencies of Continuing Educators*, no. 1. San Francisco: Jossey-Bass, 1979a.

KNOX, A. B. (Ed.). *New Directions for Continuing Education: Programming for Adults Facing Mid-Life Change,* no. 2. San Francisco: Jossey-Bass, 1979b.

KNOX, A. B. "The Nature and Causes of Professional Obsolescence." In P. P. LeBreton and others (Eds.), *The Evaluation of Continuing Education for Professionals: A Systems View.* Seattle: Continuing Education, Division of Academic and Professional Programs, University of Washington, 1979c.

KNOX, A. B. (Ed.). *New Directions for Continuing Education: Assessing the Impact of Continuing Education,* no. 3. San Francisco: Jossey-Bass, 1979d.

KNOX, A. B., and FARMER, H. S. "Overview of Counseling and Information Services for Adult Learners." *International Review of Education,* 1977, *23* (4), 387–414.

KNOX, A. B., GROTELUESCHEN, A. D., and SJOGREN, D. D. "Adult Intelligence and Learning Ability." *Adult Education,* 1968, *18* (3), 188–196.

KNOX, A. B., and SJOGREN, D. D. "Achievement and Withdrawal in University Adult Education Classes." *Adult Education,* 1964, *15* (2), 74–88.

KNOX, A. B., and others. *An Evaluation Guide for Adult Basic Education Programs.* Washington, D.C.: U.S. Government Printing Office, 1974.

KOTINSKY, R. *Adult Education and the Social Scene.* New York: Appleton-Century-Crofts, 1933.

KOTLER, P. *Marketing for Nonprofit Organizations.* Englewood Cliffs, N.J.: Prentice-Hall, 1974.

KOZOLL, C. E. *Administrator's Guide to the Use of Volunteer Teachers.* Englewood Cliffs, N.J.: Prentice-Hall, 1972.

KOZOLL, C. E. *Staff Development in Organizations.* Reading, Mass.: Addison-Wesley, 1974.

KURLAND, N. D. *Entitlement Studies.* National Institute of Education Papers in Education and Work, no. 4. Washington, D.C.: U.S. Government Printing Office, 1977.

KURLAND, N. D., and COMLY, L. T. *Financing Lifelong Education.* Albany: New York State Education Department, 1975.

LAHTI, R. E. *Innovative College Management: Implementing Proven Organizational Practice.* San Francisco: Jossey-Bass, 1973.

LASSEY, W. R. *Leadership and Social Change.* Iowa City, Iowa: University Associates, 1971.

LEAGANS, P., COPELAND, H., and KAISER, G. *Selected Concepts from Educational Psychology and Adult Education for Extension and Continuing Educators.* Notes and Essays on Education for Adults, No. 71. Syracuse, N.Y.: Publications in Continuing Education, Syracuse University, November 1971.

LEAKEY, R. E. *Origins.* New York: Dutton, 1977.

LE BRETON, P. (Ed.). *The Assessment and Development of Professionals.* Seattle: University of Washington Press. 1976.

LEE, R. E. *Continuing Education for Adults Through the American Public Library, 1833–1964.* Chicago: American Library Association, 1966.

LEVIN, H. M. "Cost-Effectiveness Analysis in Evaluation Research." In A. Guttentag and E. L. Struening (Eds.), *Handbook of Evaluation Research.* Beverly Hills, Calif.: Sage, 1975.

LINDEMAN, E. C. *The Meaning of Adult Education.* Montreal: Harvest House, 1961. (Originally published 1926.)

LINDQUIST, J. *Strategies for Change.* Berkeley, Calif.: Pacific Soundings Press, 1978.

LIVERIGHT, A. A. *A Study of Adult Education in the United States.* Boston: Center for the Study of Liberal Education for Adults, 1968.

LIVERIGHT, A. A., and MASCONI, D. L. *Continuing Education in the United States: A New Survey.* New York: Academy for Educational Development, 1971.

LLOYD, J. H. *A Handbook for Teachers of Adults.* Washington, D.C.: Federal City College, 1972.

LONDON, J. "Program Development in Adult Education." In M. S. Knowles (Ed.), *Handbook of Adult Education in the United States.* Washington, D.C.: Adult Education Association of the U.S.A., 1960.

LONDON, J., WENKERT, R., and HAGSTROM, W. O. *Adult Education and Social Class.* U.S. Office of Education Cooperative Research Project No. 1017. Berkeley: Survey Research Center, University of California, 1963.

LONDONER, C. A. "Perseverance Versus Nonperseverance Patterns Among Adult High School Students." *Adult Education,* 1972a, *22* (3), 179–195.

LONDONER, C. A. "Teacher-Student Correlates of Goal Expectations." *Adult Education,* 1972b, *22* (4), 267–281.

LONDONER, C. A. "Sources of Educational Funds as Motivators for Participating in Adult Secondary Education." *Adult Education,* 1974, *25* (1), 47–63.

Los Angeles City Schools. *Because They Want to Learn.* Los Angeles: Division of Career and Continuing Education, Los Angeles City Schools, 1977.

LUKE, R. A. "The Development of Public Support for Adult Education." In N. C. Shaw (Ed.), *Administration of Continuing Education.* Washington, D.C.: National Association for Public School Adult Education, 1969.

MC CALL, G. J., and SIMMONS, J. L. *Issues in Participant Observation.* Reading, Mass.: Addison-Wesley, 1969.

MC CLUSKY, H. Y. "Community Development." In M. S. Knowles (Ed.), *Handbook of Adult Education in the United States.* Chicago: Adult Education Association of the U.S.A., 1960.

MC DONALD, B. "Evaluation and the Control of Education." Unpublished paper. Centre for Applied Research in Education, University of East Anglia, Norwich, England, May 1974.

MC GREGOR, D. *The Human Side of Enterprise.* New York: McGraw-Hill, 1960.

MC GREGOR, D. *The Professional Manager.* New York: McGraw-Hill, 1967.

MC KINLEY, J. "Perspectives on Diagnostics in Adult Education." *Viewpoints,* (Bulletin of the School of Education, Indiana University), 1973, *49* (5), 69–83.

MAGER, R. F. *Preparing Instructional Objectives.* San Francisco: Fearon, 1962.

MATHIESON, D. E. *Correspondence Study: A Summary Review of the Research and Development Literature.* Syracuse, N.Y.: National Home Study Council and ERIC Clearinghouse on Adult Education, 1971.

MAVOR, A. S., TORO, J. O., DE PROSPO, E. R. *The Role of the Public Libraries in Adult Independent Learning.* (Final report.) New York: College Entrance Examination Board, 1976.

MAYFIELD, E. C. "The Selection Interview: A Reevaluation of Published Research." *Personnel Psychology,* 1964, *17,* 239–260.

(Ed.), *Evaluation Studies Review Annual,* Vol. 1. Beverly Hills,

MAYO, E. *The Social Problems of an Industrial Civilization.* London: Routledge & Kegan Paul, 1949.

MEZIROW, J., DARKENWALD, G., and KNOX, A. B. *Last Gamble on Education.* Washington, D.C.: Adult Education Association of the U.S.A., 1975.

MILES, M. B. "Changes During and Following Laboratory Training: A Clinical-Experimental Study." *Journal of Applied Behavioral Science,* 1965, *1* (3), 215–242.

MILLER, H. L. *Teaching and Learning in Adult Education.* New York: Macmillan, 1964.

MILLER, H. L. *Participation of Adults in Education: A Force Field Analysis.* Syracuse, N.Y.: Center for Liberal Education of Adults, Syracuse University, 1967.

MINIUM, E. W. *Statistical Reasoning in Psychology and Education.* (2nd ed.) New York: Wiley, 1978.

MINTZBERG, H. *The Nature of Managerial Work.* New York: Harper & Row, 1973.

MIRE, J. "Adult Education in Labor Unions." In M. S. Knowles (Ed.), *Handbook of Adult Education in the United States.* Washington, D.C.: Adult Education Association of the U.S.A., 1960.

MONETTE, M. L. "The Concept of Educational Need." *Adult Education,* 1977, *27* (2), 116–127.

MONETTE, M. L. "Need Assessment: A Critique of Philosophical Assumptions." *Adult Education,* 1979, *29* (2), 83–95.

MOORE, D. E., JR. (Ed.). *Proceedings, Mandatory Continuing Education: Prospects and Dilemmas for Professionals.* Urbana: Office of Continuing Education and Public Service, University of Illinois, 1976.

MOYNIHAN, D. P. "Counselor's Statement." In *Toward Balanced Growth: Quantity and Quality.* Washington, D.C.: U.S. Government Printing Office, 1970.

NADLER, L. "Business and Industry." In R. M. Smith, G. F. Aker, and J. R. Kidd (Eds.), *Handbook of Adult Education.* New York: Macmillan, 1970.

NAKAMOTO, J., and VERNER, C. *Continuing Education in the Health Professions: A Review of the Literature, 1960–1970.* Syracuse, N.Y.: ERIC Clearinghouse on Adult Education, 1973.

National Center for Education Statistics. *The Condition of Education.* Washington, D.C.: U.S. Government Printing Office, 1976.

National Council on Schoolhouse Construction. *Guide for Planning*

School Plants. East Lansing, Mich.: National Council on School-house Construction, 1964.

NAYLOR, H. H. *Volunteers Today: Finding, Training, and Working with Them.* New York: Association Press, 1967.

New York State Education Department. "New Uses for Excess Space and Unused Buildings." *Inside Education,* 1975, *61,* 4–5.

NIEMI, J. A., GRABOWSKI, S. M., and KUUSISTO, E. A. (Eds.). *Research and Investigation in Adult Education.* 1976 Annual Register. DeKalb: ERIC Clearinghouse in Career Education, Northern Illinois University, 1976.

NIEMI, J. A., and JESSEN, D. C. *Directory of Resources in Adult Education.* Washington, D.C.: Adult Education Association of the U.S.A. and ERIC Clearinghouse in Career Education, Northern Illinois University, 1976.

NORTHCUTT, N. W. *The Adult Performance Level Study.* Austin: University of Texas, 1973.

NYLEN, D. J., and Associates. *Handbook of Staff Development and Human Relations Training.* Washington, D.C.: National Training Laboratories, 1967.

OHLIGER, J. *The Mass Media in Adult Education: A Review of Recent Literature.* Syracuse, N.Y.: ERIC Clearinghouse on Adult Education, 1968.

OKES, I. *Participation in Adult Education.* National Center for Education Statistics, Final Report 1969. Washington, D.C.: U.S. Government Printing Office, 1974.

OKES, I. *Participation in Adult Education.* National Center for Education Statistics, Final Report 1972. Washington, D.C.: U.S. Government Printing Office, 1976.

OWENS, T. R. "Educational Evaluation by Adversary Proceedings." In E. R. House (Ed.), *School Evaluation: The Politics and Process.* Berkeley, Calif.: McCutchan, 1973.

PARKER, B., and PAISLEY, J. *Patterns of Adult Information Seeking.* Final Report on U.S. Office of Education Project No. 2583. Stanford, Calif.: Stanford University Press, 1966.

PARLETT, M., and HAMILTON, D. "Evaluation as Illumination: A New Approach to the Study of Innovative Programs." In G. V. Glass (Ed.), *Evaluation Studies Review Annual,* Vol. 1. Beverly Hills, Calif.: Sage, 1976.

PENNINGTON, F., and GREEN, J. "Comparative Analysis of Program Development Processes in Six Professions." *Adult Education,* 1976, *27* (1), 13–23.

PETERS, F. N. "Expanding Facilities for Adult Learners." In N. C. Shaw (Ed.), *Administration of Continuing Education.* Washington, D.C.: National Association for Public School Adult Education, 1969.

PITCHELL, R. J. "Financing Part-Time Students." In D. W. Vermilye (Ed.), *Lifelong Learners—A New Clientele for Higher Education: Current Issues in Higher Education 1974.* San Francisco: Jossey-Bass, 1974.

POPHAM, W. J. "Objectives and Instruction." In R. E. Stake (Ed.), *Instructional Objectives.* American Educational Research Association Monograph Series on Curriculum Evaluation, Vol. 3. Chicago: Rand McNally, 1969.

PORTER, L. *Faculty Perceptions of Continuing Education at Syracuse University.* Occasional Paper, Publications in Continuing Education, No. 20. Syracuse, N.Y.: Syracuse University Press, 1970a.

PORTER, L. "Adults Have Special Counseling Needs." *Adult Leadership,* 1970b, *18* (9), 275–277.

PORTWOOD, J. D., and SCHMIDT, S. M. "Beyond *Griggs* vs. *Duke Power Company:* Title VII After *Washington* vs. *Davis.*" *Labor Law Journal,* 1977, *28,* 174–181.

POSTON, R. "The Relation of Community Development to Adult Education." *Adult Education,* 1954, *4* (6), 191–196.

PROVUS, M. "Evaluation of Ongoing Programs in the Public School System." In R. W. Tyler (Ed.), *Educational Evaluation: New Roles, New Means.* 68th Yearbook of the National Society for the Study of Education, Part II. Chicago: University of Chicago Press, 1969.

REINEKE, R. A., and WELCH, W. W. *Evaluation Report: Workshops for Faculty Development in Family Medicine.* Prepared for the Society of Teachers of Family Medicine. Kansas City, Mo., May 1977.

RICHMAN, B. M., and FARMER, R. N. *Leadership, Goals, and Power in Higher Education: A Contingency and Open-Systems Approach to Effective Management.* San Francisco: Jossey-Bass, 1974.

RIPPEY, R. (Ed.). *Studies in Transactional Evaluation.* New York: McCutcheon, 1973.

RISLEY, R. F. "Adult Education in Business and Industry." In M. S. Knowles (Ed.), *Handbook of Adult Education in the United States.* Washington, D.C.: Adult Education Association of the U.S.A., 1960.

RIVLIN, A. M. *Systematic Thinking for Social Action.* Washington, D.C.: Brookings Institution, 1971.

ROBBINS, S. *The Administrative Process.* Englewood Cliffs, N.J.: Prentice-Hall, 1976.

ROETHLISBERGER, F. J., and DICKSON, W. J. *Management and the Worker.* Cambridge, Mass.: Harvard University Press, 1939.

ROGERS, C. R. *Freedom to Learn.* Columbus, Ohio: Merrill, 1969.

ROGERS, J. *Adults Learning.* Baltimore: Penguin, 1971.

ROGIN, L. "Labor Unions." In R. M. Smith, G. F. Aker, and J. R. Kidd (Eds.), *Handbook of Adult Education.* New York: Macmillan, 1970.

ROTH, R. M. (Ed.). *A Conspectus to the Self-Study Project of University College, the University of Chicago.* Center for the Study of Liberal Education for Adults Report No. 212. Syracuse, N.Y.: Syracuse University Press, 1964.

RYAN, L. V. "Lifelong Learning in Churches and Synagogues." *Journal of Research and Development in Education,* 1974, *7,* 87–96.

SAINTY, G. E. "Predicting Dropouts in Adult Education Courses." *Adult Education,* 1971, *21* (4), 223–230.

SCHECHTER, D. S. *Agenda for Continuing Education: A Challenge to Health Care Institutions.* Chicago: Hospital Research and Educational Trust, 1974.

SCHEIN, E. H. *Process Consultation: Its Role in Organization Development.* Reading, Mass.: Addison-Wesley, 1969.

SCHEIN, E. H. *Career Dynamics: Matching Individual and Organizational Needs.* Reading, Mass.: Addison-Wesley, 1978.

SCHLOSSBERG, N. K. "Community-Based Counseling." In D. W. Vermilye (Ed.), *Lifelong Learners—A New Clientele for Higher Education: Current Issues in Higher Education 1974.* San Francisco: Jossey-Bass, 1974.

SCHLOSSBERG, N. K. "The Case for Counseling Adults." *Counseling Psychologist,* 1976, *6* (1), 33–36.

School Review, 1978, *86* (3), entire issue. (Special issue on financing the learning society.)

SCHWAB, J. J. "The Practical 3: Translation into Curriculum." *School Review*, 1973, *81*, 501–522.

SCRIVEN, M. S. "The Methodology of Evaluation." In R. E. Stake (Ed.), *Perspectives of Curriculum Evaluation*. American Educational Research Association Monograph Series on Curriculum Evaluation, No. 1. Chicago: Rand McNally, 1967.

SCRIVEN, M. S. "An Introduction to Meta-Evaluation." *Educational Product Report*, 1969, *2*, 36–38.

SCRIVEN, M. S. "Pros and Cons About Goal-Free Evaluation." *Evaluation Comment* (UCLA, Center for the Study of Evaluation), 1972.

SCRIVEN, M. S. "Evaluation Bias and Its Control." In G. V. Glass (Ed.), *Evaluation Studies Review Annual*. Vol. 1. Beverly Hills, Calif.: Sage, 1976.

SEAMAN, D. F. *Preventing Dropouts in Adult Basic Education*. Tallahassee: Florida State University, 1971.

SERGIOVANNI, T. J. *Emerging Patterns of Supervision: Human Perspectives*. New York: McGraw-Hill, 1971.

SERGIOVANNI, T. J. (Ed.). *Professional Supervision for Professional Teachers*. Washington, D.C.: Association for Supervision and Curriculum Development, 1975.

SHAW, N. C. (Ed.). *Administration of Continuing Education*. Washington, D.C.: National Association for Public School Adult Education, 1969.

SHEATS, P. H. "Present Trends and Future Strategies in Adult Education." In M. S. Knowles (Ed.), *Handbook of Adult Education in the United States*. Washington, D.C.: Adult Education Association of the U.S.A., 1960.

SIMON, G. B. "What Kind of Evaluation?" *Educational Researcher Newsletter*, 1969, *20* (5), 9–10.

SIMON, H. A. *Administrative Behavior*. New York: Free Press, 1947.

SMITH, E. T. "Your Library: A College Around the Corner." *American Education*, 1976, *12*, 6–10.

SMITH, R. M., AKER, G. F., and KIDD, J. R. (Eds.). *Handbook of Adult Education*. New York: Macmillan, 1970.

SNYDER, R. E. *Recruitment in Adult Basic Education*. Tallahassee: Florida State University, 1971.

SOLOMON, D., BEZDEK, W. E., and ROSENBERG, L. *Teaching Styles and*

Learning. Chicago: Center for the Study of Liberal Education for Adults, 1963.

SPEAR, G. E. (Ed.). *Adult Education Staff Development: Selected Issues, Alternatives, and Implications.* Kansas City: Center for Resource Development in Adult Education, University of Missouri, 1976.

STAKE, R. E. "The Countenance of Educational Evaluation." *Teachers College Record,* 1967, *68,* 523–540.

STAKE, R. E. "Generalizability of Program Evaluation: The Need for Limits." *Education Product Report,* 1969, *2,* 39–40.

STAKE, R. E. "Objectives, Priorities, and Other Judgment Data." *Review of Educational Research,* 1970, *40,* 181–212.

STAKE, R. E. "Responsive Evaluation." Unpublished paper. Center for Instructional Research and Curriculum Evaluation, University of Illinois at Urbana-Champaign, 1973.

STAKE, R. E. "To Evaluate an Arts Program." In R. E. Stake (Ed.), *Evaluating Arts in Education: A Responsive Approach.* Columbus, Ohio: Merrill, 1974a.

STAKE, R. E. "Nine Approaches to Educational Evaluation." Unpublished paper. Center for Instructional Research and Curriculum Evaluation, University of Illinois at Urbana-Champaign, September 1974b.

Stanford Evaluation Consortium. "Review Essay: Evaluating the *Handbook of Evaluation Research.*" In G. V. Glass (Ed.), *Evaluation Studies Review Annual.* Vol. 1. Beverly Hills, Calif.: Sage, 1976.

STANLEY, J. C. "Principles of Scientific Research Are Not Pertinent to Educational Evaluation?" *Educational Researcher Newsletter,* 1969, *20* (5), 8–9.

STEELE, S. M. *Contemporary Approaches to Program Evaluation and Their Implications for Evaluating Programs for Disadvantaged Adults.* Syracuse, N.Y.: ERIC Clearinghouse on Adult Education, 1973.

STENZEL, A. K., and FEENEY, H. M. *Learning by the Case Method.* New York: Seabury Press, 1970.

STERN, M. R. *People, Programs, and Persuasion: Some Remarks About Promotion of University Adult Education.* Center for the Study of Liberal Education for Adults Notes and Essays No. 33. Syracuse, N.Y.: Syracuse University Press, 1961.

STOKES, K. "Religious Institutions." In R. M. Smith, G. F. Aker, and J. R. Kidd (Eds.), *Handbook of Adult Education.* New York: Macmillan, 1970.

STRINER, H. E. *Continuing Education as a National Capital Investment.* Kalamazoo, Mich.: W. E. Upjohn Institute for Employment Research, 1972.

STROBACH, S. K. "Business and Postsecondary Education Linkages." *Training and Development Journal,* 1976, *30* (12), 8–11.

STUBBLEFIELD, H. W. "Adult Civic Education in the Post World War II Period." *Adult Education,* 1974, *24* (3), 227–237.

STUFFLEBEAM, D. L. "Evaluation as Enlightenment for Decision-Making." In W. H. Beatty (Ed.). *Improving Educational Assessment & An Inventory of Measures of Affective Behavior.* Washington, D.C.: Association for Supervision and Curriculum Development, National Education Association, 1969.

STUFFLEBEAM, D. L. *Meta-Evaluation.* Kalamazoo: Evaluation Center, Western Michigan University, 1975.

STUFFLEBEAM, D. L. Untitled mimeo presented to the Evaluation Network Meeting, St. Louis, Mo., 1977.

TANNENBAUM, R., and SCHMIDT, W. H. "How to Choose a Leadership Pattern." *Harvard Business Review,* 1958, *51,* 162–164, 168.

TAYLOR, D. B. "Eeny, Meeny, Miney, Meaux: Alternative Evaluation Models." *North Central Association Quarterly,* 1976, *50* (4), 353–358.

TAYLOR, F. W. *The Principles of Scientific Management.* New York: Harper & Row, 1919.

TAYLOR, P. W. *Normative Discourse.* Englewood Cliffs, N.J.: Prentice-Hall, 1961.

Texas A & M. *The Teacher and the Adult Learner.* College Station: College of Education, Texas A & M University, 1977.

THOMAS, A. "The Concept of Program in Adult Education." In G. Jensen, A. A. Liveright, and W. Hallenbeck (Eds.), *Adult Education: Outlines of an Emerging Field of University Study.* Washington, D.C.: Adult Education Association of the U.S.A., 1964.

THOMAS, J. A., and GRIFFITH, W. S. *Adult and Continuing Education.* Special Study of the National Education Finance Project, No. 5. Chicago: Midwest Administration Center, 1970.

THOMPSON, C., and JENSEN, D. *Community-Based Educational Counseling for Adults.* Madison: University of Wisconsin Extension, 1977.

THOROMAN, E. C. *The Vocational Counseling of Adults and Young Adults.* Boston: Houghton-Mifflin, 1968.

TOMPKINS, E. W. "Public Library Joins Technical Institute." *Community College Frontiers,* 1976, *5* (1), 21–23.

TOUGH, A. M. *Learning Without a Teacher.* Educational Research Series, No. 3. Toronto: Ontario Institute for Studies in Education, 1967.

TOUGH, A. M. *Why Adults Learn: A Study of the Major Reasons for Beginning and Continuing a Learning Project.* Toronto: Ontario Institute for Studies in Education, 1968.

TOUGH, A. M. *The Adult's Learning Projects.* Research in Education Series, No. 1. Toronto: Ontario Institute for Studies in Education, 1971.

TOUGH, A. M. "Major Learning Efforts: Recent Research and Future Directions." *Adult Education,* 1978, *28* (4), 250–263.

TRAVERS, R. M. W. (Ed.). *Second Handbook of Research on Teaching* (American Educational Research Association). Chicago: Rand McNally, 1973.

TROW, M. "Notes on American Higher Education: Planning for University Access in the Context of Uncertainty." *Higher Education,* 1975, *4* (1), 1–11.

TRUESDELL, L. R. "Persisters and Dropouts in the Canada Manpower Training Program." *Adult Education,* 1975, *25* (3), 149–160.

TYE, N. B. "Process Guidelines for Adult Education Program Development." Unpublished doctoral dissertation, Teachers College, Columbia University, 1966.

TYLER, R. W. *Basic Principles of Curriculum and Instruction.* Syllabus for Education No. 305. Chicago: University of Chicago Press, 1950.

TYLER, R. W. (Ed.). *Educational Evaluation: New Roles, New Means.* 68th Yearbook of the National Society for the Study of Education, Part II. Chicago: University of Chicago Press, 1969.

ULMER, C. *Teaching the Disadvantaged Adult.* Washington, D.C.: National Association for Public School Adult Education, 1969.

University of Mid-America. *Background Paper on the University of Mid-America.* Unpublished manuscript. Lincoln, Nebr.: University of Mid-America Press, 1977.

University of Notre Dame, Center for Continuing Education. *The Learning Society: A Report on the Study on Continuing Education and the Future.* South Bend, Ind.: University of Notre Dame Press, 1973.

U.S. Department of Health, Education, and Welfare, Office of Education. *Perspectives of Adult Education in the United States and a Projection for the Future.* Washington, D.C.: U.S. Government Printing Office, 1972.

VALLEY, J. R., and HAMILTON, I. B. (Eds.). *Issues in Nontraditional Study.* Vol. I: *Matching New Needs with New Resources.* Princeton, N.J.: Office of New Degree Programs, College Entrance Examination Board, Educational Testing Service, 1976.

VERNER, C. "Definition of Terms." In G. Jensen, A. A. Liveright, and W. Hallenbeck (Eds.), *Adult Education: Outlines of an Emerging Field of University Study.* Washington, D.C.: Adult Education Association of the U.S.A., 1964.

VERNER, C., and DAVIS, S., JR. "Completions and Dropouts: A Review of Research." *Adult Education,* 1964, *14* (3), 157–176.

VON BERTALANFFY, L. "Problems of General System Theory." *Human Biology,* 1951, *23,* 302.

VOTRUBA, J. C. "Faculty Rewards for University Outreach: An Integrative Approach." *Journal of Higher Education,* 1978, *49* (6), 639–648.

WALDEN, B. L. *Recruitment and Retention of the Adult Learner.* Montgomery: Alabama State Department of Education, 1975.

WALKER, D. "A Naturalistic Model of Curriculum Development." *School Review,* 1971, *80,* 51–65.

WANN, M. D., and WOODWARD, M. V. *Participation in Adult Education 1957.* Washington, D.C.: U.S. Government Printing Office, 1959.

WARDROP, J. L. "Generalizability of Program Evaluation: The Danger of Limits." *Education Product Report,* 1969, *2,* 41–42.

WEBB, E. J., and others. *Unobtrusive Measures: Nonreactive Research in the Social Sciences.* Chicago: Rand McNally, 1966.

WERTHER, W. B., JR. "Beyond Job Enrichment to Employment Enrichment." *Personnel Journal,* 1975, *54,* 438–442.

WHIPPLE, J. B. *Especially for Adults.* Chicago: Center for the Study of Liberal Education for Adults, 1957.

WHITE, S. *Physical Criteria for Adult Learning Environments.* Syracuse, N.Y.: ERIC Clearinghouse on Adult Education, 1973.

WIENTGE, K. M., and DU BOIS, P. H. *Factors Associated with the Achieve-*

ment of Adult Students. St. Louis, Mo.: Adult Education Research Office, University College, Washington University, 1964.

WILES, D. K. *Supervision for Better Schools.* (3rd Ed.) Englewood Cliffs, N.J.: Prentice-Hall, 1967.

WILES, D. K. "Policy Adaptation in Higher Education: Fundamental Issues of Allocation and Legitimacy." *Journal of Education Finance,* 1977, *2* (3), 286–304.

WILLIAMS, F. N., and GILLHAM, L. E. "Personnel Practices in Community College Evening Programs." *Adult Leadership,* 1970, *19* (1), 5–6, 19.

WILMS, W. W. "Profile of Proprietary Students." In D. W. Vermilye (Ed.), *Lifelong Learners—A New Clientele for Higher Education: Current Issues for Higher Education 1974.* San Francisco: Jossey-Bass, 1974.

WORTHEN, B. R., and SANDERS, J. R. *Educational Evaluation: Theory and Practice.* Belmont, Calif.: Wadsworth, 1973.

ZELAN, J., and GARDNER, D. P. "Alternatives in Higher Education: Who Wants What?" *Higher Education,* 1975, *4* (3), 317–333.

ZETTERBERG, H. L. *Museums and Adult Education.* Clifton, N.J.: Augustus M. Kelly, 1969.

ZIEGLER, W. L. (Ed.). *Essays on the Future of Continuing Education.* Notes and Essays on Education for Adults, No. 66. Syracuse, N.Y.: Publications in Continuing Education, Syracuse University, 1970.

Index

Meta-evaluation, 117–119
MEZIROW, J., 40
MICHELANGELO, 13
Michigan State University, Task
   Force on Lifelong Education,
   24; Report, 33
Milestone charts, 237
MILLER, H. L., 42, 66–68, 127–128,
   136
MILLER, P. A., 24, 33
MINIUM, E. W., 102
MINTZBERG, H., 233
MIRE, J., 162
MONETTE, M. L., 4, 29
Montana University System, 184
MOONEY, J. D., 218
Motivation, 234–236
MOUTON, J. S., 219
MOYNIHAN, D. P., 80
Museums, support for education,
   157, 160

N

NADLER, L., 163
National Association for Public
   Continuing Adult Education,
   195
National Center for Education Sta-
   tistics, 27
National Council on Schoolhouse
   Construction, 158
National Institute of Education, 177
National University Extension As-
   sociation, 15, 24–25, 195
Needs assessment, 80; for program
   ideas, 14, 29–32, 34, 250–251
Network analysis, 237
New York State Education Depart-
   ment, 176
NIEMI, J. A., 26, 128, 195
North Carolina, Winston-Salem
   language program in, 177–178
NORTHCUTT, N. W., 5
NOWLEN, P., 5, 13–36
NYLEN, D. J., 69

O

Objective setting: components of,
   45–49; schema of, 46
Objectives: administrator's concern
   for, 39–42, 46–55, 251–254;

evaluation of, 51–55, 84–86, 90–
   93; form of, 49–51; leadership
   and, 224; management by,
   (MBO), 168, 227; for multiple
   audiences, 46–49; research
   needs on, 252; selection of, 52–55
OKES, I., 125
On-the-job training, 61
Open University, 157
Organizational development, 207–
   212; implementation suggestions, 243–245; leadership in,
   227–229; and program planning,
   15–17; research needs in, 260–
   261; and staffing, 9, 213, 215
Organizational theory, 228–229
Orientation, of staff, 202–206, 213–
   214
ORR, B., 4, 14, 27–28
Outcomes: first and second order,
   87; measurable and unmeasur-
   able, 49–50; questions for evaluation of, 91–93; unanticipated,
   53–54
OVERSTREET, B., 23–24
OVERSTREET, H., 23–24
OWENS, T. R., 76

P

PAISLEY, J., 126, 128, 133
Panels, 62, 65, 67
Paraprofessionals, as counselors,
   140–142, 144
Parent organization: and objective
   setting, 45–47; relations with,
   217–219, 229; and staffing decisions, 187; support from, 156–
   157, 165–166
PARKER, B., 126, 128, 133
PARLETT, M., 76, 84
Participants: evaluation questions
   for, 91–93, 105–106; with low
   education levels, 150–152; part-
   time, 154–155
Participation: administrator's concern with, 7–8, 72, 255–257;
   costs of, 8, 154–155; factors af-
   fecting, 28, 125–130; research
   needs on, 256
Peer counseling, 145